THE EDUCATION OF MODERN MAN

THE EDUCATION

Some Differences

OF MODERN MAN

of Opinion

EDITED BY

MARGARET M. STARKEY

Brooklyn College of the City University of New York

PITMAN PUBLISHING CORPORATION

New York · Toronto · London

© 1966 by Pitman Publishing Corporation
Library of Congress Catalog Card Number: 66–10182
Designed by Jeanette Young
Manufactured in the United States of America
1.987654321

Acknowledgments

The editor wishes to gratefully acknowledge the following authors and publishers for permission to reprint the selections in this book:

Jacques Barzun, "A Truce to the Nonsense on Both Sides," from the *Saturday Evening Post*, May 3, 1955, reprinted by permission of the author.

Arthur E. Bestor, "Training for a Livelihood," from *The Restoration of Learning*, New York: Alfred A. Knopf, Inc., 1955, copyright © by the author, reprinted by permission of the publisher.

Douglas Bush, "Science and the Humanities," from Brand Blanshard (ed.), *Education in the Age of Science*, New York: Basic Books, Inc., 1959, reprinted by permission of the publisher.

Clifton Fadiman, "The Case for Basic Education," from Jerome D. Koerner (ed.), *The Case for Basic Education*, Boston: Little, Brown & Co.—Atlantic Monthly Press, 1959, copyright © by the Council for Basic Education, reprinted by permission of the publisher.

John W. Gardner, "The Idea of Individual Fulfillment," from *Excellence*, New York: Harper & Row, Publishers, Inc., 1961, copyright © by the author, reprinted by permission of the publisher.

Bentley Glass, "Liberal Education in a Scientific Age," from *Science and Liberal Education*, Baton Rouge: Louisiana State University Press, 1959, reprinted by permission of the publisher.

Sidney Hook, "The Content of Education," from *Education for Modern Man*, New York: The Dial Press, 1946, reprinted by permission of the author.

Robert M. Hutchins, "A Letter to the Reader," and "The Tradition of the West," from *Great Books*, New York: Simon & Schuster, Inc., 1954, copyright by the Encyclopaedia Brittanica, reprinted by permission of the publisher.

Arthur E. Jensen, "Leadership through the Liberal Arts," from *Vital Speeches*, July 15, 1952, reprinted by permission of the publisher.

Howard Mumford Jones, "A Joy Forever," from *Reflections on Learning*, New Brunswick: Rutgers University Press, 1932, reprinted by permission of the publisher.

Joseph Wood Krutch, "If You Don't Mind My Saying So . . . ," from *The American Scholar*, Autumn 1962, reprinted by permission of the author.

F. R. Leavis, "Two Cultures? The Significance of C. P. Snow," from F. R. Leavis and Michael Yudkin, *Two Cultures? The Significance of C. P. Snow* and *An Essay on Sir Charles Snow's Rede Lecture*, New York: Random House, Inc., 1963, reprinted by permission of the publisher.

Sir Robert Livingstone, "The Rainbow Bridge," from *The Atlantic Monthly*, November 1957, reprinted by permission of the publisher.

Jacques Maritain, "Liberal Education for All," from Nelson Henry (ed.), *Modern Philosophies and Education: The Fifty-Fourth Yearbook of the National Society for the Study of Education, Part I*, Chicago: The National Society for the Study of Education, 1955, copyright by the publisher, reprinted by permission of the author, and the National Society for the Study of Education.

Ernest Nagel, "Science and the Humanities," from Brand Blanshard (ed.), *Education in the Age of Science*, New York: Basic Books, Inc., 1959, reprinted by permission of the publisher.

J. Robert Oppenheimer, "Physics in the Contemporary World," from *The Open Mind*, New York: Simon & Schuster, Inc., 1955, copyright by the author, reprinted by permission of the publisher.

José Ortega y Gasset, "The Fundamental Question," from *The Mission of a University*, Princeton: Princeton University Press, 1944, copyright by the publisher, reprinted by permission of the publisher.

Nathan M. Pusey, "The Centrality of Humanistic Study," from Julian Harris (ed.), *The Humanities*, Madison: University of Wisconsin Press, 1950, reprinted by permission of the Regents of the University of Wisconsin.

Sir Charles P. Snow, *The Two Cultures and the Scientific Revolution*, New York: Cambridge University Press, 1959, reprinted by permission of the publisher.

Alfred North Whitehead, *Technical Education and Its Relation to Science and Literature*, New York: The Macmillan Company, 1927, copyright by the publisher and renewed in 1957 by Evelyn Whitehead, reprinted by permission of the publisher.

To John,
with whom I have enjoyed
many an enlivening debate on science
and the liberal arts.

Preface

The essays in this book are part of the long and rapidly lengthening argument about the education of modern man. All commentators on the subject agree that man should be educated to cope with the problems of his age, but the nature of the education which will help him understand himself and his world is a matter for infinite analysis, speculation, and disagreement.

In Part I, "Sciences and the Humanities—Some Differences of Opinion," the essays are paired according to certain points on which the authors are at odds. The difference may be merely one of emphasis, or it may involve radically different assumptions about the nature of man and the universe. Areas of agreement do exist in all the pairs, however, and all of them, to some extent, touch upon the relative roles of the sciences and the humanities in modern education.

Joseph Wood Krutch pinpoints the limitations of scientific illumination, while Ernest Nagel defends the scientific enlightenment and deplores the pretensions of humanists. A classicist, Sir Richard Livingstone, sees a guide to modern wisdom in the study of the literature and philosophy of ancient Greece, but biologist Bentley Glass insists that it is the principles and procedures of science which hold the key to modern problems. Matthew Arnold and Thomas Henry Huxley appear as the classic protagonists of the nineteenth-century version of the humanities-versus-science debate. Physicist J. Robert Oppenheimer argues that the intrinsic values of science as a discipline carry over into other areas of life while the president of Harvard, Nathan M. Pusey, observes that the scientists he has known were, outside the laboratory, singularly bereft of the traditional "scientific" virtues. Sir Charles Snow, scientist and novelist, looks to science to teach all men to work for the good of all, while critic F. R. Leavis summarily rejects Sir Charles, and all his words and works.

The last two essays in Part I illustrate the way in which the defenders of the humanities can disagree among themselves. Douglas Bush and Jacques Barzun, ardent humanists both, differ markedly as to the *kind* of value the humanities have for man.

Part II, "The Nature of a Liberal Education—A Study in Contrasts," offers pairs of contrasting essays which are not primarily concerned with the rivalry between the sciences and the humanities. No two essays in the book are farther apart in approach than those of John Henry Newman, who argues that "knowledge is its own end," and Arthur Jensen, who finds that a liberal education is invaluable for the training of good business executives. And while Robert Hutchins stands strongly for the liberal education that for him exemplifies the "tradition of the West," Sidney Hook rejects outright most of the underlying assumptions and overlying details of Hutchins' educational proposals.

Part III, "Education in the Modern World—A Further Commentary," represents varying rather than contrasting views on such topics as the role of vocational studies, the essential elements of an education for all, and the pleasures of learning. Arthur Bestor and Alfred North Whitehead, for instance, discuss the place of vocational training in education. Clifton Fadiman and José Ortega y Gasset are concerned with the nature of the education that will best equip man to function as a citizen of the twentieth century and John W. Gardner considers the role man's education plays in his unending quest for meaning and fulfillment in life.

Finally, Howard Mumford Jones draws a sharp line between learning and pedantry and explains why the former constitutes "A Joy Forever" to the human spirit.

TO THE STUDENT

Throughout the book you will find matter for thought and material for papers. The pairing of the authors in the first section offers a particularly good opportunity to view the same points of debate from sharply different angles. And since, generally speaking, the first author of each pair represents the traditional humanistic approach to the subject of education and the second author a divergent view, you will find that the essays readily lend themselves to a variety of treatments—to comparison, to contrast, to synthesis. One reader may choose to work out his own theory of modern education on the basis of ideas given by the humanists, educators, philosophers, and scientists in the text. Another may discuss the nature of man as variously implied or described in essay after essay. Still others may deal with such recurring themes as the goal of a liberal education, the particular advantages of scientific discipline, or the breakdown in communication in our times between specialist and nonspecialist. The section "Topics for Research" at the end of the book offers suggestions both for research papers and for library-based reports. Bibliographies in the biographical headnotes and at the end of the text suggest material for further study.

As you read, analyze, criticize, and report, you will find yourself linked both to the traditions of the humanities and to the new age of science. Defenders of the liberal arts and proponents of a science-centered education would alike agree that men should exercise their minds and judgments freely, conduct research honestly, and present their findings impartially.

The liberal arts were the *artes liberales* of the ancient world, the studies that distinguish the free man from the slave. In the medieval curriculum they comprised the *trivium* (grammar, logic, and rhetoric), and the *quadrivium* (arithmetic, music, geometry, and astronomy). The humanities, variously interpreted, derive their name from the *litterae humaniores* of the Renaissance, the study of the Greek and Roman languages and literatures. In modern discussions of education, the terms are often used interchangeably. In certain of the essays, you will find the authors concerned with the ambiguities of the terms themselves.

Whether the student who uses this text is interested chiefly in science or in the humanities, he will find much here to question, analyze, consider, and debate. As a representative of modern man, he, too, has a stake in the kind of learning that will help the citizen of this century come to terms with himself and his world. The *education of modern man*—to these differences of opinion each will wish to add his own.

MARGARET M. STARKEY

A Note on the Presentation
of Material

Of the sixteen paired essays, only the Snow-Leavis, Arnold-Huxley, Hook-Hutchins pairs have authors who are actually pitted against each other in the debate on modern man and his education. And of these three only the Snow-Leavis combination is represented by pieces in which one work (Leavis') is actually an answer to the other (Snow's). The essays by Bush and Nagel, not paired in this text, were originally given as part of the same panel on science and the humanities.

Since the essays may be read in any order that suits the purpose of the class, or the research of the student, some of the questions on a given essay encourage comparison of that text with other pieces in the book, regardless of whether these come before or after the essay being discussed.

The original paging is indicated by brackets. If a word at the end of a page was hyphenated, the bracketed number has been placed before the beginning of the word. Three periods [. . .] indicate the omission of part of a sentence; four periods [. . . .] denote a longer ellipsis. Texts are reproduced exactly except for obvious typographical errors. When the author's footnotes are included, they are indicated by asterisks; editor's footnotes are numbered consecutively and are placed at the end of each essay. Dictionary definitions are quoted from *Webster's International Dictionary*, Second Edition, are marked [WID], and are set off by quotation marks.

Contents

III. EDUCATION IN THE MODERN WORLD—
A Further Commentary

THE SCIENCES AND THE HUMANITIES

Some Differences of Opinion

JOSEPH WOOD KRUTCH

If You Don't Mind
My Saying So . . .

Joseph Wood Krutch, educator, critic, naturalist, and biographer was born in 1893. Drama critic of The Nation 1924-1957, he was president of the New York Drama Critics' Circle 1940-1941. In 1924 and 1925 Professor Krutch was special lecturer at Vassar; between 1932 and 1935 he lectured at the New School for Social Research. He was professor of English at Columbia from 1937-1952, and from 1943-1952 was Brander Matthews Professor of Dramatic Literature there. He was a Guggenheim fellow 1930-1931. As an historian and critic of the theater, Professor Krutch has written such works as Comedy and Conscience after the Restoration (1924), The American Drama since 1918 (1939), and Modernism in Modern Drama (1953). His biographies include Edgar Allan Poe—a Study in Genius (1926), Samuel Johnson (1944), and Henry David Thoreau (1948). The Twelve Seasons (1949) and The Desert Year (1952) illustrate his talents as a naturalist; The Measure of Man (1954) and Human Nature and the Human Condition (1959) provide eloquent testimony to his fear that scientism may threaten not only the humanities, but humanity itself. The Measure of Man received the National Book Award for 1954.

Other provocative chapters in Professor Krutch's long-standing defense of the humanities are: "Are the Humanities Worth Saving?" (I) Saturday Review, XXXVIII (June 4, 1955), 22-24; "Are the Humanities Worth Saving?" (II) Saturday Review, XXXVIII (June 11, 1955), 22-23; "The Meaning of Meaningless Questions," "The Not So Blank Slate," and "A Meaning for Humanism," from Human Nature and the Human Condition (New York: Random House, Inc., 1959), and "The Old-Fashioned Science of Man," The Measure of Man (New York: Bobbs-Merrill Company, Inc., 1954). [This selection is taken from Joseph Wood Krutch, "If You Don't Mind My Saying So . . . ," The American Scholar (Autumn 1962), 516-19.]

[516] What used to be called the War between Science and Religion was a hot war. That now in progress between Science and the Humanities is a cold one. It is being fought somewhat more chivalrously and with many protestations of respect on both sides. The scientist doesn't want to exterminate literature, and the humanist certainly doesn't want to abolish science. Coexistence is the catchword. But, as in the case of the other cold war, the real question is, "On whose terms?" From both sides one gets something rather like the attitude of the Catholic priest who is said to have remarked to his Protestant opposite number: "After all, we are both trying to do God's work; you in your way and I—in His." There seems to be a good deal of question-begging and so many polite concessions that the terms are not usually clearly defined and the issues not squarely met.

C. P. Snow—a champion *sans peur* and *sans reproche*—seems to rest his case not so much on the superiority of science over the humanities as upon the alleged fact that scientists are better guys. There is, he argues, more good will among them, a larger common ground on which to operate and more willingness to make common cause. Probably this is true so long as they stay on this common ground. But scientists not infrequently are also patriots, adherents to this or that social philosophy and even, sometimes, loyal sons of some church. Those who are scientists and nothing else may be a bit *too* neutral—as, for instance, a famous rocket expert who appears to have been so little interested in anything except rockets that he was perfectly willing to make them for either side even in the middle of what less "objective" people regarded as Armageddon.[1]

As William James[2] said, "We may philosophize well or ill, but philosophize we must." Those who say they do not philosophize at all have usually answered philosophical questions arbitrarily and without thought. And for all the claims made that science itself can become an adequate philosophy, it seems to an unregenerate humanist like myself that such philosophy provides no answer to questions that have to be answered either thoughtfully or, as the scientist so often tends to answer them, arbitrarily. We may, says a distinguished American professor of experimental psychology, take it for granted that all ultimate questions can be reduced to one—namely, what is most likely to lead to survival? But who are the "we" who take this for granted? The better-red-than-dead boys apparently do. On the other hand, there is what some regard as good authority for "He who loseth his life shall gain it."[3] Probably there is no way of arbitrating between the two attitudes. But there is certainly no purely scientific solution, and the humanist is at least more acutely aware of the problem.

I must repeat the familiar charge that science can tell us how to do a bewildering (indeed, an alarming) number of things, but not which of them ought to be done: and I repeat it because I have never heard a satisfactory reply, and because it is perfectly evident that scientists themselves do not always agree in such decisions when called upon to make them. Of the medical practitioner it is sometimes said that medicine [517] itself supplies him with an ethic. But take, for example, the case of the German doctors who used human beings as laboratory animals. They had learned the same medical science as those of their European and American fellows who found their experiments morally and even criminally shocking. At a medical congress both groups would have met on that common ground that Sir Charles[4] regards as so important—so long as the discussion was confined to science. At a clinic they would have agreed on both diagnosis and treatment. Whatever the origin of their moral differences, it certainly did not lie in the field of the scientific knowledge that both had mastered. Their science gave them no guidance in the making of an ethical decision.

To this objection, which seems to be incontrovertible, either of two answers is usually given. One is that science, properly understood, *would* give an answer if properly attended to. The other is that "ought" implies a concept that corresponds to nothing outside the human mind and exists there only subjectively, induced by the conditioning effect of social custom; and that, therefore, we should be content to say merely that what we ought to do must be left to whatever society evolves as a result of the wise determination to devote ourselves exclusively to scientific knowledge.

Pushed into a corner, those who maintain that only science is anything more than nonsense are likely to throw the question back into the face of the humanist. "Just how much progress have philosophy, metaphysics, religion and poetry ever made toward establishing 'oughts' conclusively demonstrated or widely agreed upon for long? You blame us for our failures. What are your successes?" This *tu quoque*[5] is, to put it mildly, embarrassing—so embarrassing, in fact, that I would rather drop the subject for the moment and come back to it (if I must) a little later in this discussion.

What seems to me necessary (and lacking) to clarify any general discussion of the "case for the humanities" is some clear definition of science on the one hand and, on the other, of the subject matter that the humanist believes he alone can deal with and of the methods he uses.

Originally, of course, science meant simply knowledge of any kind, and the humanities meant merely secular learning—knowledge about human affairs is contrasted with the divine, or, more simply still, the kind of thing one found in the writings of the Greeks and Romans before the Christian revelation made knowledge of the divine possible. But the meaning of the first term narrowed, and the meaning of the second grew more vague. Science came to mean a special kind of knowledge that can be acquired by certain techniques while the humanities came to mean, well, whatever is left over. What actually is left over came to seem to many less and less important if, indeed, it was important at all.

Suppose we say that science (and the definition would certainly have been accepted at a time when scientists were more modest) deals with whatever is measurable and subject to experimental verification. I cannot think of any scientific inquiry that has gone beyond that without ceasing to be completely scientific. Accept that definition, add that the subject matter of the humanities is whatever cannot be measured or verified experimentally, and it is obvious that what is left over is extensive and important.

Take, for example, the question of contentment, happiness and joy. Pope[6] called the second "our being's end and aim." At least some scientists would agree that it is as fundamental as survival since, if science can tell us how to survive but not how to be happy, it is wasting its time. Yet happiness cannot be measured and the assumption that this man is happier than that cannot be experimentally verified. The difficulty may not be quite as thorny as that which involves the "ought," but it is thorny enough and important enough. Hedonists may say that what we ought to do is what will make us as individuals in our society most happy, but that still leaves happiness as one of the things that can neither be measured nor experimented with. And it is one of the things with which the literature or humanism is concerned in its own way.

The humanist does at least recognize the [518] importance of happiness, and he does not brush it aside like the scientist whose logic is likely to run more or less thus: happiness cannot be measured, therefore it cannot be the subject of science; but since the methods of science are the only useful ones, we will just have to assume that happiness is directly proportional to something that can be measured—say income, standard of living or even horsepower available per unit of population. That this is a monstrous assumption is made abundantly clear by the introspection and direct observation dealt with in humanistic literature. And if we are not even further than we are now down the road to radical discontent and alienation in the midst of abundance, it is largely because humane letters still affect us.

So much for the kind of subject with which the humanities can and science cannot deal. What methods does the humanist, who can neither measure nor experiment, rely upon? He cannot, of course, prove anything. All that he can do is to carry conviction. He can, for example, draw a picture of a happy man and tell a story that seems to account for that man's happiness. There is no objective test for the truth or falsity of his assumptions. For his success or failure he depends upon one thing only—the extent to which he can carry conviction, and he convinces just to the extent that our own experience confirms his. Hence my own definition of the humanities would be simply this: they are that branch of inquiry concerned with the unmeasurable and the undemonstrable and dealing with it in such a way that although nothing is proved, something is, nevertheless, believed. The truths of the humanities are, in other words, those that cannot be demonstrated but can be recognized.

Thomas De Quincey's[7] famous definition of humane literature as the literature of power, as distinguished from the literature of knowledge, is sound although sometimes misunderstood. The literature of knowledge is that which *confers* power; humane literature, that which *is* powerful. The half-sciences of psychology, sociology and history necessarily fall between two stools, and they would be both more useful and less dangerous if they always recognized the fact. So long as they deal only with what can be measured and experimentally verified, they rarely throw very much light upon the most important subjects. When, as all too often happens, they pretend to have proved something that their facts do not really prove, they can be disastrously misleading. They are most effective when they, like the nonscientist, carry conviction by statements whose truths we seem to recognize.

Sir Charles himself, when he expresses the opinion that scientists are better guys than humanists, is indulging in exactly the kind of loose, unsupported generalizations often cited as reproachable in the man of letters. He may give random examples, but he presents no hard statistics. We may agree or not, and whether we do agree will depend upon our own experience. He is speaking as a humanist, not as a scientist.

Freud offers a more striking case in point. He was so far from establishing a science that there are by now almost as many incompatible schools of psychoanalysis as there are Christian sects. Competent physicists could not possibly disagree among themselves on fundamentals as psychoanalysts disagree. But Freud probably had as much effect upon our mental climate as any man who lived during his time, because when we read what he had to say, we experienced "the shock of recognition." What he had not actually demonstrated was recognized. We believed because our past experience had prepared us to do so.

The Lonely Crowd is, I suppose, the most widely read sociological work written in the United States during the past twenty years. Yet, as sociologists with a narrower conception of their quasi-science were quick to point out, it didn't actually prove anything. There were no measurements and no experiments weighty enough to be taken seriously. The examples of "inner-directed" and "other-directed" personalities were not selected by any controlled process of sampling but were treated merely as illustrations, much as a literary essayist might have treated them. Yet, most readers did experience the shock of recognition. *The Lonely Crowd* is a contribution to "the humanities."

[519] Scientists fear (not without reason) the power that literature has to keep alive and to propagate all sorts of notions, including the pernicious. It can decline into mere rhetorical oratory and sometimes make the worse appear the better reason. Poets, said the American novelist and paragrapher Ed Howe,[8] are the only prophets who are always wrong. Exasperated by Alexander Pope, Bernard Shaw[9] exclaimed that "you can't make a lie true by putting it into an heroic couplet." But the unfortunate fact is that you can go a long way toward making it seem so. Said Mark Twain, "The history of the human race is strewn thick with evidence that a truth is

not hard to kill; but that a lie, well told, is immortal." *Well told* is the operative phrase, and since to tell well is the special province of humane letters, they are no doubt responsible for more seemingly immortal lies than erroneous science ever has been. On the other hand, it is the great body of these same humane letters that have kept alive many supremely important concepts like those of "honor," "love," "duty," "the good life," et cetera, which science dismisses or at least ignores just because it has no means of dealing with them. A scientist may be and often is also a humanist, but he can be such only insofar as he recognizes the legitimacy of problems with which he cannot, as a scientist, deal. Accept science as the only legitimate concern of the human mind, and you must cease to concern yourself with anything that cannot be measured or experimented with. And a world that disregards everything thus excluded would be a world in which the human being as we know him would cease to exist.

The humanist cannot claim any success in his enterprise comparable to that which the scientist boasts of in his. He is compelled, generation after generation, to begin all over again. It is not certain that he has made any progress since the time of Plato[10] and Aristotle[11] or the times of Homer and Shakespeare. He may even find himself carrying less and less conviction to others, perhaps even being less and less sure himself. He never has, and he probably never will have, a method that produces results as the method of science does. But that is not because he is less intelligent and less competent. It is because the human being is more complicated than the physical world—more complicated even than the atom. But it is also at least as important to all of us; and as long as we continue to ask questions, even unanswered questions, we at least continue to recognize the reality of what the scientist tends to regard as nonexistent or unimportant just because he does not know how to deal with it. Perhaps the best defense of the humanities was made by Justice Holmes[12] when he said that science teaches us a great deal about things that are not really very important, philosophy a very little bit about those that are supremely so.

NOTES

1. Armageddon. Rev. 16 : 16 names Armageddon as the place where the last great battle between good and evil will take place; the term is used figuratively for any great, terrible, final conflict.

2. William James (1842-1910). American psychologist and philosopher, brother of the novelist Henry James, his work was particularly important in the development of American pragmatism.

3. "He who loseth his life shall gain it." Luke 17 : 33.

4. Sir Charles. C. P. Snow.

5. *tu quoque.* You too! (Literally "Thou also!") The phrase enables A to charge his opponent B with the same fault that B is complaining of in A.

6. Pope. Alexander Pope (1688-1744) English neoclassical poet, especially distinguished for his satires, e.g., *The Rape of the Lock* (1714) and *The Dunciad* (1743).

7. Thomas De Quincey (1785-1859). English essayist and literary critic; his *Confessions of an English Opium Eater* (1821) is a good example of his musical and highly imaginative prose.

8. Ed Howe. Edgar Watson Howe (1853-1937), American journalist and novelist; he was the proprietor and editor of the *Atchison Daily Globe* and *E. W. Howe's Monthly*.

9. Shaw. George Bernard Shaw (1856-1950), Irish critic, dramatist, and advocate of social reform. His plays include *Man and Superman* (1903), *Pygmalion* (1912), and *St. Joan* (1923).

10. Plato. Plato (427?-347 B.C.), a pupil and friend of Socrates, has probably had more influence upon Western thought than any other Greek philosopher. Central to his philosophy is the concept of eternal, changeless Ideas or Archetypes. His dialogues include *Crito* (on the death of Socrates), *Ion* (on poetry), *Symposium* (on love), *Phaedo* (on immortality), and *Republic* (on the ideal state).

11. Aristotle. Aristotle (384-322 B.C.), a pupil of Plato, was one of Greece's greatest philosophers. His influence dominated medieval philosophy and is in our day still vitally important. His works include the *Metaphysics*, the *Nicomachean Ethics*, the *Politics*, and the *Poetics*.

12. Justice Holmes. Oliver Wendell Holmes (1841-1935), distinguished American jurist; associate justice of the United States Supreme Court 1902-1932.

TOPICS FOR DISCUSSION

1. According to Krutch, what is C. P. Snow's main argument for preferring science to the humanities? After reading *The Two Cultures* do you agree with Krutch on this point? Why or why not?

2. What widely differing concepts of human nature and human destiny underlie the psychologist's statement: "We may take it for granted that all ultimate questions can be reduced to one—namely, what is most likely to lead to survival?" and the New Testament reminder: "He who loseth his life shall gain it"? Can you cite current events which indicate that both points of view are very much alive in the contemporary world?

3. According to Krutch, what are science's strengths and limitations? With what evidence does he support his criticisms?

4. How does the author reply to the charge that the humanities have had no success in establishing "oughts" for long? How would Barzun handle this accusation? Livingstone? Arnold? Newman?

5. What is this author's definitions of science? Of the humanities? How does his definition of the latter compare with Barzun's term for them—"the misbehavioral science"?

6. Krutch argues that science cannot deal with such a concept as "happiness"; how would the essayists favoring the scientific approach reply to this charge?

7. In "A Meaning for Humanism," Chapter 11 of his book *Human Nature and the Human Condition* (1959, p. 210) Krutch writes "The ancients had a wise

motto: '*Quo Urania ducit*'—Wherever Wisdom leads. We have somehow mistranslated or perverted it. Our motto has become '*Quo Uranium ducit.*' And that, of course, is the antithesis of humanism." Explain the significance of this change in the light of "If You Don't Mind My Saying So. . . ." To give the allusion full value, check the meaning and significance of *Urania*.

ERNEST NAGEL

Science and the Humanities

Ernest Nagel, educator (b. 1901), has been John Dewey Professor of Philosophy at Columbia University since 1955. A Guggenheim fellow 1934-1935 and 1950-1951, Professor Nagel was a fellow of the Center for Advanced Studies in the Behavioral Sciences 1959-1960. From 1940-1956 he edited the Journal of Philosophy, and from 1956-1959 he was editor of Philosophy of Science. His writings include Sovereign Reason (1954), Logic Without Metaphysics (1957), with J. R. Neuman, and The Structure of Science (1960). His point of view, clearly evident in the following essay, is that of a specialist in the philosophy and methodology of science.

This essay is taken from an address given at the Tamiment Institute in 1958. On the Tamiment program it followed Douglas Bush's address, "Science and the Humanities," the greater portion of which is given on pp. 91. The Tamiment conference dealt with the roles of science and the humanities in modern education. Brand Blanshard, who participated in the program, later edited Education in the Age of Science (New York: Basic Books, 1959), a compilation of papers given at the conference and of much of the discussion that followed. The introduction contains Professor Blanshard's own reactions to the debate; you might find it interesting to compare his views with those of Professor Nagel. You might also wish to compare Professor Nagel's views with those expressed in "Educated Man in 1984" by Jacob Bronowski, an English scientist. This essay can be found in Science, CCXXII (April 27, 1956), 710-12.

[This selection is taken from Ernest Nagel, "Science and the Humanities," in Brand Blanshard (ed.), Education in the Age of Science (New York: Basic Books, 1959), pp. 188-207.]

[188] What are the distinctive contributions the study of science can make toward realizing the objectives of a liberal education? Let me outline what I regard as the three cardinal contributions.

THE THEORETICAL AND MORAL VALUE OF SCIENCE

[189] It has been the perennial aim of theoretical science to make the world intelligible by disclosing fixed patterns of regularity and orders of dependence in events. This aim may never be fully realized. But it has been partly realized in the scientific exploration of both animate and inanimate subject matter. The knowledge that is thus progressively achieved—of general truths about various sectors in nature as well as of particular processes and events in them—is intrinsically delightful to many minds. In any event, the quest for such knowledge is an expression of a basic impulse of human nature, and it represents a distinctive variety of human experience. It is a history of magnificent victories as well as of tragic defeats for human intelligence in its endless war against native ignorance, childish superstitions, and baseless fears. If to be a humanist is to respond perceptively to all dimensions of man's life, an informed study of the findings and of the development of science must surely be an integral part of a humanistic education.

There is the further point that knowledge acquired by scientific inquiry is indispensable for a responsible assessment of moral ideals and for a rational ordering of human life. Ideals and values are not self-certifying; they are not established as valid by appeals to dogmatic authority, to intuitions of moral imperatives, or to undisciplined preference. Moral ideals must be congruous with the needs and capacities of human beings, both as biological individuals and as historically conditioned members of cultural groups, if those ideals are to serve as satisfactory guides to a rich and satisfying human life. The adequacy of proposed moral norms must therefore be evaluated on the basis of reliable knowledge acquired through controlled [190] scientific inquiry. It is simply grotesque to imagine that anyone today can exercise genuine wisdom in human affairs without some mastery of the relevant conclusions of natural and social science.

I am not unaware that there have been great moral seers who possessed little if any scientific knowledge of the world or of man, and who nevertheless spoke with understanding about the paths of human virtue. However, though such men may have expressed profound insights into the ways of the human heart, merely to proclaim an insight does not establish its wisdom; and it is by no means self-evident that their vision of the human good, though generous and wise for their time, is really adequate for men living in different climes and with different opportunities for developing their powers. Insight and imagination are undoubtedly necessary conditions for moral wisdom, but they are not sufficient. For insights and visions may differ, and knowledge of the world and human circumstance must be introduced for adjudicating between conflicting moral ideas. It would be absurd to deny the exquisite perceptions and the stimuli to reflection that are often found in the pronouncements of scientifically untutored moral seers. But I do not believe their pronouncements can be taken at face value, or that in the light of the scientific knowledge we now possess those pronouncements are invariably sound. In short, apart from the intellectual joys accompanying the enlarged understanding of the world that scientific knowledge may bring, such knowledge is indispensable if the ideal and the conduct we adopt are to be based neither on illusion nor on uninformed parochial preferences. It is not an exaggeration to claim that the theoretical understanding that the sciences provide is the foundation for a liberal civilization and a humane culture.

SCIENCE AS INTELLECTUAL METHOD

[191] The conclusions of science are the products of an intellectual method, and in general they cannot be properly understood or evaluated without an adequate grasp of the logic of scientific inquiry. I am not maintaining, of course, that there are fixed rules for devising experiments or making theoretical discoveries. There are no such rules; and it is in large measure because it is commonly supposed that there are, that scientific inquiry is frequently believed to be a routine for grubbing for facts, and unlike literature and the arts to require no powers of creative imagination. Indeed, science has fallen into understandable though undeserved disrepute among many humanistic thinkers because students of human affairs have sometimes permitted this misconception to control their inquiries and their literary productions. Nor am I asserting that the sciences share a common set of techniques of inquiry, so that disciplines not employing those techniques are not properly scientific. Except for the ability to use a language, it is doubtful whether there is such a set of common techniques. Certainly the techniques required for making astronomical observations are different from those used in the study of cellular division; mathematically formulated laws are relatively recent developments in chemistry, biology, and the social sciences; and though quantitative distinctions are widely used in many sciences, the techniques of measurement are often quite different for different subject matters.

On the other hand, I am suggesting that what is distinctive of all science, not merely of natural science such as physics, and what assures the general reliability of scientific findings, is the use of a *common intellectual method* [192] for assessing the weight of the available evidence for a proposed solution of a problem, and for accepting or rejecting a tentative conclusion of an inquiry. Scientific method, in my use of this phrase, is a procedure of applying logical canons for *testing* claims to knowledge.

Those logical canons have been adopted neither as arbitrary conventions, nor because there are no conceivable alternatives to them, nor because they can be established by appeals to self-evidence. They are themselves the distilled residue of a long series of attempts to win reliable knowledge, and they may be modified and improved in the course of further inquiries. They owe their authority to the fact that conclusions obtained in accordance with their requirements have agreed better with data of observation, and have in the main withstood further critical testing more successfully, than have conclusions obtained in other ways. The use of scientific method does not guarantee the truth of every conclusion reached by that method. But scientific method does give rational assurance that conclusions conforming to its canons are more likely to approximate the truth than beliefs held on other grounds. To accept the conclusions of science without a thorough familiarity with its method of warranting them is to remain ignorant of the critical spirit that is the life of science. Not every claim to knowledge is a valid claim; and without a clear grasp of the standards that evidence for a conclusion must meet, the risk is large of becoming a slave to every rhetorical appeal, to every plausible though specious argument, and to every intellectual fashion.

A firm grasp of the logical grounds upon which the sciences rest their conclusions serves to show that the sciences can make no dogmatic claims for the finality of their findings, that their procedure nevertheless provides [193] for the progressive corrections of their cognitive claims; that they can achieve reliable knowledge even though they are fallible; and that, however impressive the achievements of science have been in giving us intellectual mastery over many segments of existence, we cannot justifiably assume that we have exhaustively surveyed the variety and the depths of nature. The critical temper, the confidently constructive rationality, and the manly intellectual humility that are essential for the practice of scientific method are not simply adornments of a well-balanced mind; they are of its essence.

SCIENCE AS THE CODE OF A COMMUNITY

This brings me to the final point I want to make in this context. Viewed in broad perspective, science is an enterprise carried on by a self-governing community of inquirers who conduct themselves in accordance with an unwritten but binding code. Each member of this republic has the right and the obligation to make the most of his capacities for original and inventive research, to make full use of his powers of imagination and insight, to be independent in his analyses and assessments, and to dissent from the views of others if in his judgment the evidence requires him to do so. In return for this he must submit his own investigations to examination by his scientific peers, and he must be prepared to defend his claims by reasoned argument against all competent critics, even if he should believe himself their superior in knowledge and insight. Accordingly, no question of fact or theory is in principle finally closed. The career of science is a continuing free exchange of ideas, and its enduring intellectual products are in the end the fruits of a refining process of [194] mutual criticism. This does not mean that individual scientists do not possess passions and vanities, which are often obstacles to dispassionate judgment and which may hamper the advance of knowledge. It does mean that the institution of science provides a mechanism for discovering the truth irrespective of personal idiosyncrasies, but without curtailing the rights of its members to develop freely their own insights and to dissent from accepted beliefs.

The organization of science as a community of free, tolerant, yet alertly critical inquirers embodies in remarkable measure the ideals of liberal civilization. The discipline that fosters these qualities of mind therefore must have an important place in an educational program designed to develop members for such a society. . . . [196]

THE FEAR OF SCIENCE AS INHUMANE

[197] I shall try to meet some of the strictures made in the name of humanism against science and its influence and to suggest what could be done to emphasize the humanistic and philosophic import of science, without depriving science instruction of substantive content.

It is undoubtedly true that the existence of mass cultures depends upon the technical fruits of theoretical and engineering research. It is also undoubtedly the case that many of these techniques have been put to reprehensible uses. On the other hand, it is absurdly unilluminating to make science therefore responsible for the failings of contemporary society, as unilluminating as it would be to place the blame for Hitler's moral inadequacies upon the procreative act of his parents. Scientific discoveries and inventions indeed have created opportunities which frequently have been misused, whether by design or by inadvertence. But an opportunity does not determine the use that men make of it. It is childish to bewail the expansion of science as the chief source of our current evils, and sheer sentimentality to look with longing to earlier days when science played a less conspicuous role in the human economy—as if living under such earlier conditions were an option now open to us, and as if societies less complex than ours exhibit no failings comparable with those of our own.

It is not possible to deny that, despite improvements [198] in the material conditions of life for an increasing fraction of the populace, much of our energy is directed toward the realization of shoddy ideals, and that relatively few men lead lives of creative self-fulfillment and high satisfaction. It is difficult to demur at such indictments without appearing to act the part of a Philistine.[1] Nevertheless, the failings noted are not unique to our own culture. Critics of American mass culture tend to forget that only comparatively small elite groups in the great civilizations of the past were privileged to share in the high achievements of those cultures, and that even those groups had only limited opportunities for appreciating the supreme products of the human spirit. In our own society, on the other hand, modern science and technology have made available to unprecedented numbers the major resources of the great literature and of the arts of the past and present, never accessible before in such variety even to the highly privileged

and cultivated members of earlier societies. I do not claim that these benefits are of passionate interest to the great majority. But there seems to me
ample evidence that an increasing number in our society has come to value
them, and that as a consequence of exposure to such things tastes have
become more discriminating and less provincial.

Discriminating tastes cannot be formed overnight. In view of the size
and heterogeneous character of the American population, and of the fact
that adequate leisure and training for developing and pursuing rational
ideals is a fairly recent acquisition for most of its members, it is perhaps
remarkable how rapid has been the growth of sensitivity in our society to
the great works of literary, scientific, and artistic imagination. It is simply
not the case that the mechanisms of our alleged mass culture are all geared
to enforcing meretricious standards of excellence, [199] or that there is
today a decreasing number of opportunities for men to cultivate their individual talents. The evidence seems to me overwhelming that the growth of
scientific intelligence has helped to bring about not only improvements in
the material circumstances of life, but also an enhancement in its quality.

HUMANISTS NOT IMMUNE TO PROVINCIALISM

If thorough exposure to the discipline of science is essential for the
development of a liberal intelligence, familiarity with the subjects tradition-
ally classified as the humanities is no less essential. The values implicit in
the study of the humanities are too well known to require extended comment. Their study acquaints us with a range of human aspirations and
passions to which we can be strangers only if we remain provincial members
of the human race; they transmit to us visions of human excellence that
have stirred men throughout the centuries and that make men kindred spir-
its despite accidents of birth and circumstance; and they make us conscious
of our cultural heritage, and so potentially more discriminatingly aware of
its virtues and limitations. But there is no inherent incompatibility between
the liberal values implicit in the study of the sciences and those fostered by
the humanities.

Nevertheless, professional humanists often display a snobbish tradi-
tionalism, a condescension toward everything modern, and an impatience
with the critical standards of scientific thought. There have been humanists
whose enthusiasm for the aqueducts of ancient Rome had no bounds, but
for whom contemporary systems of water supply were undeserving of a cultivated man's serious interest. There [200] are self-proclaimed humanists
who are profoundly affected by the tragic heroism of the Spartans at Thermopylae,[2] but who dismiss the Warsaw uprising[3] against the Nazi oppressor as merely a sordid incident. There are humanists who claim a special
kind of truth for knowledge about human values and who reject as sheer
presumption the view that ordinary canons of scientific validity are pertinent for assessing the worth of moral insights. Needless to say, I am not

suggesting that attachment to the classical tradition of humanistic thought is invariably associated with the narrowness of spirit some of these attitudes exhibit. However, the fact that they are sometimes manifested suffices to show that professional scientists have no monopoly on snobbery and provincialism, and that training in the humanities does not insure breadth of perspective.

Since the claim that the humanities represent a distinct mode of knowledge is a frequent source of antagonism between scientifically oriented thinkers and spokesmen for the humanities, I must deal with it briefly. The claim seems to me to rest partly on a misunderstanding of what is covered by the label "scientific method," partly on a confusion of knowledge with other forms of experience, and partly on what I regard as a mistaken belief in the efficacy of human reason to establish absolutely certain and necessary truths about empirical subject matter. I have already indicated that the label "scientific method" does not signify either a set of rules for making discoveries or the use of certain techniques in conducting inquiries. In any case, I am in full agreement with those who maintain that distinctive subject matters require distinct modes of investigation, that the techniques employed in the natural sciences are not paradigmatic[4] for the study of human affairs, and that though there are physical, biological, and sociopsychological [201] conditions for the occurrence of preferences and valuations, trustworthy judgments about moral ideals cannot be deduced simply from statements about those conditions.

The disciplines constituting the humanities in some cases supply instruction which is no different in kind, though it is different in specific content, from the knowledge obtained in various special areas of natural science. This is patently the case for history and biography, and for much descriptive literature about the habits, customs, and aspirations of men. The factual claims of such literature must be tested by reference to the available evidence. Though standards of proof in these inquiries may be less stringent than in other areas, cognitive claims are validated through the use of logical canons common to all discursive thought about empirical subject matter. On the other hand, there are other humanistic disciplines, among them poetry, painting, and music, which are sometimes alleged to be sources of a special kind of knowledge to which the canons of scientific method are said to be irrelevant. Now undoubtedly these disciplines can be instructive, in ways different from the way propositions are instructive. They can provide objects for reflection and perception, they can acquaint us with works of imagination that develop our sensibilities and heighten our powers of discrimination, they can present us with patterns of sound, color, and rhythm which evoke, intensify, and discipline emotional responses, and they can confront us with embodied visions of human virtue and human destiny. These are all important and instructive forms of experience. But since nothing is stated by these objects in propositional form, in no intelligible sense can they be regarded as conveying truth or falsity. They are therefore not sources of a special [202] kind of knowledge, though they may be occasions or subject matters for knowledge.

Men who are equipped by native endowment and training to be successful investigators in one area are usually not equally successful in other areas. In any event, the capacity for making contributions to moral enlightenment is not uniformly distributed; and insofar as humanists are capable conservers and purifiers of the conscience of mankind, they require powers of moral imagination and insight which are as specialized as are the powers of imagination and insight into physical processes that the competent physicist must possess. However, as has already been argued, imagination and insight are not sufficient for establishing a cognitive claim, whether in morals or in physics. For insights must be tested. In a manner analogous to the procedure in physics, a test of a moral insight consists in formulating a hypothesis, comparing the consequences of the hypothesis with alternative assumptions and with empirical data relevant to the problem, and finally evaluating the adequacy of the hypothesis as a solution of the moral problem in the light of the evidence. Those who reject this procedure as not suitable for the adjudication of moral issues, and who also reject authoritarian justifications of moral judgments, attempt to validate moral principles by appealing to an alleged rational intuition of their necessary truth. I do not think this approach is tenable, among other reasons because of the historical fact that men have claimed intuitive certainty for incompatible moral principles. Accordingly, though there are as many distinct true statements as there are situations about which predications can be made, there are not several kinds of truth, and there is only one reliable *method* for establishing claims to truth. In short, the contention that the humanities employ a [203] distinctive conception of truth and represent a mode of knowledge different from scientific knowledge seems to me to be the consequence of a failure in analysis.

NOTES

1. Philistine. One who prefers riches and material conveniences to the things of the mind. This definition derives from Arnold's use of the term, *e.g.*, in *Culture and Anarchy*.

2. Spartans at Thermopylae. Thermopylae in ancient times was the narrow pass through which stretched the only road from northern to southern Greece. Here in 480 b.c. Leonidas, the Spartan general, with three hundred Spartans and their allies, held back the invading Persian hordes until the pass was betrayed and its defenders perished.

3. Warsaw uprising. The heroic though unsuccessful attempt of August 1944 to drive the Nazis from the Polish capital. After the Germans crushed the revolt, they razed the city in retaliation.

4. paradigmatic. Suitable to serve as a model.

TOPICS FOR DISCUSSION

1. Discuss the pleasure and intellectual profit modern man can derive from the study of science and its historic development. How can a knowledge of science and the use of the scientific method contribute to man's moral life? How would Krutch join issue with Nagel on this point? How, in your opinion, would Glass and Oppenheimer respond?

2. What is Nagel's opinion of the moral wisdom enunciated in the past by men of little scientific knowledge of the world? How would Bush reply to this? Hutchins? Hook? Livingstone? Arnold?

3. Discuss the shortcomings Nagel finds in the claims and attitudes of certain humanists. To what extent do the essays by humanists in this collection meet Professor Nagel's objections? To what extent do you think they justify them?

4. "The critical temper, the confidently constructive rationality and the manly intelligent humility that are essential for the practice of the scientific method are not simply adornments of a well-balanced mind; they are its essence." Which other essays name these qualities of mind as peculiar to scientists and the scientific method? Are similar virtues mentioned by any of the humanists as typical of the scholar in nonscientific disciplines? Explain your answer.

5. Compare the pictures of the scientific community drawn by Oppenheimer, Nagel, Glass, and C. P. Snow. (A useful contrast to some of the details of these sketches is provided by the article "A Human Enterprise" by the physicist Harold K. Schilling in *Science*, CXXVII [June 7, 1956], 1324-27.)

RICHARD LIVINGSTONE

The Rainbow Bridge

Sir Richard Livingstone (1880-1960), classicist, received his formal education at Oxford. In the course of his long and distinguished scholarly career he was Vice-Chancellor of the Queen's University, Belfast (1924-1933), Vice-Chancellor of Oxford University (1944-1947), President of Corpus Christi College, Oxford (1933-1950), President of the Education Section of the British Association (1936), President of the Hellenic Society (1938), President of the Classical Association (1940-1941), member of the Prime Minister's Committee on the Classics (1920), and editor, with J. U. Sheppard, of the Classical Review (1920-1922). His speaking engagements in this country included lectures at Oberlin and Smith Colleges and Princeton University. A prolific writer, Sir Richard has defended the role of the classics in the contemporary world and has suggested reforms for modern education in such works as A Defense of Classical Education (1917), The Mission of Greece (1928), Greek Ideals and Modern Life (1935), Education for a World Adrift (1943), Some Tasks for Education (1947), Education and the Spirit of the Age (1952), and The Rainbow Bridge (1959).

The reader of The Rainbow Bridge would do well to compare this essay with the defense of the study of Greek civilization offered by another ardent classicist, Edith Hamilton, in "The Lessons of the Past," Saturday Evening Post, CCXXXI (September 27, 1958), 24-25. [This selection is taken from Richard Livingstone, "The Rainbow Bridge," Atlantic Monthly, CC (November 1957), 174-78.]

[174] The chief task of education is to make human beings, to develop the aptitudes and attitudes necessary for successful living. How can a classical education develop them? That is the subject of this article. "Of course it cannot," is the obvious and, I would add, unthinking reply. "Why, these peoples are antiquated. Their problems were different. Their civilization, compared to ours, was primitive. They had no airplanes, automobiles, railroads, no atomic power or electricity, not even steam." All these things can also be said of the New Testament, of Shakespeare, of Molière,[1] even of Goethe.[2] But are they, for that reason, antiquated? The criticism of the

classics which I have mentioned is due to a failure to distinguish knowledge and wisdom. Knowledge gets out-of-date—often very quickly—especially scientific knowledge. But wisdom does not. Like gold, it keeps its value, however long ago some human mind dug it up. . . .

But what is the explanation of this paradox? How can the study of two long-dead peoples be [175] any preparation for living in our modern age? This is an interesting problem, not only in itself but because it raises the general questions: What is a good education? What ought we to be seeking when we go to school or college or when we educate ourselves? What insights, what outlook, what training of the mind?

There are two types of teachers to whom we have reason to be grateful. There are those who teach us facts, who introduce us in a methodical way to a subject, lay solid foundations in it, and on these foundations raise the tower of knowledge, foursquare and firmly built. We owe much to them. But there is another, rarer type, to whom we owe more still—those teachers who have an attitude to life, an outlook on the world, that we have not met before, who open our eyes to a new point of view and teach us to see life in a new way. That is the most valuable education one ever gets and one can recognize it not so much perhaps by the impression it makes at the moment as by the way in which the mind recurs with growing understanding and gratitude to an inspiration which the passage of time does nothing to dim. The Greeks belong to this rarer type of teachers. They give, or can give, two things which everyone needs, two things which education must give if it is to be education at all; first, a certain intellectual habit and attitude of mind; second, a view of life. If education can give these two things, a right view of life and the right mental habits, it will have given us the chief equipment which we need for our voyage through the world. My suggestion is that Greek can give these two things. If so, it has a very important connection with the modern world, and it is the connection between ancient Greece and modern civilization with which this article deals—the mental habits and the attitude to life which can be learned from the Greeks. First their mental habits. What were they?

If we wish to know the nature and quality of a man's mind, we can discover it by studying his life and observing what he has achieved. So too with a nation. If we wish to know its quality, capacity, nature, genius, we have only to study what it has done, and then to ask what that nation must have been like to do this. What did the Greeks do?

In Norse mythology there is a legend of a rainbow bridge, made by the gods so that men who had earned the right could cross the deep and sundering gulf between Midgard, which is the earth, and Asgard, which is heaven. That legend reflects man's sense of the two worlds, human and superhuman, to both of which he belongs, and his instinct, often sleeping, never dead, to pass from the lower to the higher world. Earth and heaven, barbarism and civilization; these are worlds between which a deep gulf lies. But the gulf can be bridged. In Norse mythology the bridge is built by Odin[3] and the Aesir;[4] in history and fact it was built by the Greeks with a double span, the bridge of goodness and the bridge of wisdom, by which men pass from barbarism to civilization, if not from earth to heaven.

It was not an easy bridge to build. Consider, very briefly, the Greek achievement—in the form of two contrasts. If we had lived in Greece in 650 B.C., we would have thought that the sun and moon were gods, that thunder and lightning were divine weapons, that the arrows of Apollo caused influenza, that corn was the gift of Demeter, that each mountain, tree, and river was the home of a spirit. Four hundred years later, we would have known that the earth was a sphere rotating on its own axis and revolving round the sun; the circumference of the earth had been determined accurately within fifty miles; a recent astronomer had catalogued eight hundred fixed stars; and two hundred years earlier a scientist had argued that the universe was constructed of atoms in infinite space. There we have one of the great transformations of the world, one of the great steps forward in the history of man: the creation of a rational, scientific attitude to the universe. That is a bridge which the Greeks built between 600 and 300 B.C.

Human history shows nothing comparable. It is not of course the actual amount of knowledge achieved, of facts discovered. It is to have created, out of ignorance and superstition, the idea of science, the notion of a rational world. We have done infinitely more in detailed scientific discovery. But ours has been development; theirs was origination. Greek science—by which I mean the idea that the universe is rational and is capable of being explained and understood—was created in a world in which science, as we understand the word, did not exist; and to have originated science is greater than to have developed it.

That, to recur to my metaphor, is one span of the bridge leading from barbarism to civilization which the Greeks built for us—the span of reason which leads to knowledge. Now let me turn to the other span. The fact that in the dark chaos of ignorance and superstition the Greeks conceived the idea of looking at the universe and life with the eye of reason shows that they must have had unique intellectual genius. But they created something else besides science and philosophy: they created a great human ideal; and from that fact we can divine that they had a rare spiritual genius too. We have seen the contrast between man's attitude to the universe before and after Greek [176] thought, and how the Greeks built the bridge by which mankind crossed from a nonscientific view of the world to a scientific view. But they built an even more important bridge—the bridge by which it passed from barbarism to the life which caused Goethe to say that of all men the Greeks had dreamed the dream of life best.

Think of the early Greek world as we see it in the poems of Homer, a world with its splendid virtues but also full of injustice, cruelty, and superstition, a world that knew human sacrifice and believed in gods who, even as men, would have been discreditable. And then contrast with it the Greek world of the fifth century B.C., and see how in the interval the Greeks had created out of a primitive society a great spiritual life. It may seem a surprising suggestion that Greece can help us in the field of conduct, of morals. People don't always think of her in that light; art, literature, thought—yes; morality—no. But Greece and Christianity are the two supreme masters of the ethical, the spiritual life. There and nowhere else in Western civilization do we find what the modern world has largely lost: a clear philosophy of living.

Think, as I suggested, of the world of Homer; then look at two pictures: the first an ideal for the state, the second an ideal for the individual. The first, from the second book of Thucydides,[5] is Pericles'[6] political ideal for Athens:

> Our constitution is called a democracy because it is in the hands not of the few but of the many. But the laws secure equal justice for all in their private disputes. As for social standing, our practice is that a citizen who has recognized ability in some field gets public preferment— it is a question of his abilities, not of his rank. As for poverty, our practice is that if a man can do good work for the community, humbleness of condition is no bar. . . . Open and friendly in our private intercourse, in our public conduct we keep strictly within the control of law . . . we are obedient to those in authority and to the laws, more especially to those which offer protection to the oppressed.

Has any finer definition of the democratic ideal ever been written? Has any nation gone beyond that? Or contrast with the ideals of the Homeric age this conception, from the *Theaetue*[7] of Plato, of what human life should be.

> Evil, Theodorus, can never pass away, for there must always be an opposite to good. It has no place in heaven, so of necessity it haunts the mortal nature and this earthly sphere. Therefore we ought to escape from earth to heaven as quickly as we can; and the way to escape is to become like God, as far as this is possible; and the way to become like him is to become holy, good and wise.

Between 700 and 400 B.C., beside the transformation of human outlook by the creation of the scientific spirit, is another of the great transformations of the world—the creation of a rational and worthy spiritual ideal for men. During these years a real civilization emerged with incredible rapidity; amid heavy clouds a patch of the clearest sky appeared, in which of the three great lights of the human firmament—Goodness, Beauty, Truth —two at least, Beauty and Truth, shine as brightly as they have ever shone since. There is only one other movement in the spiritual history of Western civilization in any degree comparable to it in importance—what was done in Palestine between the age of the Book of Judges and the age of the New Testament.

What qualities make the Greek achievement possible? How could a people pass, in a few centuries, from Homeric to Platonic morality, from primitive views about the universe to thinking that it was composed of atoms in infinite space?

Two qualities do much to explain this achievement; and they can be divined in some Greek sayings taken from the sixth and fifth centuries B.C., if we look behind the saying to the outlook of the man who said it. "I would rather discover one scientific fact than be King of Persia" (as we might say, a Rockefeller or a Ford). "Why are we born? To contemplate the works of Nature." What sort of men were the speakers of these words, Democritus[8] and Anaxagoras?[9] What do these phrases reveal? A passionate interest in the world and curiosity about it—their own word to describe their feeling, "wonder," is better. These men do not want money or fame or pleasure, but they find the world about them extraordinarily interesting, and it seems to them a sufficient occupation to contemplate and study it. People who felt like that were singularly well-equipped to create science and philosophy. We recognize in those sayings the secret of perpetual youth, and feel in them the greatness of man—something divine and immortal emerging in this frail, sensuous, mundane, petty creature. The Greeks say in effect about the pursuit of knowledge what Antony in Shakespeare says about something very different: "The nobleness of life is to do thus."[10] That attitude of wonder in the presence of the world is a continuous quality of Greek thought.

Then there is a second quality, which again is revealed in two sentences, if, as before, we look behind the words to the spirit of the man who uttered them. "The greatness of man consists in saying what is true, and in acting according to Nature, listening to her" (Heraclitus, sixth century B.C.).[11] The second instance is a sentence from Plato:

> [177] I am one of the people who would like to be proved wrong if they say anything which is not correct, and would like to prove others wrong if they are in error; and I should not find it more disagreeable to have my own errors pointed out than to prove others wrong, for it is a greater gain to be set free from the greatest of evils [error] than to set others free.

The speaker of these words was not a common type—how many of us think it an advantage to be shown wrong? In those two passages another secret of how the Greeks came to create science and philosophy and a rational view of life is apparent. They found the world and life intensely interesting, but also they desired to see both as they really are. That again is a continuous quality of Greek literature, the instinct to see things accurately—not to rest in prejudices and preconceptions. How difficult, how salutary, how liberating! Few things are more needed in politics, amid the cant of Party, in the work of education or administration—indeed everywhere—than this desire, without bitterness or cynicism, to see things as they are. There again we see the divine in man, something human and also superhuman.

These attitudes: curiosity, the capacity for intense interest, and the power

> To bear all naked truths,
> And to envisage circumstance, all calm,

are the essential qualities for achievement in science and philosophy. (But in what field of life are they not of supreme importance?) No people have ever used the eye of the mind so steadily and effectively as the Greeks. It meets us everywhere from Homer to Epictetus.[12] Even the earliest Greek literature shows that instinct to see things without prejudice or prepossession, which is a forerunner of reason. Thus Homer writes of a war between Greeks and barbarians, but we could not tell from the *Iliad* whether he was Greek or Trojan. Thus Thucydides narrates the war in which his country was ruined; but it would be difficult to tell, except for the rare passages in which he speaks in the first person, whether he was an Athenian or a Spartan.

It is by the use of reason that the Ionians broke loose from a savage's view of the universe and argued their way through a series of hypotheses to the atomism of Democritus. It is by reason that the Greeks achieved the most difficult of all tasks, that of seeing further than the accepted conventions of their age; thus Plato, in a state where women had no education or share in public life, declared that they should have the same upbringing as men and follow the same pursuits and occupations; thus, in an age when slavery was universally accepted, Alcidamas (fifth century B.C.)[13] wrote, "God has set all men free; nature has made no one a slave"; thus, two centuries later in a world divided by race, culture, and government, Diogenes,[14] when asked what was his country, replied, "I am a citizen of the world"; and Zeno, the founder of Stoicism,[15] said, "Let us look to all men as fellow countrymen and fellow citizens, and let there be unity in our life, like that of a flock feeding together in a common pasture."

The Greeks reached these truths—Plato, the emancipation of women, Alcidamas, the abolition of slavery, Zeno, the unity of mankind—not under the pressure of social or economic trends, but by the power of reason, breaking the thought barrier of their time. It has taken mankind a long time to see as far; even today we have not seen as far as Zeno.

A trinity of virtues shines throughout Greek literature. I have mentioned two; the Greek writers find the world intensely interesting, and they try to see it as it is. The third virtue is *sophrosyne*. The word is untranslatable—the most interesting words in any language are always the words which cannot be translated, like *spirituel* in French, or "comfortable" and "gentleman" in English, for such words are characteristic of their creators and give a glimpse of their inner selves. We generally render it as "temperance"; "self-mastery" is better, but "balance" perhaps would come nearest to its meaning. It is the virtue which keeps men in the middle of the road, checks their waywardness and extravagance, saves them from the falsehood of extremes, and gives their life and thought the harmony of a fine piece of music. The literal meaning of the word is "soundness of mind"; if you have *sophrosyne*, you have health of spirit and intellect and character. Really it is reason in another aspect—the power to see things as a whole, each in its place and proportion. It is not a common virtue in human beings, as Shakespeare knew when he made Hamlet praise Horatio:

> *A man that Fortune's buffets and rewards*
> *Hast ta'en with equal thanks; and blest are these*
> *Whose blood and judgment are so well commingled*
> *That they are not a pipe for Fortune's finger*
> *To sound what stop she pleas. Give me the man*
> *That is not passion's slave, and I will wear him*
> *In my heart's core.*

That is a good description of *sophrosyne*.

Nor is *sophrosyne* a common virtue in peoples: witness the excesses of the French Revolution and the Nazi madness. But, apart from such spectacular instances of popular delirium, the history of most nations shows less destructive but equally irrational lapses from sanity. We can all think of such cases. There are plenty in Greek history, for [178] the Greeks were a passionate people; *sophrosyne*, supreme in their thought and literature, did not rule their political life. One would not recommend the study of Greek history to anyone who wished to know what *sophrosyne* is in action. If anyone wishes to see *sophrosyne* in a statesman, he could not find a better example than Abraham Lincoln.

Sophrosyne is as necessary a virtue in literature and in thought as in practical life. Can we see clearly if our eyes are bloodshot with prejudice or passion? If one of them is blind, are we likely to get things in focus? There is plenty of unbalance in the literature of the last hundred years. It is obvious in the sentimentality and facile optimism of the weaker Victorian writers; but, in a different form, it is quite as common in the generation which reacted against the Victorians, practiced the art of debunking, and, in a world often dreary and sordid, was blind to the countervailing goodness.

The irony of it is that these modern writers of whom I am speaking profess to look at the world with clear eyes, to see things as they are. But no one's eyes are clear unless they see the good in life as well as the evil. To miss the good is unbalance too, unbalance of a more dangerous kind. It is not to be found in the great Greek writers. There is plenty of gloom in them, in Homer or Pindar[16] or the tragic poets; but always, shining in the gloom, there is a sense of beauty and splendor in the world no less real than the tragedy and evil. It is best to see life as the Greeks saw it—for they saw it as it is—and to go into the world with eyes open indeed to its darker side, so that we may know what we have to face, but not to ignore the other aspect in which its growing good resides.

Yes, it may be said, but what exactly do we get by reading this literature and studying this civilization? In what way does it prepare us to live in the modern world? No doubt the Greek achievement was remarkable, indeed unique. But how does it help us now?

My reply would be that the people who did these things must have been a very remarkable people, a people with extraordinary qualities of mind, the sort of people one likes to meet, the sort of people one cannot meet without learning something from them; and when one reflects that the Greeks brought into the world the idea of science and the ideal of democracy, and when one considers their achievement in philosophy, in political thought, in poetry, in sculpture, in architecture, in the creation of an ideal of life, are not the men who did these things worth meeting? Are they not likely to be able to teach us much, not in actual facts, but if we ask from them what Elisha asked from Elijah[17]—a portrait of their spirit?. . .

NOTES

1. Molière. Pseudonym of Jean Baptiste Pocquelin (1622-1673), the greatest French writer of comedies. Among his masterpieces are *Le Misanthrope, Tartuffe, Les Précieuses Ridicules,* and *Le Malade Imaginaire.*

2. Goethe. Johann Wolfgang von Goethe (1749-1832), German poet, dramatist, novelist, philosopher, statesman, and scientist. His *Faust* (Part I, 1808; Part II, 1832) is one of the world's greatest poems.

3. Odin. The Norse name for Woden, the chief god of Teutonic mythology. He was the god of poetry, agriculture, wisdom, war, and also god of the dead.

4. Aesir. The chief gods of Scandinavian mythology; they dwelt in Asgard.

5. Thucydides. Thucydides (c. 471-400 B.C.). An Athenian historian; his great work is the *History of the Peloponnesian War.*

6. Pericles. Athenian statesman (c. 495-429 B.C.), general, orator, and patron of the arts. Leader of Athens during its Golden Age; the Parthenon was begun under his direction.

7. *Theaetue.* A Platonic dialogue on the definition of knowledge.

8. Democritus (c. 460-370 B.C.). Greek philosopher who conceived of the universe as being composed of atoms, eternal, invisible, indivisible, and indestructible.

9. Anaxagoras (500-428 B.C.). Ionian philosopher and scientist, he taught Euripides, Pericles, and possibly Socrates.

10. "The nobleness of life is to do thus." Shakespeare's *Antony and Cleopatra,* I, i; as Antony speaks these words, he embraces Cleopatra.

11. Heraclitus (fl. c. 513 B.C.). A philosopher of Ephesus; his most memorable contribution was the concept of change (flux) as the essential nature of all things.

12. Epictetus. A Stoic philosopher of the first century A.D.

13. Alcidamas (fl. fourth century B.C.). Greek rhetorician. A Sophist, he taught rhetoric in Athens. The passage to which Livingstone refers is taken from a speech in which Alcidamas urged freedom for the Messenians.

14. Diogenes (c. 412-323 B.C.). "The cynic," as this Greek philosopher was called, preached simplicity and self-control. When Alexander the Great asked what boon the philosopher craved, Diogenes requested that the monarch get out of his light.

15. Stoicism. A school of philosophy founded in the fourth century B.C., it stressed the ideal of duty and the wisdom of a life free from passion.

16. Pindar (c. 518-448 B.C.). Considered the greatest of the Greek lyric poets, he is particularly known for his mastery of the choral ode. Unfortunately, only fragments of his work are extant.

17. Elisha and Elijah. Elijah, a Hebrew prophet of the ninth century B.C., was swept, the story tells us, from this world to the next in a fiery chariot. His mantle fell upon his disciple Elisha, who asked of the older prophet, "I pray thee, let a double portion of thy spirit be upon me" (II *Kings* 2 : 9).

TOPICS FOR DISCUSSION

1. According to Livingstone, what is the goal of education? How does the study of the ancient Greeks relate to this goal?

2. In developing his case for classical studies, what distinction does this author draw between knowledge and wisdom? Discuss the symbolism of the phrase "rainbow bridge." Describe the two spans of that bridge which stretched from the age of barbarism in Greece to the age of civilization.

3. What examples does Livingstone cite of the wisdom of ancient Greece? Discuss the relevance of these for modern readers. Describe the three qualities of mind which illuminated the thinking and attitudes of the people of classical Greece. Discuss the extent to which these attributes can be useful to a citizen or a civilization beset by the crises of the twentieth century.

4. Jacob Bronowski, an English scientist, has likened a future in which a few scientific specialists would hold all power to Athens in the days of its decline, when a minority of educated men held sway over 300,000 slaves. Do you think Livingstone would consider this analogy to be valid? Why or why not?

5. Compare Livingstone's defense of classical studies with that of Matthew Arnold's. Which do you find more convincing? Why?

6. Compare Livingstone's fervent defense of the study of the past with Hook's equally fervent defense of the study of the present. Do special values lie in either study? Why or why not?

Liberal Education
in a Scientific Age

H. Bentley Glass (b. 1906) biologist and specialist on the genetic effects of atomic radiation, was born in China in 1906 of American parents. Educated at Decatur Texas Baptist College, Baylor University, and the University of Texas, he was National Research Council fellow at the University of Oslo, Norway, 1932-1933, and studied at the Kaiser-Wilhelm Institute für Biologie in Berlin in 1933. From 1936 to 1937 he was research associate of the bureau of educational research in science at Teachers College, Columbia. Currently professor of biology of Johns Hopkins University, Professor Glass has also taught at Baylor University, Stephens College, and Goucher. In 1950-1951 he was consultant to the State Department in West Germany, and from 1953 to 1955 he served as United States Delegate to the International Union of Biological Sciences. President of the American Institute of Biological Sciences 1954-1958, he has also been chairman of the advisory commission for biology and medicine of the Atomic Energy Commission as well as a member of the committee on the genetic effects of atomic radiation of the National Academy of Sciences. His writings include Genes and the Man *(1943) and* Science and Liberal Education *(1959). Professor Glass has been editor of the* Quarterly Review of Biology *and a member of the editorial board of* Science, Science Monthly, Isis, *and* Human Biology.

An interesting counterpoint to Professor Glass is provided by "Science as Cliché, Fable, and Faith," by D. J. Dooley, Bulletin of the Atomic Scientists, *XV (November 1959), 372-75. An article which sharply challenges many of the biologists' assumptions. Certain differences in tone and point of view are evident, too, in the comments of another biologist, Warren Weaver, in "Science for Everybody,"* Saturday Review, *XLV (July 7, 1962), 45-46 and in "Science and Complexity," Warren Weaver (ed.),* The Scientists Speak *(New York: Boni and Gaer, 1947), pp. 1-13. [This selection is taken from Bentley Glass, "Liberal Education in a Scien-*

tific Age," Science and Liberal Education (*Baton Rouge: Louisiana State University Press,* 1959) *pp.* 54-85.]

[60] . . . The enlargement of freedom by the technical, empirical side of science is, on the other hand, an enlargement through the extension of choice and opportunity. Man, to paraphrase Lyman Bryson,[1] is not free to choose what he has never heard of or what doesn't exist. Prior to writing and printing he could not choose to read a book; and prior to the invention of television he was not free to choose between reading a [61] book and watching a television program. Nor can he choose wisely what he has never been free to think about, whence derives the importance of freedom of the mind in a truly liberal education.

The thought may be made even more implicit [*sic*]. Science is the one most powerful means devised by the mind of man for arriving at truth in respect to the world of matter and energy, and indeed also the realm of mind and behavior. Science is the great force in human life making for change in ways of living, through increased power to alter and control the environment. Science is the greatest liberating, liberalizing force in human thought. It is obvious that in the modern world the strength of a nation, whether in war or in peace, resides in its science. The future solutions of the most critical problems of society—the problems of uncontrolled population increase and insufficient food and water, sources of energy and supplies of raw materials, and the imperative task of the mobilization of skills—lie in the applications of science. The western frontier that once challenged adventurous and imaginative youth exists no longer; the frontier of today and tomorrow is that of science—as Vannevar Bush has called it, the "Endless Horizons."*

Education, which transmits from each generation to the next the heritage of the past and the seeds of new powers yet to be, ought then to reflect the central reality of modern life. If we agree with the pragmatist that "life adjustment" is the goal of education, then paramount in such adjustment [62] must be the reckoning with science and the technology which is based upon it, as the sources of continual change in the conditions of life. If we agree with the proponents of a liberal education, we must equally recognize that science is inescapably the core of a truly liberal education.

It is a basic fault of our present theory and practice of education in the United States that the natural sciences stand apart from the social and humanistic studies, as if they were a fearsome body of technical facts and mathematical concepts, and that only. If the natural sciences are to become indeed the core of the curriculum, they must unquestionably sacrifice something of their forbidding character. Much effort must be expended to develop science courses that will avoid unnecessary jargon and that will aim

---

* Vannevar Bush, *Endless Horizons*, Public Affairs Press, Washington (1946).

not so much at the training of the technical expert as at the liberal education of the citizen. I fully agree with Mr. Conant[2] and with my predecessor
in the Mitchell Lectures, Dean DeVane, in this respect.† To understand
science one must see a problem unfold from its beginnings, see progress
impeded by traditional ways of thought, learn that scientists make mistakes
as well as achieve successes, and observe what experiments brought illumination, and why. One must ask continually, What is the evidence? One
must observe how frequently the truth of today is a synthesis of opposing
counterviews and countertheories held in their time to be irreconcilable.
And one must learn from the study of cases how varied and refractory to
definition are the methods of science. As [63] to its spirit, there is little of
that in either the conventional textbook or lecture. One meets it better in
Arrowsmith or the *Life of Pasteur*. It is born by contagion: its home is the
laboratory, the observatory, or the field, wherever the inexperienced person
can observe experience, and the novitiate partake of the zest of discovery.

In teaching science we must not forget, in other words, that it is simul-
taneously social study and creative art, a history of ideas, a philosophy, and
a supreme product of esthetic ingenuity. The graduate who has missed this
experience, whether science major or non-major, has missed the basis for a
rational judgment of today's crucial problems. He has likewise lost a revelation deep in meaning and of unending beauty. . . .

[64] We have reached a point in human history where the structure
of our civilization and its staggering technology depend [sic] vitally on the
sciences for support (the skeleton) and for new ideas and concepts (the
seeds of progress). Education, to reflect modern life, to prepare for life, to
adjust to life, must reckon with this clear reality.

A friend of mind, Dr. Warren Weaver of the Rockefeller Foundation,
argues with me that he does not "want to see science as the central core,
with the arts, letters, philosophy, and ethics, and all the rest relegated to a
less central, less dominant, less significant position. I want," he continues,
"to see science in a full partnership with other approaches to the order and
beauty of meaning of life. Science (to me) contributes *most* to our understanding of 'order,' a good deal of 'beauty' (largely via order), and still less
to 'meaning.' The humane arts start with the middle one of these three
words, contribute chiefly at that point, and spill over in each direction.
Moral philosophy starts with the third, and diffuses back to the second and
the first. If I had to assign priorities, it would be to moral philosophy."*

This is an admirable statement, and one with which I [65] could
scarcely disagree. But the argument misses my point. I have no wish to
assign priorities, but rather to emphasize the essentiality of the sciences to
modern man's concepts of beauty and meaning no less than to those of

---

† William Clyde DeVane, *The American University in the Twentieth Century*,
Louisiana State University Press, Baton Rouge (1957), pp. 51-55.
* Personal letter, March 31, 1958. [Quoted by permission.]

order. Alfred North Whitehead touched on the former when he wrote: "In his youth, the born poet often wavers between science and literature [he had mentioned Shelley]; and his choice is determined by the chance attraction of one or other of the alternative modes of expressing his imaginative joy in nature. It is essential to keep in mind, that science and poetry have the same root in human nature."† . . .

One more thing must be said. Beauty and meaning—ecstasy and apprehension of truth—may as always in the past be grasped intuitively. More and more, however, as science occupies a larger place in human life and as it transforms the condition of our existence, the area of beauty and meaning which scientific understanding reveals becomes magnified relative to the intuitive. One example may make this apparent. It requires no scientific understanding to take delight in the green of woods and meadows and the rustle of leaves in spring. But the deeper insight into the significance of green leaves which the scientific understanding of leaf structure, photosynthesis, and the ecological interdependence of living things can generate in the mind detracts not at all from intuitive appreciation, while it adds immeasurably to it. . . .

[68] To sum up the thought so far: Human life is now permeated with science; civilization rests upon scientific foundations. The sciences are the greatest educational forces in generating true freedom of the mind, and thus must in fact constitute the heart of truly liberal education. Yet the vast majority of our people have little understanding of science as a way of thinking or a method of seeking answers to problems. Superstitious awe of the magician—yes, we have far too much of that—but of the avowed adoption of a scientific approach to all sorts of human problems, how woefully little! Nor have the great scientific principles, concepts, and theories fully replaced the primitive superstitions and traditional beliefs of most men. Advertising and propaganda, based on the reiteration of obvious falsities, still dominate economic life and international relations.

Politically it has been demonstrated that a house divided against itself cannot stand. I affirm that it must also be true that a nation of microscopically few scientists molding and altering people's lives, and a populace uncomprehending, superstitious, and resistant to the novel ideas of the scientist while blandly accepting the technological fruits of these very ideas, likewise cannot endure. Somehow, and soon, [69] mankind must become truly scientific in spirit and in endeavor. Otherwise we face oligarchy, and eventual collapse of our form of civilization, our way of life. . . .

[84] The whole of nature is far beyond man's present comprehension, the edifice of science and philosophy a mere foundation, and not the completed structure it will some day be. For we hope to build of our ideas and

† Alfred North Whitehead, "Science in General Education" (1921) *Science and Philosophy* (New York: Wisdom Library, Philosophical Library, 1948), p. 207.

conceptions a cathedral, vast and beautiful, time-tested, wherein the human spirit may find strength and courage, peace and wisdom.

For this, science has its limitation as well as powers. It tells us much, but hardly everything. It can deal with matter and energy, space and form and time. It scarcely measures values; it is thwarted by intangibles. Science reveals truths, [85] but perhaps never the whole of truth. Its grandest conceptual schemes and theories may fail and have to be replaced. It is objective, not subjective, and the inner life of man is, and must always remain, subjective. Science is the product of the human mind, but what the mind is we do not know.

Science, as Bertrand Russell[3] has said, can enhance among men two great evils, war and tyranny. For the powers of science can be used for evil as well as good ends. How ironical that what I have declared to be the greatest force in liberating the mind might be turned to enslave man and destroy him! Yet this is true of all power. As man, with previously unimagined physical and biological powers in his grasp, stands lonely and afraid in the universe, it is of himself that he is afraid, of the choice he must make between good and evil.

Science, in ever greater measure, must permeate the study and teaching of each of the arts, humanities, and social studies. These, on their side, must mollify, enrich, and protect the sciences.

NOTES

1. Lyman Bryson (1888-1959), educator, author, director of CBS *Invitation to Learning*, consultant on public affairs to CBS, popularizer of the public forum.

2. Conant. James Bryant Conant (1893-   ), American educator. Professor of chemistry at Harvard (1913-1933), President of Harvard (1933-1953), United States High Commissioner in Germany (1953-1955), United States Ambassador to the Federal Republic of Germany (1955-1957). From 1957 to 1962 he conducted a study of the American high school and from 1962 to the present, he has been engaged in a study of the education of American teachers. His works include *Science and Common Sense* (1921), *Modern Science and Modern Man* (1952), *The American High School Today* (1959), *Slums and Suburbs* (1961), and *The Education of American Teachers* (1963).

3. Bertrand Russell. Bertrand Arthur William Russell, Third Earl (1872-   ), English mathematician and philosopher. Recipient of the Nobel Prize for Literature 1950. His many works include *Principia Mathematica* with A. N. Whitehead (1910-1913), *Outline of Philosophy* (1927), *Mysticism and Logic* (1918), and *The ABC of Relativity* (1925). [*Author's Note*: Bertrand Russell, *The Impact of Science on Society*, Columbia University Press, New York (1951), p. 51.]

TOPICS FOR DISCUSSION

1. Compare Glass' view of the effects of increased communication through the progress of technology with Bush's. Which view seems the more reasonable to you? Why?

2. The theme of this essay is that "science is the greatest liberating, liberalizing force in human thought." What support is offered for this statement? What support do other essayists offer? What objections may be made to the claim?

3. Does Glass feel that the core of modern man's education should be vocational or liberal? Why?

4. The author says he agrees with Professor Weaver's comment and that he has no "wish to assign priorities." Does the rest of his essay bear out this assertion in content and tone? Explain.

5. What is your reaction to Glass' belief that "the deeper insight into the significance of green leaves which the scientific understanding of leaf structure, photosynthesis, and the ecological interdependence of living things can generate in the mind" adds "immeasurably" to the individual's intuitive appreciation of the woods in spring?

6. "Civilization rests upon a scientific foundation." How would Bush reply to this assertion? Krutch? Livingstone? Nagel?

7. What are the dangers which may result from a society in which a scientifically educated few are not in communication with the nonscientifically educated many? How do other essayists treat this peculiarly modern problem of communication?

8. Does this author see any limitations to the realm of science? If so, what and why?

9. Glass writes that the arts, humanities, and social studies "must mollify, enrich, and protect the sciences." Basing your answer on the essays in this book and on your own experience, what suggestions can you make concerning interaction between the humanities and the sciences?

MATTHEW ARNOLD

Literature and Science

Matthew Arnold (1822-1888), the English poet and critic, was edu-
cated at Rugby and Oxford. Arnold served for thirty-five years as an inspec-
tor in the Education Department. His major work, however, lay in his liter-
ary and social criticism, and from 1857 to 1867 he was professor of poetry
at Oxford. His own poetry, including The Strayed Reveller and Other Poems *and* Empedocles on Etna, *was published between 1849 and 1856. Its*
lyric mood is elegiac; it speaks of a loss of a power to feel, to communicate
that is the peculiar torment of the modern world. Arnold sought through
his criticism to awaken his contemporaries from the "philistinism" of the
day—concentration on material goods to the exclusion of intellectual and
spiritual values. He preached the gospel of "culture"—the desire to know
the best that had been thought and said and to make this best prevail
among all men. He suggested "touchstones" of magnificent lines as stand-
ards for testing the value of other pieces of poetry. His influential essays
include "The Function of Criticism at the Present Time" (1864), "Sweet-
ness and Light" (1867), "The Study of Poetry" (1880), and "Literature
and Science" (1882).

This address, which Lionel Trilling calls "perhaps the classic defense
of the humanistic tradition against the attacks of positivism and science,"
was given by Arnold on his American tour (1883-1884). It is a revision of
his Rede Lecture given at Cambridge in 1882—the chief revisions occur in
the first five paragraphs. In England Arnold had used allusions particularly
suited to a Cambridge audience; in the American version he substituted the
comment on Plato and the supposed impracticality of his ideas, and added
occasional allusions to life in the United States. Arnold's Rede Lecture was
a reply to Thomas Huxley's "Science and Culture," the address given in
1882 at the opening of Sir Josiah Mason's Science College in Birmingham.
[This selection is taken from Matthew Arnold, "Literature and Science,"
The Portable Matthew Arnold, *Lionel Trilling, ed. (New York: The Vik-*
ing Press, 1962), *pp. 405-29.]*

[405] Practical people talk with a smile of Plato and of his absolute ideas;
and it is impossible to deny that Plato's ideas do often seem unpractical and

impracticable, and especially when one views them in connection with the life of a great work-a-day world like the United States. The necessary staple of the life of such a world Plato regards with disdain; handicraft and trade and the working professions he regards with disdain; but what becomes of the life of an industrial modern community if you take handicraft and trade and the working professions out of it? The base mechanic arts and handicrafts, says Plato, bring about a natural weakness in the principle of excellence in a man, so that he cannot govern the ignoble growths in him, but nurses them, and cannot understand fostering any other. Those who exercise such arts and trades, as they have their bodies, he says, marred by their vulgar businesses, so they have their souls, too, bowed and broken by them. And if one of these uncomely people has a mind to seek self-culture and philosophy, Plato compares him to a [406] bald little tinker, who has scraped together money, and has got his release from service, and has had a bath, and bought a new coat, and is rigged out like a bridegroom about to marry the daughter of his master who has fallen into poor and helpless estate.

Nor do the working professions fare any better than trade at the hands of Plato. He draws for us an inimitable picture of the working lawyer, and of his life of bondage; he shows how this bondage from his youth up has stunted and warped him, and made him small and crooked of soul, encompassing him with difficulties which he is not man enough to rely on justice and truth as means to encounter, but has recourse, for help out of them, to falsehood and wrong. And so, says Plato, this poor creature is bent and broken, and grows up from boy to man without a particle of soundness in him, although exceedingly smart and clever in his own esteem.

One cannot refuse to admire the artist who draws these pictures. But we say to ourselves that his ideas show the influence of a primitive and obsolete order of things, when the warrior caste and the priestly caste were alone in honour, and the humble work of the world was done by slaves. We have now changed all that; the modern majority consists in work, as Emerson declares; and in work, we may add, principally of such plain and dusty kind as the work of cultivators of the ground, handicraftsmen, men of trade and business, men of the working professions. Above all is this true in a great industrious community such as that of the United States.

Now education, many people go on to say, is still mainly governed by the ideas of men like Plato, who lived when the warrior caste and the priestly or philosophical class were alone in honour, and the really useful part of the community were slaves. It is an education for persons of leisure in such a community. This [407] education passed from Greece and Rome to the feudal communities of Europe, where also the warrior caste and the priestly caste were alone held in honour, and where the really useful and working part of the community, though not nominally slaves as in the pagan world, were practically not much better off than slaves, and not more seriously regarded. And how absurd it is, people end by saying, to inflict this education upon an industrious modern community, where very few indeed are persons of leisure, and the mass to be considered has not leisure, but is bound, for its own great good, and for the great good of the world at large, to plain labour and to industrial pursuits, and the education in question tends necessarily to make men dissatisfied with these pursuits and unfitted for them!

That is what is said. So far I must defend Plato, as to plead that his view of education and studies is in the general, as it seems to me, sound enough, and fitted for all sorts and conditions of men, whatever their pursuits may be. "An intelligent man," says Plato, "will prize those studies which result in his soul getting soberness, righteousness, and wisdom, and will less value the others." I cannot consider *that* a bad description of the aim of education, and of the motives which should govern us in the choice of studies, whether we are preparing ourselves for a hereditary seat in the English House of Lords or for the pork trade in Chicago.

Still I admit that Plato's world was not ours, that his scorn of trade and handicraft is fantastic, that he had no conception of a great industrial community such as that of the United States, and that such a community must and will shape its education to suit its own needs. If the usual education handed down to it from the past does not suit it, it will certainly before long drop this and try another. The usual education in the past has been mainly [408] literary. The question is whether the studies which were long supposed to be the best for all of us are practically the best now; whether others are not better. The tyranny of the past, many think, weighs on us injuriously in the predominance given to letters in education. The question is raised whether to meet the needs of our modern life, the predominance ought not now to pass from letters to science; and naturally the question is nowhere raised with more energy than here in the United States. The design of abasing what is called "mere literary instruction and education," and of exalting what is called "sound, extensive, and practical scientific knowledge," is, in this intensely modern world of the United States, even more perhaps than in Europe, a very popular design, and makes great and rapid progress.

I am going to ask whether the present movement for ousting letters from their old predominance in education, and for transferring the predominance in education to the natural sciences, whether this brisk and flourishing movement ought to prevail, and whether it is likely that in the end it really will prevail. An objection may be raised which I will anticipate. My own studies have been almost wholly in letters, and my visits to the field of the natural sciences have been very slight and inadequate, although those sciences have always strongly moved my curiosity. A man of letters, it will perhaps be said, is not competent to discuss the comparative merits of letters and natural science as means of education. To this objection I reply, first of all, that his incompetence, if he attempts the discussion but is really incompetent for it, will be abundantly visible; nobody will be taken in; he will have plenty of sharp observers and critics to save mankind from that danger. But the line I am going to follow is, as you will soon discover, so extremely simple, that perhaps it may be followed [409] without failure even by one who for a more ambitious line of discussion would be quite incompetent.

Some of you may possibly remember a phrase of mine which has been the object of a good deal of comment; an observation to the effect that in our culture, the aim being *to know ourselves and the world*, we have, as the means to this end, *to know the best which has been thought and said in the world*. A man of science, who is also an excellent writer and the very prince of debaters, Professor Huxley,[1] in a discourse at the opening of Sir Josiah Mason's[2] college at Birmingham, laying hold of this phrase, expanded it by quoting some more words of mine, which are these: "The civilised world is to be regarded as now being, for intellectual and spiritual purposes, one great confederation, bound to a joint action and working to a common result; and whose members have for their proper outfit a knowledge of Greek, Roman, and Eastern antiquity, and of one another. Special local and temporary advantages being put out of account, that modern nation will in the intellectual and spiritual sphere make most progress, which most thoroughly carries out this programme."

Now on my phrase, thus enlarged, Professor Huxley remarks that when I speak of the above-mentioned knowledge as enabling us to know ourselves and the world, I assert *literature* to contain the materials which suffice for thus making us know ourselves and the world. But it is not by any means clear, says he, that after having learnt all which ancient and modern literatures have to tell us, we have laid a sufficiently broad and deep foundation for that criticism of life, that knowledge of ourselves and the world, which constitutes culture. On the contrary, Professor Huxley declares that he finds himself "wholly unable to admit that either nations or individuals will really advance, if their outfit draws nothing [410] from the stores of physical science. An army without weapons of precision, and with no particular base of operations, might more hopefully enter upon a campaign on the Rhine, than a man, devoid of a knowledge of what physical science has done in the last century, upon a criticism of life."

This shows how needful it is for those who are to discuss any matter together, to have a common understanding as to the sense of the terms they employ,—how needful, and how difficult. What Professor Huxley says, implies just the reproach which is so often brought against the study of *belles lettres*, as they are called: that the study is an elegant one, but slight and ineffectual; a smattering of Greek and Latin and other ornamental things, of little use for any one whose object is to get at truth, and to be a practical man. So, too, M. Renan[3] talks of the "superficial humanism" of a school-course which treats us as if we were all going to be poets, writers, preachers, orators, and he opposes this humanism to positive science, or the critical search after truth. And there is always a tendency in those who are remonstrating against the predominance of letters in education to understand by letters *belles lettres*, and by *belles lettres* a superficial humanism, the opposite of science or true knowledge.

But when we talk of knowing Greek and Roman antiquity, for instance, which is the knowledge people have called the humanities, I for my part mean a knowledge which is something more than a superficial humanism, mainly decorative. "I call all teaching *scientific*," says Wolf,[4] the critic of Homer, "which is systematically laid out and followed up to its original sources. For example: a knowledge of classical antiquity is scientific when the remains of classical antiquity are correctly studied in the original languages." There can be no [411] doubt that Wolf is perfectly right; that all learning is scientific which is systematically laid out and followed up to its original sources, and that a genuine humanism is scientific.

When I speak of knowing Greek and Roman antiquity, therefore, as a help to knowing ourselves and the world, I mean more than a knowledge of so much vocabulary, so much grammar, so many portions of authors in the Greek and Latin languages. I mean knowing the Greeks and Romans, and their life and genius, and what they were and did in the world; what we get from them, and what is its value. That, at least, is the ideal: and when we talk of endeavouring to know Greek and Roman antiquity, as a help to knowing ourselves and the world, we mean endeavouring so to know them as to satisfy this ideal, however much we may still fall short of it.

The same also as to knowing our own and other modern nations, with the like aim of getting to understand ourselves and the world. To know the best that has been thought and said by the modern nations is to know, says Professor Huxley, "only what modern *literatures* have to tell us; it is the criticism of life contained in modern literature." And yet "the distinctive character of our times," he urges, "lies in the vast and constantly increasing part which is played by natural knowledge." And how, therefore, can a man, devoid of knowledge of what physical science has done in the last century, enter hopefully upon a criticism of modern life?

Let us, I say, be agreed about the meaning of the terms we are using. I talk of knowing the best which has been thought and uttered in the world; Professor Huxley says this means knowing *literature*. Literature is a large word; it may mean everything written with letters or printed in a book. Euclid's *Elements*[5] and Newton's *Principia* are thus literature. All knowledge that [412] reaches us through books is literature. But by literature Professor Huxley means *belles lettres*. He means to make me say, that knowing the best which has been thought and said by the modern nations is knowing their *belles lettres* and no more. And this is no sufficient equipment, he argues, for a criticism of modern life. But as I do not mean, by knowing ancient Rome, knowing merely more or less of Latin *belles lettres*, and taking no account of Rome's military, and political, and legal, and administrative work in the world; and as, by knowing ancient Greece, I understand knowing her as the giver of Greek art, and the guide to a free and right use of reason and to scientific method, and the founder of our mathematics and physics and astronomy and biology,—I understand knowing her as all this, and not merely knowing certain Greek poems, and histories, and treatises, and speeches,—so as to the knowledge of modern nations also. By knowing modern nations, I mean not merely knowing their *belles lettres*, but knowing also what has been done by such men as Copernicus,[6] Galileo,[7] Newton,[8] Darwin.[9] "Our ancestors learned," says Professor Huxley, "that the earth is the centre of the visible universe, and that man is the cynosure of things terrestrial; and more especially was it inculcated that the course of nature had no fixed order, but that it could be, and constantly was, altered." But for us now, continues Professor Huxley, "the notions of the beginning and the end of the world entertained by our forefathers are no longer credible. It is very certain that the earth is not the chief body in the material universe, and that the world is not subordinated to man's use. It is even more certain that nature is the expression of a definite order, with which nothing interferes. And yet," he cries, "the purely classical education advocated by the representatives of the humanists in our day gives no inkling of all this!"

[413] In due place and time I will just touch upon that vexed question of classical education; but at present the question is as to what is meant by knowing the best which modern nations have thought and said. It is not knowing their *belles lettres* merely which is meant. To know Italian *belles lettres* is not to know Italy, and to know English *belles lettres* is not to know England. Into knowing Italy and England there comes a great deal more, Galileo and Newton, amongst it. The reproach of being a superficial humanism, a tincture of *belles lettres*, may attach rightly enough to some other disciplines; but to the particular discipline recommended when I proposed knowing the best that has been thought and said in the world it does not apply. In that best I certainly include what in modern times has been thought and said by the great observers and knowers of nature.

There is, therefore, really no question between Professor Huxley and me as to whether knowing the great results of the modern scientific study of nature is not required as a part of our culture, as well as knowing the products of literature and art. But to follow the processes by which those results are reached, ought, say the friends of physical science, to be made the staple of education for the bulk of mankind. And here there does arise a question between those whom Professor Huxley calls with playful sarcasm "the Levites[10] of culture," and those whom the poor humanist is sometimes apt to regard as its Nebuchadnezzars.[11]

The great results of the scientific investigation of nature we are agreed upon knowing, but how much of our study are we bound to give to the processes by which those results are reached? The results have their visible bearing on human life. But all the processes, too, all the items of fact, by which those results are reached and established, are interesting. All knowledge is interesting [414] to a wise man, and the knowledge of nature is interesting to all men. It is very interesting to know, that, from the albuminous white of the egg, the chick in the egg gets the materials for its flesh, bones, blood, and feathers; while, from the fatty yolk of the egg, it gets the heat and energy which enable it at length to break its shell and begin the world. It is less interesting, perhaps, but still it is interesting, to know that when a taper burns, the wax is converted into carbonic acid and water. Moreover, it is quite true that the habit of dealing with facts, which is given by the study of nature, is, as the friends of physical science praise it for being, an excellent discipline. The appeal, in the study of nature, is constantly to observation and experiment; not only is it said that the thing is so, but we can be made to see that it is so. Not only does a man tell us that when a taper burns the wax is converted into carbonic acid and water, as a man may tell us, if he likes, that Charon[12] is punting his ferry-boat on the river Styx, or that Victor Hugo[13] is a sublime poet, or Mr. Gladstone[14] the most admirable of statesmen; but we are made to see that the conversion into carbonic acid and water does actually happen. This reality of natural knowledge it is, which makes the friends of physical science contrast it, as a knowledge of things, with the humanist's knowledge, which is, say they, a knowledge of words. And hence Professor Huxley is moved to lay it down that, "for the purpose of attaining real culture, an exclusively scientific education is at least as effectual as an exclusively literary education." And a certain President of the Section for Mechanical Science in the British Association is, in Scripture phrase, "very bold," and declares that if a man, in his mental training, "has substituted literature and history for natural science, he has chosen the less useful alternative." But whether we go these lengths [415] or not, we must all admit that in natural science the habit gained of dealing with facts is a most valuable discipline, and that every one should have some experience of it.

More than this, however, is demanded by the reformers. It is proposed to make the training in natural science the main part of education, for the great majority of mankind at any rate. And here, I confess, I part company with the friends of physical science, with whom up to this point I have been agreeing. In differing from them, however, I wish to proceed with the utmost caution and diffidence. The smallness of my own acquaintance with the disciplines of natural science is ever before my mind, and I am fearful of doing these disciplines an injustice. The ability and pugnacity of the partisans of natural science makes them formidable persons to contradict. The tone of tentative inquiry, which befits a being of dim faculties and bounded knowledge, is the tone I would wish to take and not to depart from. At present it seems to me, that those who are for giving to natural knowledge, as they call it, the chief place in the education of the majority of mankind, leave one important thing out of their account: the constitution of human nature. But I put this forward on the strength of some facts not at all recondite, very far from it; facts capable of being stated in the simplest possible fashion, and to which, if I so state them, the man of science will, I am sure, be willing to allow their due weight.

Deny the facts altogether, I think, he hardly can. He can hardly deny, that when we set ourselves to enumerate the powers which go to the building up of human life, and say that they are the power of conduct, the power of intellect and knowledge, the power of beauty, and the power of social life and manners,—he can hardly deny that this scheme, though drawn in rough [416] and plain lines enough, and not pretending to scientific exactness, does yet give a fairly true representation of the matter. Human nature is built up by these powers; we have the need for them all. When we have rightly met and adjusted the claims of them all, we shall then be in a fair way for getting soberness and righteousness, with wisdom. This is evident enough, and the friends of physical science would admit it.

But perhaps they may not have sufficiently observed another thing: namely, that the several powers just mentioned are not isolated, but there is, in the generality of mankind, a perpetual tendency to relate them one to another in divers ways. With one such way of relating them I am particularly concerned now. Following our instinct for intellect and knowledge, we acquire pieces of knowledge; and presently, in the generality of men, there arises the desire to relate these pieces of knowledge to our sense for conduct, to our sense for beauty,—and there is weariness and dissatisfaction if the desire is baulked. Now in this desire lies, I think, the strength of that hold which letters have upon us.

All knowledge is, as I said just now, interesting; and even items of knowledge which from the nature of the case cannot well be related, but must stand isolated in our thoughts, have their interest. Even lists of exceptions have their interest. If we are studying Greek accents, it is interesting to know that *pais* and *pas*, and some other monosyllables of the same form of declension, do not take the circumflex upon the last syllable of the genitive plural, but vary, in this respect, from the common rule. If we are studying physiology, it is interesting to know that the pulmonary artery carries dark blood and the pulmonary vein carries bright blood, departing in this respect from the common rule for the division of labour between the veins and the arteries. But [417] every one knows how we seek naturally to combine the pieces of our knowledge together, to bring them under general rules, to relate them to principles; and how unsatisfactory and tiresome it would be to go on for ever learning lists of exceptions, or accumulating items of fact which must stand isolated.

Well, the same need of relating our knowledge, which operates here within the sphere of our knowledge itself, we shall find operating, also, outside that sphere. We experience, as we go on learning and knowing,—the vast majority of us experience,—the need of relating what we have learnt and known to the sense which we have in us for conduct, to the sense which we have in us for beauty.

A certain Greek prophetess of Mantineia in Arcadia, Diotima by name, once explained to the philosopher Socrates that love, and impulse, and bent of all kinds, is, in fact, nothing else but the desire in men that good should for ever be present to them. This desire for good, Diotima assured Socrates, is our fundamental desire, of which fundamental desire every impulse in us is only some one particular form. And therefore this fundamental desire it is, I suppose,—this desire in men that good should be for ever present to them,—which acts in us when we feel the impulse for relating our knowledge to our sense for conduct and to our sense for beauty. At any rate, with men in general the instinct exists. Such is human nature. And the instinct, it will be admitted, is innocent, and human nature is preserved by our following the lead of its innocent instincts. Therefore, in seeking to gratify this instinct in question, we are following the instinct of self-preservation in humanity.

But, no doubt, some kinds of knowledge cannot be made to directly serve the instinct in question, cannot be directly related to the sense for beauty, to the sense [418] for conduct. These are instrument-knowledges; they lead on to other knowledges, which can. A man who passes his life in instrument-knowledges is a specialist. They may be invaluable as instruments to something beyond, for those who have the gift thus to employ them; and they may be disciplines in themselves wherein it is useful for every one to have some schooling. But it is inconceivable that the generality of men should pass all their mental life with Greek accents or with formal logic. My friend Professor Sylvester,[15] who is one of the first mathematicians in the world, holds transcendental doctrines as to the virtue of mathematics, but those doctrines are not for common men. In the very Senate House and heart of our English Cambridge I once ventured, though not without an apology for my profaneness, to hazard the opinion that for the majority of mankind a little of mathematics, even, goes a long way. Of course this is quite consistent with their being of immense importance as an instrument to something else; but it is the few who have the aptitude for thus using them, not the bulk of mankind.

The natural sciences do not, however, stand on the same footing with these instrument-knowledges. Experience shows us that the generality of men will find more interest in learning that when a taper burns, the wax is converted into carbonic acid and water, or in learning the explanation of the phenomenon of dew, or in learning how the circulation of the blood is carried on, than they find in learning that the genitive plural of *pais* and *pas* does not take the circumflex on the termination. And one piece of natural knowledge is added to another, and others are added to that, and at last we come to propositions so interesting as Mr. Darwin's famous proposition that "our ancestor was a hairy quadruped furnished with a tail and pointed ears, probably arboreal in his [419] habits." Or we come to propositions of such reach and magnitude as those which Professor Huxley delivers, when he says that the notions of our forefathers about the beginning and the end of the world were all wrong, and that nature is the expression of a definite order with which nothing interferes.

Interesting, indeed, these results of science are, important they are, and we should all of us be acquainted with them. But what I now wish you to mark is, that we are still, when they are propounded to us and we receive them, we are still in the sphere of intellect and knowledge. And for the generality of men there will be found, I say, to arise, when they have duly taken in the proposition that their ancestor was "a hairy quadruped furnished with a tail and pointed ears, probably arboreal in his habits," there will be found to arise an invincible desire to relate this proposition to the sense in us for conduct, and to the sense in us for beauty. But this the men of science will not do for us, and will hardly even profess to do. They will give us other pieces of knowledge, other facts, about other animals and their ancestors, or about plants, or about stones, or about stars; and they may finally bring us to those great "general conceptions of the universe, which are forced upon us all," says Professor Huxley, "by the progress of physical science." But still it will be *knowledge* only which they give us; knowledge not put for us into relation with our sense for conduct, our sense for beauty, and touched with emotion by being so put; not thus put for us, and therefore, to the majority of mankind, after a certain while, unsatisfying, wearying.

Not to the born naturalist, I admit. But what do we mean by a born naturalist? We mean a man in whom the zeal for observing nature is so uncommonly strong and eminent, that it marks him off from the bulk of man- [420] kind. Such a man will pass his life happily in collecting natural knowledge and reasoning upon it, and will ask for nothing, or hardly anything, more. I have heard it said that the sagacious and admirable naturalist whom we lost not very long ago, Mr. Darwin, once owned to a friend that for his part he did not experience the necessity for two things which most men find so necessary to them,—religion and poetry; science and the domestic affections, he thought, were enough. To a born naturalist, I can well understand that this should seem so. So absorbing is his occupation with nature, so strong his love for his occupation, that he goes on acquiring natural knowledge and reasoning upon it, and has little time or inclination for thinking about getting it related to the desire in man for conduct, the desire in man for beauty. He relates it to them for himself as he goes along, so far as he feels the need; and he draws from the domestic affections all the additional solace necessary. But then Darwins are extremely rare. Another great and admirable master of natural knowledge, Faraday,[16] was a Sande-manian. That is to say, he related his knowledge to his instinct for conduct and to his instinct for beauty, by the aid of that respectable Scottish sec-tary, Robert Sandeman. And so strong, in general, is the demand of religion and poetry to have their share in a man, to associate themselves with his knowing, and to relieve and rejoice it, that, probably, for one man amongst us with the disposition to do as Darwin did in this respect, there are at least fifty with the disposition to do as Faraday.

Education lays hold upon us, in fact, by satisfying this demand. Profes-sor Huxley holds up to scorn mediaeval education, with its neglect of the knowledge of nature, its poverty even of literary studies, its formal logic devoted to "showing how and why that which the Church said was true must be true." But the great [421] mediaeval Universities were not brought into being, we may be sure, by the zeal for giving a jejune and contemptible education. Kings have been their nursing fathers, and queens have been their nursing mothers, but not for this. The mediaeval Universi-ties came into being, because the supposed knowledge, delivered by Scrip-ture and the Church, so deeply engaged men's hearts, by so simply, easily, and powerfully relating itself to their desire for conduct, their desire for beauty. All other knowledge was dominated by this supposed knowledge and was subordinated to it, because of the surpassing strength of the hold which it gained upon the affections of men, by allying itself profoundly with their sense for conduct, their sense for beauty.

But now, says Professor Huxley, conceptions of the universe fatal to the notions held by our forefathers have been forced upon us by physical science. Grant to him that they are thus fatal, that the new conceptions must and will soon become current everywhere, and that every one will finally perceive them to be fatal to the beliefs of our forefathers. The need of humane letters, as they are truly called, because they serve the para-mount desire in men that good should be for ever present to them,—the need of humane letters, to establish a relation between the new concep-tions, and our instinct for beauty, our instinct for conduct, is only the more visible. The Middle Age could do without humane letters, as it could do without the study of nature, because its supposed knowledge was made to engage its emotions so powerfully. Grant that the supposed knowledge dis-appears, its power of being made to engage the emotions will of course disappear along with it,—but the emotions themselves, and their claim to be engaged and satisfied, will remain. Now if we find by experience that humane letters have an undeniable power of [422] engaging the emotions, the importance of humane letters in a man's training becomes not less, but greater, in proportion to the success of modern science in extirpating what it calls "mediaeval thinking."

Have humane letters, then, have poetry and eloquence, the power here attributed to them of engaging the emotions, and do they exercise it? And if they have it and exercise it, *how* do they exercise it, so as to exert an influence upon man's sense for conduct, his sense for beauty? Finally, even if they both can and do exert an influence upon the senses in question, how are they to relate to them the results,—the modern results,—of natural science? All these questions may be asked. First, have poetry and eloquence the power of calling out the emotions? The appeal is to experience. Experience shows that for the vast majority of men, for mankind in general, they have the power. Next, do they exercise it? They do. But then, *how* do they exercise it so as to affect man's sense for conduct, his sense for beauty? And this is perhaps a case for applying the Preacher's words: "Though a man labour to seek it out, yet he shall not find it; yea, farther, though a wise man think to know it, yet shall he not be able to find it."* Why should it be one thing, in its effect upon the emotions, to say with Homer,

τλητὸν γὰρ Μοῖραι θυμὸν θέσαν ἀνθρώποισιν—

"for an enduring heart have the destinies appointed to the children of men"?† Why should it be one thing, in its effect upon the emotions, to say with the philosopher Spinoza,[17] *Felicitas in eo consistit quod homo suum esse* [423] *conservare potest*—"Man's happiness consists in his being able to preserve his own essence," and quite another thing, in its effect upon the emotions, to say with the Gospel, "What is a man advantaged, if he gain the whole world, and lose himself, forfeit himself?" How does this difference of effect arise? I cannot tell, and I am not much concerned to know; the important thing is that it does arise, and that we can profit by it. But how, finally, are poetry and eloquence to exercise the power of relating the modern results of natural science to man's instinct for conduct, his instinct for beauty? And here again I answer that I do not know *how* they will exercise it, but that they can and will exercise it I am sure. I do not mean that modern philosophical poets and modern philosophical moralists are to come and relate for us, in express terms, the results of modern scientific research to our instinct for conduct, our instinct for beauty. But I mean that we shall find, as a matter of experience, if we know the best that has been thought and uttered in the world, we shall find that the art and poetry and eloquence of men who lived, perhaps, long ago, who had the most limited natural knowledge, who had the most erroneous conceptions about many important matters, we shall find that this art, and poetry, and eloquence, have in fact not only the power of refreshing and delighting us, they have also the power,—such is the strength and worth, in essentials, of their authors' criticism of life,—they have a fortifying, and elevating, and quickening, and suggestive power, capable of wonderfully helping us to relate the results of modern science to our need for conduct, our need for beauty. Homer's conceptions of the physical universe were, I imagine, gro-

* Ecclesiastes viii, 17.
† *Iliad* xxiv, 49.

tesque; but really, under the shock of hearing from modern science that
"the world is not subordinated to [424] man's use, and that man is not the
cynosure of things terrestrial," I could, for my own part, desire no better
comfort from Homer's line which I quoted just now,

τλητὸν γὰρ Μοῖραι θυμὸν θέσαν ἀνθρώποισιν—

"for an enduring heart have the destinies appointed to the children of
men!"

And the more that men's minds are cleared, the more that the results
of science are frankly accepted, the more that poetry and eloquence come to
be received and studied as what in truth they really are,—the criticism of
life by gifted men, alive and active with extraordinary power at an unusual
number of points;—so much the more will the value of humane letters, and
of art also, which is an utterance having a like kind of power with theirs, be
felt and acknowledged, and their place in education be secured.

Let us therefore, all of us, avoid indeed as much as possible any invidi-
ous comparison between the merits of humane letters, as means of education, and the merits of the natural sciences. But when some President of a
Section for Mechanical Science insists on making the comparison, and tells
us that "he who in his training has substituted literature and history for
natural science has chosen the less useful alternative," let us make answer to
him that the student of humane letters only, will, at least, know also the
great general conceptions brought in by modern physical science; for science, as Professor Huxley says, forces them upon us all. But the student of
the natural sciences only, will, by our very hypothesis, know nothing of
humane letters; not to mention that in setting himself to be perpetually
accumulating natural knowledge, he sets himself to do what only specialists
have in general the gift for doing genially. And so he will probably be unsat-
isfied, or at any rate incomplete, and even [425] more incomplete than the
student of humane letters only.

I once mentioned in a school-report, how a young man in one of our
English training colleges having to paraphrase the passage in *Macbeth* beginning,

Can'st thou not minister to a mind diseased?

turned this line into, "Can you not wait upon the lunatic?" And I remarked
what a curious state of things it would be, if every pupil of our national
schools knew, let us say, that the moon is two thousand one hundred and
sixty miles in diameter, and thought at the same time that a good paraphrase for

Can'st thou not minister to a mind diseased?

was, "Can you not wait upon the lunatic?" If one is driven to choose, I
think I would rather have a young person ignorant about the moon's diame-

ter, but aware that "Can you not wait upon the lunatic?" is bad, than a young person whose education had been such as to manage things the other way.

Or to go higher than the pupils of our national schools. I have in my mind's eye a member of our British Parliament who comes to travel here in America, who afterwards relates his travels, and who shows a really masterly knowledge of the geology of this great country and of its mining capabilities, but who ends by gravely suggesting that the United States should borrow a prince from our Royal Family, and should make him their king, and should create a House of Lords of great landed proprietors after the pattern of ours; and then America, he thinks, would have her future happily and perfectly secured. Surely, in this case, the President of the Section for Mechanical Science would himself hardly say that our member of Parliament, by concentrating himself [426] upon geology and mineralogy, and so on, and not attending to literature and history, had "chosen the more useful alternative."

If then there is to be separation and option between humane letters on the one hand, and the natural sciences on the other, the great majority of mankind, all who have not exceptional and overpowering aptitudes for the study of nature, would do well. I cannot but think, to choose to be educated in humane letters rather than in the natural sciences. Letters will call out their being at more points, will make them live more.

I said that before I ended I would just touch on the question of classical education, and I will keep my word. Even if literature is to retain a large place in our education, yet Latin and Greek, say the friends of progress, will certainly have to go. Greek is the grand offender in the eyes of these gentlemen. The attackers of the established course of study think that against Greek, at any rate, they have irresistible arguments. Literature may perhaps be needed in education, they say; but why on earth should it be Greek literature? Why not French or German? Nay, "has not an Englishman models in his own literature of every kind of excellence?" As before, it is not on any weak pleadings of my own that I rely for convincing the gainsayers; it is on the constitution of human nature itself, and on the instinct of self-preservation in humanity. The instinct for beauty is set in human nature, as surely as the instinct for knowledge is set there, or the instinct for conduct. If the instinct for beauty is served by Greek literature and art as it is served by no other literature and art, we may trust to the instinct of self-preservation in humanity for keeping Greek as part of our culture. We may trust to it for even making the study of Greek more prevalent than it is now. Greek will come, I hope, some day to be studied [427] more rationally than at present; but it will be increasingly studied as men increasingly feel the need in them for beauty, and how powerfully Greek art and Greek literature can serve this need. . . .

[428] And so we at last find, it seems, we find flowing in favour of the

humanities the natural and necessary stream of things, which seemed against them when we started. The "hairy quadruped furnished with a tail and pointed ears, probably arboreal in his habits," this good fellow carried hidden in his nature, apparently, something destined to develop into a necessity for humane letters. Nay, more; we seem finally to be even led to the further conclusion that our hairy ancestor carried in his nature, also, a necessity for Greek.

And therefore, to say the truth, I cannot really think that humane letters are in much actual danger of being thrust out from their leading place in education, in spite of the array of authorities against them at this moment. So long as human nature is what it is, their attractions will remain irresistible. As with Greek, so with letters generally: they will some day come, we may hope, to be studied more rationally, but they will not lose their place. What will happen will rather be that there will be crowded into education other matters besides, far too many; there will be, perhaps, a period of unsettlement and confusion and false tendency; but letters will not in the end lose their leading place. If they lose it for a time, they will get it back again. We shall be brought back to them by our wants and aspirations. And a poor humanist may possess his soul in patience, neither strive nor cry, admit the energy and brilliancy of the partisans of physical science, and their present favour with the public, to be far greater than his own, and still have a [429] happy faith that the nature of things works silently on behalf of the studies which he loves, and that, while we shall all have to acquaint ourselves with the great results reached by modern science, and to give ourselves as much training in its disciplines as we can conveniently carry, yet the majority of men will always require humane letters; and so much the more, as they have the more and the greater results of science to relate to the need in man for conduct, and to the need in him for beauty.

NOTES

1. Professor Huxley. Thomas Henry Huxley.
2. Sir Josiah Mason (1795-1881). English manufacturer and philanthropist. His Scientific College in Birmingham, which opened in 1880, cost him £180,000. Other of his philanthropies included almshouses for the aged and orphanages.
3. M. Renan. Ernest Renan (1823-1892), French philologist and historian, particularly famous for his *Vie de Jésus*, a rationalistic treatment of Christ as a most admirable human being.
4. Wolf. Friedrich August Wolf (1759-1824), German philologist and critic. His *Prolegomena ad Homerum* (1795) gave rise to the "Homeric question" by denying the unity of Homer, and initiated the "higher criticism" by using textual and philological evidence to support its position.
5. Euclid's *Elements*. Euclid (fl. c. 300 B.C.), Greek mathematician; the geometrical problems and theorems that comprise his *Elements* form the basis of traditional geometry.

6. Copernicus (1473-1543). Polish astronomer. His *De Revolutionibus Orbium Coelestium* (1543), with its description of a heliocentric system, became the foundation of modern astronomy.

7. Galileo (1564-1642). Italian astronomer and physicist. Famous for his treatise on the specific gravity of solid bodies, his construction of the first complete astronomical telescope, his observations with the new, improved telescope, and his defense of the Copernican system which brought him into conflict with the Inquisition.

8. Newton. Sir Isaac Newton (1642-1727), English mathematician and philosopher. Particularly influential were his contributions to the study of light and his formulation of the law of universal gravitation and of the laws of motion.

9. Darwin. Charles Robert Darwin (1809-1882), English naturalist. His *Origin of Species* (1859), which sets forth his theory of evolution (Darwinism), aroused considerable controversy in the nineteenth century and has exerted tremendous influence from his time to the present day.

10. Levites of culture. The Levites, descendents of Levi (a son of Jacob and Leah) were dedicated to religious service; the Old Testament describes their services as priests and as teachers of the law.

11. Nebuchadnezzers. Nebuchadnezzer (c. 604-562 B.C.), king of Babylon, conqueror and oppressor of the Jewish people. By this allusion Arnold is suggesting ironically that the scientists may prove the conquerors and oppressors of the humanities.

12. "Charon . . . Styx." In Greek mythology Charon, son of Erebos, ferried the shades of the dead across the Styx, the principal river in Hades, the Greek underworld.

13. Victor Hugo (1802-1885). French poet (*La Légende des Siècles* [1859-1883], *Les Châtiments* [1853], *Les Contemplations* [1856]); dramatist (*Hernani* [1830]); novelist (*Les Misérables* [1862]), leader of the French romanticists and, as the reference in the text makes clear, no favorite of Matthew Arnold's.

14. Mr. Gladstone. William Gladstone (1809-1898), English statesman, leader of the Liberal Party; prime minister 1868-1874; 1880-1885; 1886 (briefly); 1892-1893. Arnold, who called himself a "liberal of the future," differed considerably from and with the liberals of his time.

15. Professor Sylvester. James Joseph Sylvester (1814-1897), English mathematician. Professor at the University of Virginia, at the Royal Military Academy in England, first professor of mathematics at Johns Hopkins, and (1883-1894) professor of geometry at Oxford.

16. Faraday. Michael Faraday (1791-1867), English physicist and chemist; among his notable discoveries were electromagnetic induction (1831), the magnetization of light (1845), and diamagnetism. The discovery of electromagnetic induction made possible in time the modern dynamo and the electric motor.

17. Spinoza. Baruch or Benedict Spinoza (1632-1677) was born in Holland to a family of Spanish or Portuguese Jews. Though he earned his modest living as a lens grinder, he yet became so esteemed for his learning and philosophical speculation that in 1673 he was offered a professorship at the University of Heidelberg. He did not accept. His greatest philosophical work, *Ethics*, completed in 1675, was first published in 1677 as part of his *Opera Posthuma*. It was later admired by such literary men as Lessing, Herder, and Goethe, and, through the teaching

of such philosophers as Fichte, Schelling, and Hegel it was to exert enormous influence on modern German philosophy.

TOPICS FOR DISCUSSION

1. What is the relevance of Plato to Arnold's topic and to his audience? How do Plato's ideas of the aim of education compare with Huxley's? Maritain's? Ortega y Gasset's? Hutchins'?

2. Define the term *belles lettres*. Discuss the different meanings which underlie Arnold's and Huxley's use of the term *literature*.

3. In what sense does Arnold [p. 410] use the term *scientific*?

4. What assumption underlies Arnold's claim that the humanities are absolutely essential to man? What place, if any, does he make for science in his scheme of education? Compare his opinion on this point with Huxley's.

5. C. P. Snow in the Rede Lecture for 1959 is concerned with the gap between the scientific and nonscientific world. Does Arnold, in his 1882 lecture, indicate that he is conscious of such a problem? Does he offer any solution?

6. What strategy does Arnold use to make it seem that Huxley—indeed, that everyone—must come to agree with his estimate of humanistic studies? What variations of tone (e.g., irony, self-deprecation, indignation) does the essay use? What details seem particularly appropriate for the audience he is addressing?

7. Keeping in mind the comments of other essayists on modern man's relationship to the humanities and to the sciences, discuss Arnold's concluding statement: ". . . yet the majority of men will always require humane letters; and so much the more, as they have the more and the greater results of science to relate to the need in man for conduct, and to the need in him for beauty."

THOMAS HENRY HUXLEY

On Science and Art
in Relation to Education

Thomas Henry Huxley (1825-1895), English biologist, writer, teacher, and lecturer. For thirty-one years Huxley taught at the Royal School of Mines. From 1874 to 1877 he was rector of Aberdeen University. In 1883 he was Rede lecturer at Cambridge, and for four years (1881-1885) President of the Royal Society. Called "Darwin's bull-dog" because of his enthusiasm in defending and popularizing Darwin's evolutionary theory, Huxley was particularly notable in his genius for conveying scientific material to nonscientific audiences. His works include texts in physiology and biology, Essays upon some Controverted Questions, *and* Evolution and Ethics *(1893).*

The following address was given by Huxley in 1882 to members of the Liverpool Institution. It is included here in preference to the 1880 lecture "Science and Culture" (the address that challenged Arnold and that Arnold in turn answered in "Literature and Science") because this later piece shows Huxley taking into consideration the extremes to which some supporters of the sciences may go in their plans for education and carefully differentiating his own stand from that of the "scientific Goths and Vandals." He begins the 1882 address by noting that fourteen years earlier he had given a speech in Liverpool on the subject of Scientific Education, and that he will now elaborate on three or four propositions he discussed at that time. Then follows the address given here, with the exception of seven autobiographical paragraphs. [This selection is taken from Thomas Henry Huxley, "On Science and Art in Relation to Education," *Selected Works of Thomas H. Huxley (New York: D. Appleton and Company, 1893), VIII, pp. 160-88.]*

[162] Now, the points to which I directed particular attention on that occasion[1] were these: in the first place, that instruction in physical science supplies information of a character of especial value, both in a practical and a speculative point of view—information which cannot be obtained other-

wise; and, in the second place, that, as educational discipline, it supplies, in a better form than any other study can supply, exercise in a special form of logic, and a peculiar method of testing the validity of our processes of inquiry. I said further, that, even at that time, a great and increasing attention was being paid to physical science in our schools and colleges, and that, most assuredly, such attention must go on growing and increasing, until education in these matters occupied a very much larger share of the time which is given to teaching and training, than had been the case heretofore. And I threw all the strength of argumentation of which I was possessed into the support of these propositions. But I venture to remind you, also, of some other words I used at that time, and which I ask permission to read to you. They were these: "There are other forms of culture besides physical science, and I should be profoundly sorry to see the fact forgotten, or even to observe a tendency to starve or cripple literary or aesthetic culture for the sake of science. Such a narrow view of the nature of education has nothing to do with my firm conclusion that a complete and thorough [163] scientific culture ought to be introduced into all schools."

I say I desire, in commenting upon these various points, and judging them as fairly as I can by the light of increased experience, to particularly emphasize this last, because I am told, although I assuredly do not know it of my own knowledge—though I think if the fact were so I ought to know it, being tolerably well acquainted with that which goes on in the scientific world, and which has gone on there for the last thirty years—that there is a kind of sect, or horde, of scientific Goths and Vandals,[2] who think it would be proper and desirable to sweep away all other forms of culture and instruction except those in physical science, and to make them the universal and exclusive, or, at any rate, the dominant training of the human mind of the future generation. This is not my view—I do not believe it is anybody's view,—but it is attributed to those who, like myself, advocate scientific education. I therefore dwell strongly upon the point, and I beg you to believe that the words I have just now read were by no means intended by me as a sop to the Cerberus[3] of culture. I have not been in the habit of offering sops to any kind of Cerberus; but it was an expression of profound conviction on my own part—a conviction forced upon me not only by my mental constitution, but by the lessons of what is now becoming a [164] somewhat long experience of varied conditions of life. . . .

[174] I take it that the whole object of education is, in the first place, to train the faculties of the young in such a manner as to give their possessors the best chance of being happy and useful in their generation; and, in the second place, to furnish them with the most important portions of that immense capitalised experience of the human race which we call knowledge of various kinds. I am using the term knowledge in its widest possible sense; and the question is, what subjects to select by training and discipline, in which the object I have just defined may be best attained.

I must call your attention further to this fact, [175] that all the subjects of our thoughts—all feelings and propositions (leaving aside our sensations as the mere materials and occasions of thinking and feeling), all our mental furniture—may be classified under one of two heads—as either within the province of the intellect, something that can be put into propositions and affirmed or denied; or as within the province of feeling, or that which, before the name was defiled, was called the aesthetic side of our nature, and which can neither be proved nor disproved, but only felt and known.

According to the classification which I have put before you, then, the subjects of all knowledge are divisible into the two groups, matters of science and matters of art; for all things with which the reasoning faculty alone is occupied, come under the province of science; and in the broadest sense, and not in the narrow and technical sense in which we are now accustomed to use the word art, all things feelable, all things which stir our emotions, come under the term of art, in the sense of the subject-matter of the aesthetic faculty. So that we are shut up to this—that the business of education is, in the first place, to provide the young with the means and the habit of observation; and, secondly, to supply the subject-matter of knowledge either in the shape of science or of art, or of both combined.

Now, it is a very remarkable fact—but it is [176] true of most things in this world—that there is hardly anything one-sided, or of one nature; and it is not immediately obvious what of the things that interest us may be regarded as pure science, and what may be regarded as pure art. It may be that there are some peculiarly constituted persons who, before they have advanced far into the depths of geometry, find artistic beauty about it; but, taking the generality of mankind, I think it may be said that, when they begin to learn mathematics, their whole souls are absorbed in tracing the connection between the premises and the conclusion, and that to them geometry is pure science. So I think it may be said that mechanics and osteology[4] are pure science. On the other hand, melody in music is pure art. You cannot reason about it; there is no proposition involved in it. So, again, in the pictorial art, an arabesque, or a "Harmony in grey," touches none but the aesthetic faculty. But a great mathematician, and even many persons who are not great mathematicians, will tell you that they derive immense pleasure from geometrical reasonings. Everybody knows mathematicians speak of solutions and problems as "elegant," and they tell you that a certain mass of mystic symbols is "beautiful, quite lovely." Well, you do not see it. They do see it, because the intellectual process, the process of comprehending the reasons symbolised by these figures and these signs, confers upon them a sort [177] of pleasure, such as an artist has in visual symmetry. Take a science of which I may speak with more confidence, and which is the most attractive of those I am concerned with. It is what we call morphology, which consists in tracing out the unity in variety of the infinitely diversified structures of animals and plants. I cannot give you any example of a thorough aesthetic pleasure more intensely real than a pleasure of this kind—the pleasure which arises in one's mind when a whole mass of different structures run into one harmony as the expression of a central law. That is where the province of art overlays and embraces the province of intellect. And, if I may venture to express an opinion on such a subject, the great majority of forms of art are not in the sense what I just now defined them to be—pure art; but they derive much of their quality from simultaneous and even unconscious excitement of the intellect.

When I was a boy, I was very fond of music, and I am so now; and it so happened that I had the opportunity of hearing much good music. Among other things, I had abundant opportunities of hearing that great old master, Sebastian Bach.[5] I remember perfectly well—though I knew nothing whatever about music then, and, I may add, know nothing whatever about it now—the intense satisfaction and delight which I had in listening, by the hour together, to Bach's fugues. It is a pleasure [178] which remains with me, I am glad to think; but of late years, I have tried to find out the why and wherefore, and it has often occurred to me that the pleasure derived from musical compositions of this kind is essentially of the same nature as that which is derived from pursuits which are commonly regarded as purely intellectual. I mean, that the source of pleasure is exactly the same as in most of my problems in morphology[6]—that you have the theme in one of the old master's works followed out in all its endless variations, always appearing and always reminding you of unity in variety. So in painting; what is called "truth to nature" is the intellectual element coming in, and truth to nature depends entirely upon the intellectual culture of the person to whom art is addressed. If you are in Australia, you may get credit for being a good artist—I mean among the natives—if you can draw a kangaroo after a fashion. But, among men of higher civilisation, the intellectual knowledge we possess brings its criticism into our appreciation of works of art, and we are obliged to satisfy it, as well as the mere sense of beauty in colour and in outline. And so, the higher the culture and information of those whom art addresses, the more exact and precise must be what we call its "truth to nature."

If we turn to literature, the same thing is true, and you find works of literature which may be [179] said to be pure art. A little song of Shakespeare or of Goethe is pure art; it is exquisitely beautiful, although its intellectual content may be nothing. A series of pictures is made to pass before your mind by the meaning of words, and the effect is a melody of ideas. Nevertheless, the great mass of the literature we esteem is valued, not merely because of having artistic form, but because of its intellectual content; and the value is the higher, the more precise, distinct, and true is that intellectual content. And, if you will let me for a moment speak of the very highest forms of literature, do we not regard them as highest simply because the more we know the truer they seem, and the more competent we are to appreciate beauty the more beautiful they are? No man ever understands Shakespeare until he is old, though the youngest may admire him, the reason being that he satisfies the artistic instinct of the youngest and harmonises with the ripest and richest experience of the oldest.

I have said this much to draw your attention to what, in my mind, lies at the root of all this matter, and at the understanding of one another by the men of science on the one hand, and the men of literature, and history, and art, on the other. It is not a question whether one order of study or another should predominate. It is a question of what topics of education you shall select which will combine all the needful elements [180] in such due proportion as to give the greatest amount of food, support, and encouragement to those faculties which enable us to appreciate truth, and to profit by those sources of innocent happiness which are open to us, and, at the same time, to avoid that which is bad, and coarse, and ugly, and keep clear of the multitude of pitfalls and dangers which beset those who break through the natural or moral laws.

I address myself, in this spirit, to the consideration of the question of the value of purely literary education. Is it good and sufficient, or is it insufficient and bad? Well, here I venture to say that there are literary educations and literary educations. If I am to understand by that term the education that was current in the great majority of middle-class schools, and upper schools too, in this country when I was a boy, and which consisted absolutely and almost entirely in keeping boys for eight or ten years at learning the rules of Latin and Greek grammar, construing certain Latin and Greek authors, and possibly making verses which, had they been English verses would have been condemned as abominable doggerel,—if that is what you mean by liberal education, then I say it is scandalously insufficient and almost worthless. My reason for saying so is not from the point of view of science at all, but from the point of view of literature. I say the thing professes to be literary education that is [181] not a literary education at all. It was not literature at all that was taught, but science in a very bad form. It is quite obvious that grammar is science and not literature. The analysis of a text by the help of the rules of grammar is just as much a scientific operation as the analysis of chemical compound by the help of the rules of chemical analysis. There is nothing that appeals to the aesthetic faculty in that operation; and I ask multitudes of men of my own age, who went through this process, whether they ever had a conception of art or literature until they obtained it for themselves after leaving school. Then you may say, "If that is so, if the education was scientific, why cannot you be satisfied with it?" I say, because although it is a scientific training, it is of the most inadequate and inappropriate kind. If there is any good at all in scientific education it is that men should be trained, as I said before, to know things for themselves at first hand, and that they should understand every step of the reason of that which they do.

I desire to speak with the utmost respect of that science—philology[7]—of which grammar is a part and parcel; yet everybody knows that grammar, as it is usually learned at school, affords no scientific training. It is taught just as you would teach the rules of chess or draughts. On the other hand, if I am to understand by a literary education the study of the literatures of either [182] ancient or modern nations—but especially those of antiquity, and especially that of ancient Greece; if this literature is studied, not merely from the point of view of philological science, and its practical application to the interpretation of texts, but as an exemplification of and commentary upon the principles of art; if you look upon the literature of a people as a chapter in the development of the human mind, if you work out this in a broad spirit, and with such collateral references to morals and politics, and physical geography, and the like as are needful to make you comprehend what the meaning of ancient literature and civilisation is,—then, assuredly, it affords a splendid and noble education. But I still think it is susceptible of improvement, and that no man will ever comprehend the real secret of the difference between the ancient world and our present time, unless he has learned to see the difference which the late development of physical science has made between the thought of this day and the thought of that, and he will never see that difference, unless he has some practical insight into some branches of physical science; and you must remember that a literary education such as that which I have just referred to, is out of the reach of those whose school life is cut short at sixteen or seventeen.

But, you will say, all this is fault-finding; let us hear what you have in the way of positive [183] suggestion. Then I am bound to tell you that, if I could make a clean sweep of everything—I am very glad I cannot because I might, and probably should make mistakes,—but if I could make a clean sweep of everything and start afresh, I should, in the first place, secure that training of the young in reading and writing, and in the habit of attention and observation, both to that which is told them, and that which they see, which everybody agrees to. But in addition to that, I should make it absolutely necessary for everybody, for a longer or shorter period, to learn to draw. Now, you may say, there are some people who cannot draw, however much they may be taught. I deny that *in toto*, because I never yet met with anybody who could not learn to write. Writing is a form of drawing; therefore if you gave the same attention and trouble to drawing as you do to writing, depend upon it, there is nobody who cannot be made to draw, more or less well. Do not misapprehend me. I do not say for one moment you would make an artistic draughtsman. Artists are not made; they grow. You may improve the natural faculty in that direction, but you cannot make it; but you can teach simple drawing, and you will find it an implement of learning of extreme value. I do not think its value can be exaggerated, because it gives you the means of training the young in attention and accuracy, which are the two things in which all [184] mankind are more deficient than in any other mental quality whatever. The whole of my life has been spent in trying to give my proper attention to things and to be accurate, and I have not succeeded as well as I could wish; and other people, I am afraid, are not much more fortunate. You cannot begin this habit too early, and I consider there is nothing of so great a value as the habit of drawing, to secure those two desirable ends.

Then we come to the subject-matter, whether scientific or aesthetic, of education, and I should naturally have no question at all about teaching the elements of physical science of the kind that I have sketched, in a practical manner; but among scientific topics, using the word scientific in the broadest sense, I would also include the elements of the theory of morals and of that of political and social life, which, strangely enough, it never seems to occur to anybody to teach a child. I would have the history of our own country, and of all the influences which have been brought to bear upon it, with incidental geography, not as a mere chronicle of reigns and battles, but as a chapter in the development of the race, and the history of civilisation.

Then with respect to aesthetic knowledge and discipline, we have happily in the English language one of the most magnificent storehouses of artistic beauty and of models of literary excellence [185] which exists in the world at the present time. I have said before, and I repeat it here, that if a man cannot get literary culture of the highest kind out of his Bible, and Chaucer,[8] and Shakespeare, and Milton,[9] and Hobbes,[10] and Bishop Berkeley,[11] to mention only a few of our illustrious writers—I say, if he cannot get it out of those writers, he cannot get it out of anything; and I would assuredly devote a very large portion of the time of every English child to the careful study of the models of English writing of such varied and wonderful kind as we possess, and, what is still more important and still more neglected, the habit of using that language with precision, with force, and with art. I fancy we are almost the only nation in the world who seem to think that composition comes by nature. The French attend to their own language, the Germans study theirs; but Englishmen do not seem to think it is worth their while. Nor would I fail to include, in the course of study I am sketching, translations of all the best works of antiquity, or of the modern world. It is a very desirable thing to read Homer in Greek; but if you don't happen to know Greek, the next best thing we [sic] can do is to read as good a translation of it as we have recently been furnished with in prose. You won't get all you would get from the original, but you may get a great deal; and to refuse to know that great deal because you cannot get all, seems to be as sensible [186] as for a hungry man to refuse bread because he cannot get partridge. Finally, I would add instruction in either music or painting, or, if the child should be so unhappy, as sometimes happens, as to have no faculty for either of those, and no possibility of doing anything in any artistic sense with them, then I would see what could be done with literature alone; but I would provide, in the fullest sense, for the development of the aesthetic side of the mind. In my judgment, those are all the essentials of education for an English child. With that outfit, such as it might be made in the time given to education which is within the reach of nine-tenths of the population—with that outfit, an Englishman, within the limits of English life, is fitted to go anywhere, to occupy the highest positions, to fill the highest offices of the State, and to become distinguished in practical pursuits, in science, or in art. For, if he have the opportunity to learn all those things, and have his mind disciplined in the various directions the teaching of those topics would have necessitated, then, assuredly, he will be able to pick up, on his road through life, all the rest of the intellectual baggage he wants.

If the educational time at our disposition were sufficient there are one or two things I would add to those I have just now called the essentials; and perhaps you will be surprised to hear, though I hope you will not, that I should add, not more [187] science, but one, or, if possible, two languages. The knowledge of some other language than one's own is, in fact, of singular intellectual value. Many of the faults and mistakes of the ancient philosophers are traceable to the fact that they knew no language but their own, and were often led into confusing the symbol with the thought which it embodied. I think it is Locke[12] who says that one-half of the mistakes of philosophers have arisen from questions about words; and one of the safest ways of delivering yourself from the bondage of words is, to know how ideas look in words to which you are not accustomed. That is one reason for the study of language; another reason is that it opens new fields in art and in science. Another is the practical value of such knowledge; and yet another is this, that if your languages are properly chosen, from the time of learning the additional languages you will know your own language better than ever you did. So, I say, if the time given to education permits, add Latin and German. Latin, because it is the key to nearly one-half of English and to all the Romance languages; and German, because it is the key to almost all the remainder of English, and helps you to understand a race from whom most of us have sprung, and who have a character and a literature of a fateful force in the history of the world, such as probably has been allotted to those of no other people, except the Jews, the Greeks, and ourselves. [188] Beyond these, the essential and the eminently desirable elements of all education, let man take up his special line—the historian devote himself to his history, the man of science to his science, the man of letters to his culture of that kind, and the artist to his special pursuit.

Bacon[13] has prefaced some of his works with no more than this; *Franciscus Bacon sic cogitavit;*[14] let *"sic cogitavi"* be the epilogue to what I have ventured to address to you to-night.

NOTES

1. The occasion to which Huxley refers is an address on scientific education he had given in Liverpool in 1868.

2. Goths and Vandals. Germanic tribes who attacked and eventually overthrew the Roman Empire. Since they took pleasure in destroying works of art, Huxley uses them as a symbol of those scientists who are reported to have no appreciation of the humanities.

3. Cerberus. The three-headed dog that guarded the entrance to Hades; at funerals in ancient Greece, a honey cake was buried with the corpse so that the spirit might throw it to Cerberus and thus get safely past him.

4. osteology. "The science dealing with the bones of vertebrates" [WID].

5. Sebastian Bach. Johann Sebastian Bach (1685-1750), sometimes called the "Father of German Music"; among his works are forty-eight preludes and fugues for "The Well-Tempered Clavier," the Brandenberg concertos, the Mass in B Minor, and the Passion according to St. John.

6. morphology. "The branch of biology dealing with the form and structure of animals and plants" [WID].

7. philology. "Linguistic science; Linguistics" [WID].

8. Chaucer. Geoffrey Chaucer (c. 1340-1400), the greatest English poet before Shakespeare. His most famous work is the stories-in-a-framework poem The Canterbury Tales (1385-1400).

9. Milton. John Milton (1608-1674). One of the greatest poets of the English language; his Paradise Lost and Paradise Regained are the nearest equivalents in English to the Homeric epic. Samson Agonistes is another of his famous poetic works, and his prose tract Areopatigica is a classic argument for freedom of the press.

10. Hobbes. Thomas Hobbes (1588-1679), English philosopher, famous for his work The Leviathan (1651), which, predicating that men are naturally selfish and anarchic, held that absolute power, strongly centralized (usually in a monarch), is necessary to any society.

11. Bishop Berkeley. George Berkeley (1685-1753), Irish idealist, philosopher, and Anglican bishop who denied the independent existence of matter.

12. Locke. John Locke (1632-1704), English philosopher, "founder of British empiricism," whose most famous work is Essay Concerning the Human Understanding (1690). His political philosophy, embodied in Two Treatises of Government (1690), greatly influenced the framers of the Declaration of Independence and the American Constitution.

13. Bacon. Francis Bacon (1561-1626), English philosopher and statesman. His works include Essays (1597), The Advancement of Learning (1605), and Novum Organum (1620).

14. Franciscus Bacon sic cogitavit. "Francis Bacon thought thus."

TOPICS FOR DISCUSSION

1. Which of his earlier views on the value of scientific education is Huxley prepared to reiterate on this occasion? Who are the "scientific Goths and Vandals"? Why does he deplore their activities?

2. Do you find Huxley's concept of the goal of education to be liberal, vocational, or both? Explain your conclusion.

3. How does Huxley divide the provinces of learning? Are they mutually exclusive dominions? Why or why not? Do you agree with Huxley on this point?

4. According to Huxley, what sort of pleasure do men, himself included, derive from music and art and literature? What does he mean by "pure art"? Would he establish a hierarchy of studies in human education and, if so, how would he determine the selection of subjects in the curriculum? How do his thoughts on this matter compare with Fadiman's discussion of "master subjects" in "basic education"?

5. What faults does Huxley find with traditional literary education and the "scientific" approach to literature? How close do you think he is to Arnold on the value of studying ancient literature and civilization?

6. Huxley was a vigorous fighter for the inclusion of scientific studies in the nineteenth-century curriculum. What evidence does this essay give that he is not one of the "scientific Goths and Vandals" who would exclude everything but physical science from the course of studies?

7. In "Literature and Science" Arnold claims that human nature itself demands studies which man can relate to his sense of beauty and his sense of conduct. Does the curriculum Huxley suggests provide for such studies?

8. Huxley was a master of the art of communicating specialized information to audiences of nonspecialists. In this essay, what means does he use to catch and hold the interest of his audience? What, for example, is his tone? His plan of exposition? His devices to arouse the audience's sympathy? How do his methods of appealing to his listeners compare, in your opinion, with Arnold's?

NATHAN M. PUSEY

The Centrality
of Humanistic Study

Nathan M. Pusey (b. 1907), president of Harvard University since 1953, is currently a trustee of the Carnegie Foundation for the Advancement of Teaching. Before coming to Harvard Dr. Pusey served as president of Lawrence College, Appleton, Wisconsin. When he speaks on the humanities, he speaks from experience; before work as an administrator claimed him, Dr. Pusey was a professor of history, literature, and the classics. In his book The Age of the Scholar (1963) *he has given some of his "Observations on education in a troubled decade."*

This essay can be characterized as a humanist's protest against what he considers to be the unsupportable claims made by certain ardent supporters of the sciences. In Chapter 7 of Education in a Divided World *(Cambridge, Massachusetts: Harvard University Press, 1948), James Bryant Conant, himself a scientist, offers a more dispassionate, but still coolly skeptical treatment of similar pro-science enthusiasts. [This selection is taken from Nathan M. Pusey, "The Centrality of Humanistic Study," in Julian Harris (ed.),* The Humanities *(Madison: University of Wisconsin Press, 1950), pp. 75-82.]*

[75] I am sure, if we are honest, that all of us who belong to the trade can only smile wryly when we hear the word "community" applied to anything as atomistic as a college or university faculty. For the fact seems to be that members of faculties as a rule are less concerned to work amiably and selflessly with their colleagues in other disciplines than to assert the preeminent and superior worth of their own, and to establish and magnify its merits by belittling the less important, perhaps even faintly ridiculous, fields of study that somehow earlier caught the eccentric interests and mediocre talents of their less able colleagues.

So do we all feel more important in the world and achieve apparently some kind of necessary catharsis. It is in such a spirit of partisanship, quite frankly that I [76] wish to speak today—as a partisan primarily of the liberal arts curriculum, but within this, more especially of the humanities (in which classification I include history) and to make my case I will first, following the professional practice I have just deplored, speak *against* two other kinds of intellectual activity.

But perhaps this is not too bad, for the areas of knowledge the handling of which I should like to criticize are those least in need of apologetic treatment at the present time, namely, the natural and the social sciences. The relevance of their subject matters to present-day life is obvious to almost everyone, and their attainments—cumulative, multiform, impressive —beyond the reach of fault finding. And I would point out circumspectly that I have no quarrel with the importance of either of these fields of study or with their achievements. I am not that benighted or irresponsible. But I do want to say something critical concerning the educational value of these disciplines as recently, and even in some places currently, practiced.

The partisans of the natural sciences rightly urge the importance to higher education of the body of knowledge which is theirs to keep alive, augment, and teach, and emphasize the importance of some familiarity with and understanding of the physical world to every one of us. It is impossible for me to see how anyone could object to this. The need for such knowledge is beyond dispute. But when they go further and make claims concerning the by-products which come with the acquisition of the knowledge, i.e., when they set out to insist upon the peculiar and necessary importance of their studies in producing certain traits of mind and sets of character (and these claims [77] are made again and again), I confess that it is here that experience has made me frankly skeptical. I wish that all the claims of this kind that I have heard were true, but I just do not think they are.

Teachers of science in their apologetic literature are likely to say, for example, that the study of their subjects, experience in their disciplines, is of indispensable value in teaching people to think effectively and in inculcating certain desirable traits of mind. Their studies, it is claimed, will teach people, if anything can, to see and observe; to examine data; to analyze, weigh, measure; to withhold judgment; to think precisely, exactly, carefully from observed facts; to observe general principles and relationships, to formulate tentative explanations and to test them. They also teach habits of industry and fortitude, and, mounting higher, it is maintained that such studies engender a love for truth and respect for evidence. They teach young people to put aside their personal feelings and all other irrelevant considerations, to look at facts or at least at certain ranges of fact and to take the broad, impersonal, objective, honest, scientific view of them.

This is where my question comes, for I do not think they do. That is, I do not think the study of the sciences as widely practiced in the last generation, and at some places even now, does accomplish these things. I cannot speak of how the person trained largely, if not exclusively, on a diet of science behaves at work within his own field: I am willing to admit that he practices all these virtues there, for I cannot check him. But if the study of science did pre-eminently produce these very desirable traits of mind, one could reasonably expect to find them most conspicuously displayed in general discussion by individuals [78] who had been longest engaged in the study of courses in science, let us say, by their teachers. And it would follow that on college and university faculties the teachers of science, as a class, could therefore be counted on especially for intellectual curiosity, for objectivity and a passion for truth wherever it leads, for humility and freedom from the desire for personal triumph. And I offer it as one man's opinion that this simply is not so. The point that I want to make now is that there is much evidence, if we look at the behavior of teachers of science outside their laboratories, as compared with that of other teachers, to suggest that courses in science by themselves are patently inadequate to produce the educational results commonly claimed for them. And a similar indictment, if this word is admissible, can be brought on the record against any similar claims that may be put forth by teachers of social science. Again let me say there can be no reservations concerning the importance of their subject matters nor with their earnest and commendable aim of understanding modern society in all its ramifications with a view to improving human relationships (though we may perhaps have some reservations concerning their too ready proclivity for the hortatory mood). The only quarrel I wish to make is with any claim made for their study to an exclusive, or even to a primary, value in developing certain desirable intellectual qualities, among which are respect for fact, objectivity, initial withholding of judgment, and finally, judgment in accord with and in proportion to the evidence. Again it is my claim, supported by such observations as I have been able to make in the educational world, that the social studies, when tested [79] by the general intellectual behavior of their teachers outside their field, can no more be relied upon to insure critical, unbiased, impersonal reflections and imaginative thinking than can the natural sciences.

The point of this paper is simply to present the testimony of one individual who has worked with teachers from various disciplines in several institutions of higher learning, and so has had an opportunity of observing those in a number more, that if there is any generalization possible concerning the acquisition of desirable mental qualities from the study of particular subject matters—and I am not sure that there is—then it is that the humanities, concerned primarily with the conduct, the behavior, the aspirations and achievements, the reasons and rationalizations of individual human beings as recorded and preserved by our artists, are more apt than either of the other major areas of the curriculum to give them, even (and this is where my statement will seem most incredible to some), even and especially those virtues which we generally assume to characterize the scientific mentality—humility, accuracy, judgment in proportion to the facts.

"By their fruits ye shall know them." I have in my way tried continually to apply this test, and I find that the case for the humanities becomes clearer and clearer. I find, ironically and curiously, that those qualities of mind thought to accrue from the study of the sciences are most likely to be found in teachers of the sciences in proportion to their experience in other than their own disciplines.

The educated man and the man of judgment will ignore any of the chief divisions of knowledge to his cost, but [80] it would almost seem that lack of experience with the humanities can be virtually fatal. This is the testimony I offer for what it is worth.

It is an initial and indispensable, if not exclusive, function of higher education not merely to impart knowledge, but in doing this, to transform personality by transforming minds. It is an essential aim of education to call into quickened responsiveness the recalcitrant, darkened, and confused learning apparatus—imaginative, mental, emotional—with which we are each endowed. Our natural minds need to be transformed and developed, but they can be neither transformed nor developed by the mere passage of time, or merely by uninspired exercise, or by materials that do not speak directly to the human soul. True mental growth, it seems, can come only from contact with great and original ideas as they have operated in the minds of exceptional individuals and from vivid experience with exceptionally meaningful bits of human experience.

Every human being needs direct personal contact with the great stories, myths, and fictions of the human race, and with history, to begin to know himself and to sense the potentialities—of all sorts, for good and for bad—that lie within his reach and the reach of other men. The reaches of the human soul and the distortions the human mind is capable of, the meanness that often mars our judgments and the great liberations we can achieve, what it is to be a man and what it can be, these things are known to us by means of art and in the pages of history. Not the scientific exploration of things, not the scientific examination of the behavior of groups of people, but the [81] living, vivid acquaintance with the adventures of the human spirit, this it is which especially can stretch the humanity that lies in a man from birth and needle it into its fullest growth.

But the curious fact is that it is also this experience, this imaginative acquaintance with what I. A. Richards[1] so aptly called our "storehouse of recorded values," that seems to be most efficacious in producing those qualities of mind which we feel are essential to the scientific way of doing things, the way our world so desperately needs today. He who has followed man's story in history and who has lived long with the great fictions men have produced, whether he be scientist, social scientist, or some other, can be relied on, if anyone can, for humaneness, for temperate judgment, for respect for fact, for awareness of kinds of facts, for objectivity and judiciousness, and for concern.

A man can live, we may suppose, though not very well or very long, without an extensive acquaintance with the natural sciences. He could probably get on, though as a group we shall certainly not get ahead, without much experience in the social sciences. But he cannot be a good natural scientist or social scientist without first being a fully developed man, and he will not be that if he is not acquainted, richly acquainted, with humanistic studies.

I hope it will not destroy the effect of what I have said if I now add that in my opinion both the natural and social sciences can be and should be made a part of the humanistic studies. But they will be so incorporated only as they are cultivated by men who have worked also in the narrower field which we call the humanities, including history.

It is often argued that philosophy or religion [82] permeates every department of a curriculum, and I think there is much to be said to support this view. But in the same way I feel that literary and historical studies should affect the minds and hearts and emotions of everyone working in any branch of knowledge, for he will function to the best advantage both public and private wherever he is, of this I am convinced, only as he has been awakened and disciplined by the quickening, transforming, and perfecting power of humanistic study.

Many years ago Matthew Arnold,[2] speaking in this country, closed a discussion of this subject with these words:

> While we shall all have to acquaint ourselves with the great results reached by modern science, and to give ourselves as much training in its disciplines as we can conveniently carry, yet the majority of men will always require humane letters; and so much the more, as they have the more and the greater results of science to relate to the need in man for conduct, and to the need in him for beauty.

The years that have elapsed since seem only to have underscored the truth of this early observation.

NOTES

1. I. A. Richards (1893-   ). Literary critic, professor of English at Harvard University. Among his notable works are *The Meaning of Meaning* (1923), *Principles of Literary Criticism* (1924), and *Coleridge on Imagination* (1934).

2. Matthew Arnold. The passage quoted is from "Literature and Science"; see page 49.

TOPICS FOR DISCUSSION

1. Is this essay an attack on science? On scientists? If neither, then what, in your opinion, is being attacked?

2. To what extent does Pusey agree with the proponents of the natural sciences and where, exactly, does he part company with them? On what does he base his differing opinion?

3. What does this author believe to be the function of higher education? How does his view compare with Newman's distinction between "education" and "instruction"? Compare his praises of the humanities with those of Bush, Arnold, and Krutch.

4. "But . . . [man] cannot be a good natural scientist or social scientist without first being a fully developed man, and he will not be that if he is not acquainted, richly acquainted, with humanistic studies." Do any of the essays in this book agree with Pusey on this point? Explain.

5. Do you find any areas of agreement between Pusey and Oppenheimer?

J. ROBERT OPPENHEIMER

Physics in the Contemporary World

J. Robert Oppenheimer (b. 1904), a physicist, was educated at Harvard, Cambridge, and the University of Göttingen, Germany. Professor Oppenheimer was a National Research Fellow 1927-1928 and an International Education Board Fellow at the Universities of Leyden and Zürich 1928-1929. He taught physics at the University of California and at the California Institute of Technology until 1947. From 1943 to 1945 he was Director of the Los Alamos Science Laboratory, Los Alamos, New Mexico; he is currently Director of the Institute for Advanced Study at Princeton University, a post he first held in 1947. Between 1946 and 1952 Professor Oppenheimer was chairman of the general advisory commission of the United States Atomic Energy Commission. In 1953, in a decision which aroused considerable controversy, the AEC suspended him for security reasons; a review of the case in 1954 declared him loyal but did not reinstate him. Oppenheimer contributed importantly to the development of atomic energy for military purposes, though he has warned repeatedly of the responsibility such power imposes on scientist and nonscientist alike. In April 1963 President John F. Kennedy presented Professor Oppenheimer the Enrico Fermi Award, granted annually by the Atomic Energy Commission "for especially meritorious contribution to the development, use or control of atomic energy." His writings for laymen include The Open Mind *(1955) and* Science and the Common Understanding *(1954).*

At least three other chapters in The Open Mind *(from which the present selection is taken)—"The Encouragement of Science," "The Scientist in Society," and "Prospects in the Arts and Sciences"—stress Professor Oppenheimer's belief that the procedures of the scientific community may well serve the contemporary world as a model way of life. The physicist returns to this theme in "Science and the Human Community" in* Issues in University Education, *edited by Charles Frankel (New York: Harper & Row, 1959), pp. 48-62. [This selection is taken from J. Robert*

Oppenheimer, "Physics in the Contemporary World," The Open Mind (New York: Simon & Schuster, 1955) pp. 81-102].

[91] The true responsibility of a scientist, as we all know, is to the integrity and vigor of his science. And because most scientists, like all men of learning, tend in part also to be teachers, they have a responsibility for the communication of the truths they have found. This is at least a collective if not an individual responsibility. That we should see in this any insurance that the fruits of science will be used for man's benefit, or denied to man when they make for his distress or destruction, would be a tragic naïveté.

[92] There is another side of the coin. This is the question of whether there are elements in the way of life of the scientist which need not be restricted to the professional, and which have hope in them for bringing dignity and courage and serenity to other men. Science is not all of the life of reason; it is a part of it. As such, what can it mean to man?

Perhaps it would be well to emphasize that I am talking neither of the wisdom nor of an elite of scientists, but precisely of the kind of work and thought, of action and discipline, that makes up the everyday professional life of the scientist. It is not of any general insight into human affairs that I am talking. It is not the kind of thing we recognize in our greatest statesmen, after long service devoted to practical affairs and to the public interest. It is something very much more homely and robust than that. It has in it the kind of beauty that is inseparable from craftsmanship and form, but it has in it also the vigor that we rightly associate with the simple, ordered lives of artisans or of farmers, that we rightly associate with lives to which limitations of scope, and traditional ways, have given robustness and structure.

Even less would it be right to interpret the question of what there is in the ways of science that may be of general value to mankind in terms of the creation of an elite. The study of physics, and I think my colleagues in the other sciences will let me speak for them too, does not make philosopher-kings. It has not, until now, made kings. It almost never makes fit philosophers—so rarely that they must be counted as exceptions. If the professional pursuit of science makes good scientists, if it makes men with a certain serenity in their lives, who yield perhaps a little more slowly than others [93] to the natural corruptions of their time, it is doing a great deal, and all that we may rightly ask of it. For if Plato believed that in the study of geometry a man might prepare himself for wisdom and responsibility in the world of men, it was precisely because he thought so hopefully that the understanding of men could be patterned after the understanding of geometry. If we believe that today, it is in a much more recondite sense, and a much more cautious one.

Where, then, is the point? For one thing, it is to describe some of the features of the professional life of the scientist, which make of it one of the great phenomena of the contemporary world. Here again I would like to speak of physics; but I have enough friends in the other sciences to know how close their experience is to ours. . . .

What are some of these points? There is, in the first instance, a total lack of authoritarianism, which is hard to comprehend or to admit unless one has lived with it. This is accomplished by one of the most exacting of intellectual disciplines. In physics the worker learns the possibility of error very early. He learns that there are ways to correct his mistakes; he learns the futility of trying to conceal them. For it is not a field in which error awaits death and subsequent generations for verdict—the next issue of the journals will take care of it. The refinement of techniques for the prompt [94] discovery of error serves as well as any other as a hallmark of what we mean by science.

In any case, it is an area of collective effort in which there is a clear and well-defined community whose canons of taste and order simplify the life of the practitioner. It is a field in which the technique of experiment has given an almost perfect harmony to the balance between thought and action. In it we learn, so frequently that we could almost become accustomed to it, how vast is the novelty of the world, and how much even the physical world transcends in delicacy and in balance the limits of man's prior imaginings. We learn that views may be useful and inspiring although they are not complete. We come to have a great caution in all assertions of totality, of finality or absoluteness.

In this field quite ordinary men, using what are in the last analysis only the tools which are generally available in our society, manage to unfold for themselves and all others who wish to learn, the rich story of one aspect of the physical world, and of man's experience. We learn to throw away those instruments of action and those modes of description which are not appropriate to the reality we are trying to discern, and in this most painful discipline, find ourselves modest before the world.

The question which is so much in our mind is whether a comparable experience, a comparable discipline, a comparable community of interest, can in any way be available to mankind at large. I suppose that all the professional scientists together number some one one-hundreth of a per cent of the men of the world—even this will define rather [95] generously what we mean by scientists. Scientists as professionals are, I suppose, rather sure to constitute a small part of our people.

Clearly, if we raise at all this question that I have raised, it must be in the hope that there are other areas of human experience that may be discovered or invented or cultivated, and to which the qualities which distinguish scientific life may be congenial and appropriate. It is natural that serious scientists, knowing of their own experience something of the quality of their profession, should just today be concerned about its possible extension. For it is a time when the destruction and the evil of the last quarter century make men everywhere eager to seek all that can contribute to their intellectual life, some of the order and freedom and purpose which we conceive the great days of the past to have. Of all intellectual activity, science alone has flourished in the last centuries, science alone has turned out to have the kind of universality among men which the times require. I shall be disputed in this; but it is near to truth.

If one looks at past history, one may derive some encouragement for the hope that science, as one of the forms of reason, will nourish all of its forms. One may note how integral the love and cultivation of science were with the whole awakening of the human spirit which characterized the Renaissance. Or one may look at the late seventeenth and eighteenth centuries in France and England and see what pleasure and what stimulation the men of that time derived from the growth of physics, astronomy and mathematics.

What perhaps characterizes these periods of the past, [96] which we must be careful not to make more heroic because of their remoteness, was that there were many men who were able to combine in their own lives the activities of a scientist with activities of art and learning and politics, and were able to carry over from the one into the others this combination of courage and modesty which is the lesson that science always tries to teach to anyone who practices it.

And here we come to a point we touched earlier. It is very different to hear the results of science, as they may be descriptively or even analytically taught in a class or in a book or in the popular talk of the time; it is very different to hear these and to participate even in a modest way in the actual attainment of new knowledge. For it is just characteristic of all work in scientific fields that there is no authority to whom to refer, no one to give canon, no one to blame if the picture does not make sense. . . .

[99] Thus it would seem at least doubtful that the spiritual fruits of science could be made generally available, either by the communication of its results, or by the study of its history, or by the necessarily somewhat artificial re-enactment of its procedures. Rather it would seem that there are general features of the scientists' work the direct experience of which in any context could contribute more to this end. All of us, I suppose, would list such features and find it hard to define the words which we found it necessary to use in our lists. But on a few, a common experience may enable us to talk in concert.

In the first instance the work of science is co-operative; a scientist takes his colleagues as judges, competitors and collaborators. That does not mean, of course, that he loves his colleagues; but it gives him a way of living with them which would be not without its use in the contemporary world. The work of science is discipline in that its essential inventiveness is most of all dedicated to means for promptly revealing error. One may think of the rigors of mathematics and the virtuosity of physical experiment as two examples. Science is disciplined in its rejection of questions that cannot be answered and in its grinding pursuit of methods for answering [100] all that can. Science is always limited, and is in a profound sense unmetaphysical, in that it necessarily bases itself upon the broad ground of common human experience, tries to refine it within narrow areas where progress seems possible and exploration fruitful. Science is novelty and change. When it closes it dies. These qualities constitute a way of life which of course does not make wise men from foolish, or good men from wicked, but which has its beauty and which seems singularly suited to man's estate on earth.

If there is to be any advocacy at all in this talk, it would be this; that we be very sensitive to all new possibilities of extending the techniques and the patterns of science into other areas of human experience. Even in saying this we must be aware how slow the past development of science has in fact been, how much error there has been, and how much in it that turned out to be contrary to intellectual health or honesty.

We become fully aware of the need for caution if we look for a moment at what are called the social problems of the day and try to think what one could mean by approaching them in the scientific spirit, of trying to give substance, for example, to the feeling that a society that could develop atomic energy could also develop the means of controlling it. Surely the establishment of a secure peace is very much in all our minds. It is right that we try to bring reason to bear on an understanding of this problem; but for that there are available to us no equivalents of the experimental techniques of science. Errors of conception can remain undetected and even undefined. No means of appropriately narrowing the [101] focus of thinking is known to us. Nor have we found good avenues for extending or deepening our experience that bears upon this problem. In short, almost all the preconditions of scientific activity are missing, and in this case, at least, one may have a melancholy certainty that man's inventiveness will not rapidly provide them. All that we have from science in facing such great questions is a memory of our professional life, which makes us somewhat skeptical of other people's assertions, somewhat critical of enthusiasms so difficult to define and to control.

Yet the past century has seen many valid and inspiriting examples for the extension of science to new domains. As even in the case of physics, the initial steps are always controversial; probably we should not as a group be unanimous in saying which of these extensions were hopeful, and which not, for the science of the future. But one feature which I cannot fail to regard as sound—particularly in the fields of biology and psychology—is that they provide an appropriate means of correlating understanding and action, and involve new experimental procedures in terms of which a new conceptual apparatus can be defined; above all, they give us means of detecting error. In fact, one of the features which must arouse our suspicion of the dogmas some of Freud's followers have built up on the initial brilliant works of Freud is the tendency toward a self-sealing system, a system, that is, which has a way of almost automatically discounting evidence which might bear adversely on the doctrine. The whole point of science is to do just the opposite; to invite the detection of error and to welcome it. Some of you may [102] think that in another field a comparable system has been developed by the recent followers of Marx.

Thus we may hope for an ever-widening and more diverse field of application of science. But we must be aware how slowly these things develop and how little their development is responsive to even the most desperate of man's needs. For me it is an open question, and yet not a trivial one, whether in a time necessarily limited by the threats of war and of chaos these expanding areas in which the scientific spirit can flourish may yet contribute in a decisive way to man's rational life.

I have had to leave this essential question unanswered: I am not at all proud of that. In lieu of apology perhaps I may tell a story of another lecturer, speaking at Harvard, a few miles from here, two decades ago. Bertrand Russell had given a talk on the then new quantum mechanics, of whose wonders he was most appreciative. He spoke hard and earnestly in the New Lecture Hall. And when he was done, Professor Whitehead, who presided, thanked him for his efforts, and not least for "leaving the vast darkness of the subject unobscured."

TOPICS FOR DISCUSSION

1. Oppenheimer feels that science and the scientific community provide a valuable model of conduct for the nonscientific world. Of the essayists represented in this volume, which ones, other than C. P. Snow, share this opinion? Using Oppenheimer, Snow, and these others as a basis for your answer, draw up a list of "scientific" attitudes, qualities, and methods which you feel the nonscientific world might well imitate.

2. Which eras in the past found in science a "form of reason" that "nourished" all other forms of reason? Discuss the conditions which may inhibit such a development today.

3. What is the author's view of the possibility of the extension of the methods of science to other fields? Which of the other essayists would agree with him wholly in this matter? Partly? Not at all? Explain your answers.

4. Explain the paradox of the closing anecdote and comment on its relevance.

5. To what degree does Oppenheimer feel that the scientist's professional experience influences him in fields outside his sphere of professional competence? How would Pusey answer such a claim?

F. R. LEAVIS

Two Cultures? The Significance of C. P. Snow

Frank Raymond Leavis (1895-   ), Cambridge-educated English teacher and critic, he was one of the founders of the influential literary quarterly Scrutiny, *in 1932, and remained its editor until it ceased publication in 1953. A controversial and formidable literary critic, Professor Leavis combines close textual criticism with moral principles of evaluation. From 1938 to 1962 he was a fellow of Downing College, Cambridge, and a lecturer in English. In 1962, having reached retirement age, he was made an honorary fellow of Downing. His writings include* New Bearings in English Poetry *(1932),* Revaluation *(1936),* The Great Tradition *(1948),* The Common Pursuit *(1952)* and *D. H. Lawrence, Novelist *(1956). His "Two Cultures? The Significance of C. P. Snow" was given as the Richmond Lecture at Cambridge in February 1962 and was first printed in* The Spectator *for March 9, 1962.*

The vigorous attack on Snow contained in the Richmond lecture provoked equally vigorous counterattack in England and America. The controversy still crackles. See Lionel Trilling, "Science, Literature and Culture: A Comment on the Snow-Leavis Controversy," Commentary, *XXXIII (June 1962), 461-77; Martin Green, "A Literary Defense of the Two Cultures,"* Kenyon Review, *XXIV (Autumn 1962), 731-39; Richard Wolheim, "London Letter,"* Partisan Review, *XXIX (Spring 1962), 263-69. [This selection is taken from F. R. Leavis,* Two Cultures? The Significance of C. P. Snow *and Michael Yudkin, An Essay on Sir Charles Snow's Rede Lecture (New York: Panthéon Books, 1963), pp. 13-50.]*

. . . [33] And I have to say now that in *The Two Cultures and the Scientific Revolution* there is no evidence, either.[1] The only presence science has is as a matter of external reference, entailed in a show of knowledgeableness. Of qualities that one might set to the credit of a scientific training there are none. As far as the internal evidence goes, the lecture was conceived and written by someone who had not had the advantage of an intellectual [34] discipline of any kind. I was on the point of illustrating this truth from Snow's way with the term "culture"—a term so important for his purposes. By way of enforcing his testimony that the scientists "have their own culture," he tells us: "This culture contains a great deal of argument, usually much more rigorous, and almost always at a higher conceptual level, than literary persons' arguments." But the argument of Snow's Rede Lecture is at an immensely *lower* conceptual level, and incomparably more loose and inconsequent, than any I myself, a literary person, should permit in a group discussion I was conducting, let alone a pupil's essay.

Thought, it is true, in the field in which Snow challenges us, doesn't admit of control by strict definition of the key terms; but the more fully one realises this the more aware will one be of the need to cultivate a vigilant responsibility in using them, and an alert consciousness of any changes of force they may incur as the argument passes from context to context. And what I have to say is that Snow's argument proceeds with so extreme a *naïveté* of unconsciousness and irresponsibility that to call it a movement of thought is to flatter it. . . .

[43] It is characteristic of Snow that "believe" for him should be a very simple word. "Statistically," he says, "I suppose slightly more scientists are in religious terms unbelievers, compared with the rest of the intellectual world." There are believers and unbelievers; we all know what "religious terms" are; and everything relevant in relation to the adjective has been said. Snow goes on at once: "Statistically, I suppose slightly more scientists are on the Left in open politics." The *naïveté* is complete; it is a *naïveté* indistinguishable from the portentous ignorance. The ignorance is that which appears as historical ignorance in his account of the Industrial Revolution, and its consequences, in the nineteenth century. It manifests itself as a terrifying confidence of simplification—terrifying because of the distortions and falsifications it entails, and the part it plays in that spirit of practical wisdom about the human future of which Snow's Rede Lecture might be called a classic. Disposing with noble scorn of a wholly imaginary kind of opposition to his crass Wellsianism, he says (and *this* is his history—and his logic): "For, with singular unanimity, in any country where they have had the chance, the poor have walked off the land into the factories as fast as the factories could take them." This, of course, is mere brute assertion, callous in its irresponsibility. But it is essential to Snow's wisdom. If one points out that the actual history [44] has been, with significance for one's apprehension of the full human problem, incomparably and poignantly more complex than that, Snow dismisses one as a "natural Luddite." He dismisses so—sees no further significance in—Dickens and Ruskin,[2] and all the writers leading down to Lawrence. Yet—to confine myself to the non-creative writer, about whom the challenged comment is more easily made—it was Ruskin who put into currency the distinction between wealth and well-

being, which runs down through Morris[3] and the British Socialist movement for the Welfare State.

But for Ruskin "well-being" or "welfare" could not conceivably be matters of merely material standard of living, with the advantages of technology and scientific hygiene. And there we have the gap—the gap that is the emptiness beneath Snow's ignorance—between Snow and not only Ruskin, but the great creative writers of the century before Snow: they don't exist for him; nor does civilisation. Pressing on this ancient university his sense of the urgency of the effort to which we must give ourselves, he says: "Yet"—in spite, that is, of the "horror" which, he says, is "hard to look at straight"—"yet they've proved that common men can show astonishing fortitude in chasing jam tomorrow. Jam today, and men aren't at their most exciting: jam tomorrow, and one often sees them at their noblest. The transformations have also proved something which only the scientific culture can take in its stride. Yet, when we don't take it in our stride, it makes us look silly."

The callously ugly insensitiveness of the mode of expression is wholly significant. It gives us Snow, who is wholly representative of the world, or culture, to which it belongs. It is the world in which Mr. Macmillan said—or might, taking a tip from Snow, have varied his [45] phrase by saying—"You never had so much jam"; and in which, if you are enlightened, you see that the sum of wisdom lies in expediting the processes which will ensure the Congolese, the Indonesians, and Bushmen (no, not the Bushmen —there aren't enough of them), the Chinese, the Indians, *their* increasing supplies of jam. It is the world in which the vital inspiration, the creative drive, is "Jam tomorrow" (if you haven't any today) or (if you have it today) "*More* jam tomorrow." It is the world in which, even at the level of the intellectual weeklies, "standard of living" is an ultimate criterion, its raising an ultimate aim, a matter of wages and salaries and what you can buy with them, reduced hours of work, and the technological resources that make your increasing leisure worth having, so that productivity—the supremely important thing—must be kept on the rise, at whatever cost to protesting conservative habit.

Don't mistake me. I am not preaching that we should defy, or try to reverse, the accelerating movement of external civilisation (the phrase sufficiently explains itself, I hope) that is determined by advancing technology. Nor am I suggesting that Snow, in so far as he is advocating improvements in scientific education, is wrong (I suspect he isn't very original). What I *am* saying is that such a concern is not enough—disastrously not enough. Snow himself is proof of that, product as he is of the initial cultural consequences of the kind of rapid change he wants to see accelerated to the utmost and assimilating all the world, bringing (he is convinced), provided we are foresighted enough to perceive that no one now will long consent to be without abundant jam, salvation and lasting felicity to all mankind.

It must be recognised, though, that he doesn't *say* "salvation" or "felicity," but "jam." And if "jam" means [46] (as it does) the prosperity and leisure enjoyed by our well-to-do working class, then the significant fact not noticed by Snow is that the felicity it represents cannot be regarded by a fully human mind as a matter for happy contemplation. Nor is it felt by the beneficiaries to be satisfying. I haven't time to enlarge on this last point. I will only remark that the observation is not confined to "natural Luddites": I recently read in the *Economist*[4] a disturbed review of a book by a French sociologist of which the theme is (not a new idea to us) the incapacity of the industrial worker, who—inevitably—looks on real living as reserved for his leisure, to use his leisure in any but essentially passive ways. And this, for me, evokes that total vision which makes Snow's "social hope" unintoxicating to many of us—the vision of our imminent tomorrow in today's America: the energy, the triumphant technology, the productivity, the high standard of living and the life-impoverishment—the human emptiness; emptiness and boredom craving alcohol—of one kind or another. Who will assert that the average member of a modern society is more fully human, or more alive, than a Bushman, an Indian peasant, or a member of one of those poignantly surviving primitive peoples, with their marvellous art and skills and vital intelligence?

But I will come to the explicit positive note that has all along been my goal (for I am not a Luddite) in this way: the advance of science and technology means a human future of change so rapid and of such kinds, of tests and challenges so unprecedented, of decisions and possible non-decisions so momentous and insidious in their consequences, that mankind —this is surely clear—will need to be in full intelligent possession of its full humanity (and "possession" here means, not confident ownership of that which belongs to *us*—our property, [47] but a basic living deference towards that to which, opening as it does into the unknown and itself unmeasurable, we know we belong). I haven't chosen to say that mankind will need all its traditional wisdom; that might suggest a kind of conservatism that, so far as I am concerned, is the enemy. What we need, and shall continue to need not less, is something with the livingness of the deepest vital instinct; as intelligence, a power—rooted, strong in experience, and supremely human—of creative response to the new challenges of time; something that is alien to either of Snow's cultures.

His blankness comes out when, intimating (he supposes) that his concern for university reform envisages the total educational function, he tells us how shocking it is that educated people should not be able to appreciate the Shakespeare of science. It simply hasn't occurred to him that to call the master scientific mind (say Rutherford) a Shakespeare is nothing but a cheap journalistic infelicity. He enforces his intention by telling us, after reporting the failure of his literary friends to describe the second law of thermodynamics: "yet I was asking something which is about the equivalent of *Have you read a work of Shakespeare's?*" There *is* no scientific equivalent of that question; equations between orders so disparate are meaningless—which is not to say that the Neo-Wellsian assurance that proposes them hasn't *its* significance. More largely, Snow exclaims: "As though the scientific edifice of the physical world were not, in its intellectual depth, complexity and articulation, the most beautiful and wonderful collective work of the mind of man."

It is pleasant to think of Snow contemplating, daily perhaps, the intellectual depth, complexity and articulation in all their beauty. But there is a prior human [48] achievement of collaborative creation, a more basic work of the mind of man (and more than the mind), one without which the triumphant erection of the scientific edifice would not have been possible: that is, the creation of the human world, including language. It is one we cannot rest on as on something done in the past. It lives in the living creative response to change in the present. I mentioned language because it is in terms of literature that I can most easily make my meaning plain, and because of the answer that seems to me called for by Snow's designs on the university. It is in the study of literature, the literature of one's own language in the first place, that one comes to recognise the nature and priority of the third realm (as, unphilosophically, no doubt, I call it, talking with my pupils), the realm of that which is neither merely private and personal nor public in the sense that it can be brought into the laboratory or pointed to. You cannot point to the poem; it is "there" only in the re-creative response of individual minds to the black marks on the page. But—a necessary faith—it is something in which minds can meet. The process in which this faith is justified is given fairly enough in an account of the nature of criticism. A judgment is personal or it is nothing; you cannot take over someone else's. The implicit form of a judgment is: This is so, isn't it? The question is an appeal for confirmation that the thing *is* so; implicitly that, though expecting, characteristically, an answer in the form, "yes, but ——," the "but" standing for qualifications, reserves, corrections. Here we have a diagram of the collaborative-creative process in which the poem comes to be established as something "out there," of common access in what is in some sense a public world. It gives us, too, the nature of [49] the existence of English literature, a living whole that can have its life only in the living present, in the creative response of individuals, who collaboratively renew and perpetuate what they participate in—a cultural community or consciousness. More, it gives us the nature in general of what I have called the "third realm" to which all that makes us human belongs.

Perhaps I need say no more by way of enforcing my conviction that, for the sake of our humanity—our humanness, for the sake of a human future, we must do with intelligent resolution and with faith, all we can to maintain the full life in the present—and life is growth—of our transmitted culture. Like Snow I look to the university. Unlike Snow, I am concerned to make it really a university, something (that is) more than a collection of specialist departments—to make it a centre of human consciousness: perception, knowledge, judgment and responsibility. And perhaps I have sufficiently indicated on what lines I would justify my seeing the centre of a university in a vital English School. I mustn't say more now about what I mean by that, I will only say that the academic is the enemy and that the academic *can* be beaten, as we who ran *Scrutiny* for twenty years proved. We were, and knew we were, Cambridge—the essential Cambridge in spite of Cambridge: that gives you the spirit of what I have in mind. Snow gets on with what he calls "the traditional culture" better than I do. To impress us with his anti-academic astringency, he tells us of the old Master of Jesus who said about trains running into Cambridge on Sunday: "It is equally displeasing to God and to myself." More to the point is that *that*, I remember, was very much the attitude of the academic powers when, thirty years ago, [50] I wrote a pioneering book on modern poetry that made Eliot[5] a key figure and proposed a new chart, and again when I backed Lawrence as a great writer.

It is assumed, I believe, that work in the scientific departments must be in close touch with the experimental-creative front. In the same way, for the university English School there is a creative front with which, of its function and nature, the School must be in the closest relation. I am not thinking of the fashionable idea that the right qualification for a teaching post is to be a poet—or a commercially successful novelist. I am thinking again of what *Scrutiny* stood—and stands—for: of the creative work it did on the contemporary intellectual-cultural frontier in maintaining the critical function. I must not try now to say more about the way in which such a school would generate in the university a centre of consciousness (and conscience) for our civilisation. I will merely insist that it is not inconceivable that Cambridge might become a place where the culture of the Sunday papers was not taken to represent the best that is thought and known in our time.

If so, it is conceivable, perhaps, that the journalistic addiction of our academic intellectuals—and journalism (in one form or another) is now the menacing disease of university "English"—might, at Cambridge, be pretty generally recognised for the thing it is. In such a Cambridge the attention I have paid to a Snow would be unnecessary.

NOTES

1. ". . . there is no evidence, either." Leavis has just been saying of Snow "That he has really *been* a scientist, that science as such has ever, in any important inward way, existed for him, there is no evidence in his fiction."

2. Ruskin. John Ruskin (1819-1900), English essayist and critic. His aesthetic criticism includes *Modern Painters* (1843-1869), *Seven Lamps of Architecture*

(1849), and *The Stones of Venice* (1881-1883). After 1860 most of his criticism was directed at social conditions, e.g. *Fors Clavigera* (1871-1884).

3. Morris. William Morris (1834-1896), English poet, painter, craftsman, and socialist leader. The Arthurian tales inspired much of his poetry, e.g. "The Defense of Guinevere"; his paintings belong to the Pre-Raphaelite school; his *News from Nowhere* (1891), a utopian romance, describes his vision of an ideal community. In behalf of socialism he worked with such groups as the Socialist Democratic Federation, the Socialist League (he was one of its founders), and the Hammersmith Socialist Society.

4. *Economist.* English weekly; founded in 1843, it deals with business and industry.

5. Eliot. Thomas Stearns Eliot (1888-1965), English poet and critic. His writings include such enormously influential works as *The Love Song of J. Alfred Prufrock* (1917), *The Waste Land* (1922), *Four Quartets* (1944) (poetry), and *The Sacred Wood* (1920), *The Use of Poetry and the Use of Criticism* (1933), and *What Is a Classic* (1945) (prose).

TOPICS FOR DISCUSSION

1. What are Leavis' chief criticisms of Snow? What support does he offer for each of these criticisms?

2. What basic flaw does Leavis discover in the kind of scientific education Snow would encourage? Why does he find Snow's "jam" image and his willingness to call a "master scientific mind" a "Shakespeare" so disturbing?

3. Describe the "third realm" which Leavis considers essential to man? Does this resemble any concepts offered by other essayists?

4. How can the university help equip modern man to cope with the infinitely complex and changing conditions of the present age?

5. "And this, for me, evokes that total vision which makes Snow's 'social hope' unintoxicating to many of us—the vision of our imminent tomorrow in today's America: the energy, the triumphant technology, the productivity, the high standard of living and the life-impoverishment—the human emptiness; emptiness and boredom craving alcohol—of one kind or another. Who will assert that the average member of a modern society is more fully human, or more alive, than a Bushman, an Indian peasant, or a member of one of those poignantly surviving primitive peoples, with their marvellous art and skills and vital intelligence?" Support or refute Leavis' statement about contemporary American life by reference to current articles and headlines. Why does he consider the primitive, e.g. the Bushman, more fully alive than a member of a modern "civilized" society? Do you agree? Why or why not?

6. Leavis has been censured for the tone of this essay. Do you find it overly personal? Overly harsh? Both? Neither? What devices does Leavis use to rouse the reader? Does he succeed? Might he have gained his end by means that would have escaped criticism? Does it matter?

C. P. SNOW

The Two Cultures
and the Scientific Revolution

C. P. Snow, Charles Percy Snow (1905-   ), English author and physicist, was educated at Cambridge. He was a fellow of Christ's Church, Cambridge 1930-1950 and a Civil Service Commissioner 1945-1960. In 1959 he gave the Rede Lecture at Cambridge; this was The Two Cultures and the Scientific Revolution *printed the same year. In 1960 he gave the Godkin Lectures at Harvard, a series printed in 1961 as* Science and Government. *He was Regent's Professor at the University of California, Berkeley, 1961. A fellow of The Royal Society of London, he was knighted in 1957 for special services to his country during World War II. Since 1961 Sir Charles has been Rector of the University of St. Andrews, Scotland. His novels include* Strangers and Brothers, *a novel sequence which, when completed, will have twelve books. Some of the works of the sequence that have already appeared are* Strangers and Brothers (1940), The Masters (1951), The Conscience of the Rich (1958), *and* The Affair (1960). *His fictional portraits of the scientist as he traverses the "Corridors of Power," as well as the academic scene, and his concern with the breakdown of communication between scientists and nonscientists and with the place of science in a liberal education have won him a wide audience.*

In 1964, C. P. Snow reprinted his original essay The Two Cultures and the Scientific Revolution *and added forty-seven pages of comment on the original essay, calling this section "A Second Look," and the book itself* The Two Cultures and a Second Look (New York: Cambridge University Press, 1964). *The excerpts given below are taken from the original* Two Cultures, *since this is the material on which F. R. Leavis based his criticism. Suggestions for further readings in the Snow-Leavis controversy precede the Leavis essay. [This selection is taken from C. P. Snow,* The Two Cultures and the Scientific Revolution (New York: Cambridge University Press, 1959).]*

[4] . . . I believe the intellectual life of the whole western society is increasingly being split into two polar[1] groups. When I say the intellectual life, I mean to include also a large part of our practical life, because I should be the last person to suggest the two can at the deepest level be distinguished. I shall come back to the practical life a little later. Two polar groups: at one pole we have the literary intellectuals, who incidentally while no one was looking took to referring to themselves as "intellectuals" as though there were no others. . . .

Literary intellectuals at one pole—at the other scientists, and as the most representative, the physical scientists. Between the two a gulf of mutual incomprehension—sometimes (particularly among the young) hostility and dislike, but most of all lack of understanding. They have a curious distorted image of each other. Their attitudes are so [5] different that, even on the level of emotion, they can't find much common ground. Non-scientists tend to think of scientists as brash and boastful. They hear T. S. Eliot, who just for these illustrations we can take as an archetypal figure, saying about his attempts to revive verse-drama, that we can hope for very little, but that we feel content if he and his co-workers could prepare the ground for a new Kyd[2] or a new Greene.[3] That is the tone, restricted and constrained, with which literary intellectuals are at home: it is the subdued voice of their culture. Then they hear a much louder voice, that of another archetypal figure, Rutherford,[4] trumpeting: "This is the heroic age of science! This is the Elizabethan age!" Many of us heard that, and a good many other statements beside which that was mild; and we weren't left in any doubt whom Rutherford was casting for the role of Shakespeare. What is hard for the literary intellectuals to understand, imaginatively or intellectually, is that he was absolutely right. . . .

The non-scientists have a rooted impression that the scientists are shallowly optimistic, unaware of man's condition. On the other hand, the scientists [6] believe that the literary intellectuals are totally lacking in foresight, peculiarly unconcerned with their brother men, in a deep sense anti-intellectual, anxious to restrict both art and thought to the existential moment. And so on. Anyone with a mild talent for invective could produce plenty of this kind of subterranean back-chat. On each side there is some of it which is not entirely baseless. It is all destructive. Much of it rests on misinterpretations which are dangerous. I should like to deal with two of the most profound of these now, one on each side.

First, about the scientists' optimism. This is an accusation which has been made so often that it has become a platitude. It has been made by some of the acutest non-scientific minds of the day. But it depends upon a confusion between the individual experience and the social experience, between the individual condition of man and his social condition. Most of the scientists I have known well have felt—just as deeply as the non-scientists I have known well—that the individual condition of each of us is tragic. Each of us is alone: sometimes we escape from solitariness, through love or affection or perhaps creative moments, but those triumphs of life are pools of light we make for ourselves while the edge of the road is black: each of us dies alone. Some scientists I have known have had faith in revealed religion. Perhaps with them the sense of the tragic condition is not so strong. I don't [7] know. With most people of deep feeling, however high-spirited and happy they are, sometimes most with those who are happiest and most high-spirited, it seems to be right in the fibres, part of the weight of life. That is as true of the scientists I have known best as of anyone at all.

But nearly all of them—and this is where the colour of hope genuinely comes in—would see no reason why, just because the individual condition is tragic, so must the social condition be. Each of us is solitary: each of us dies alone: all right, that's a fate against which we can't struggle—but there is plenty in our condition which is not fate, and against which we are less than human unless we do struggle.

Most of our fellow human beings, for instance, are underfed and die before their time. In the crudest terms, *that* is the social condition. There is a moral trap which comes through the insight into man's loneliness: it tempts one to sit back, complacent in one's unique tragedy, and let the others go without a meal.

As a group, the scientists fall into the trap less than others. They are inclined to be impatient to see if something can be done: and inclined to think that it can be done, until it's proved otherwise. That is their real optimism, and it's an optimism that the rest of us badly need.

In reverse, the same spirit, tough and good and determined to fight it out at the side of their [8] brother men, has made scientists regard the other culture's social attitudes as contemptible. That is too facile: some of them are, but they are a temporary phase and not to be taken as representative. . . .

[10] At one pole, the scientific culture really is a culture, not only in an intellectual but also in an anthropological sense. That is, its members need not, and of course often do not, always completely understand each other; biologists more often than not will have a pretty hazy idea of contemporary physics; but there are common attitudes, common standards and patterns of behaviour, common approaches and assumptions. This goes surprisingly wide and deep. It cuts across other mental patterns, such as those of religion or politics or class.

Statistically, I suppose slightly more scientists are in religious terms unbelievers, compared with the rest of the intellectual world—though there are plenty who are religious, and that seems to be increasingly so among the young. Statistically also, slightly more scientists are on the Left in open politics—though again, plenty always have called themselves conservatives, and that also seems to be more common among the young. Compared with [11] the rest of the intellectual world, considerably more scientists in this country and probably in the U.S. come from poor families. Yet, over the whole range of thought and behaviour, none of that matters very much. In their working, and in much of their emotional life, their attitudes are closer to other scientists than to non-scientists who in religion or politics or class have the same labels as themselves. If I were to risk a piece of shorthand, I should say that naturally they had the future in their bones. . . .

At the other pole, the spread of attitudes is wider. It is obvious that between the two, as one moves through intellectuals, there are all kinds of tones of feeling on the way. But I believe the pole of total incomprehension of science radiates its influence on all the rest. That total incomprehension gives, much more pervasively than we realise, living in it, an unscientific flavour to the whole [12] "traditional" culture, and that unscientific flavour is often, much more than we admit, on the point of turning anti-scientific. The feeling of one pole becomes the anti-feeling of the other. If the scientists have the future in their bones, then the traditional culture responds by wishing the future did not exist. It is the traditional culture, to an extent remarkably little diminished by the emergency of the scientific one, which manages the western world.

This polarisation is sheer loss to us all. To us as people, and to our society. It is at the same time practical and intellectual and creative loss, and I repeat that it is false to imagine that those three considerations are clearly separable. But for a moment I want to concentrate on the intellectual loss.

The degree of incomprehension on both sides is the kind of joke which has gone sour. There are about fifty thousand working scientists in the country and about eighty thousand professional engineers or applied scientists. During the war and in the years since, my colleagues and I have had to interview somewhere between thirty to forty thousand of these—that is, about 25 per cent. The number is large enough to give us a fair sample, though of the men we talked to most would still be under forty. We were able to find out a certain amount of what they read and thought about. I confess that even I, who am fond of them and respect them, was a bit shaken. We hadn't quite expected that [13] the links with the traditional culture should be so tenuous, nothing more than a formal touch of the cap.

As one would expect, some of the very best scientists had and have plenty of energy and interest to spare, and we came across several who had read everything that literary people talk about. But that's very rare. Most of the rest, when one tried to probe for what books they had read, would modestly confess, "Well, I've *tried* a bit of Dickens,"[5] rather as though Dickens were an extraordinary esoteric, tangled and dubiously rewarding writer, something like Rainer Maria Rilke.[6] In fact that is exactly how they do regard him: we thought that discovery, that Dickens had been transformed into the type-specimen of literary incomprehensibility, was one of the oddest results of the whole exercise.

But of course, in reading him, in reading almost any writer whom we should value, they are just touching their caps to the traditional culture. They have their own culture, intensive, rigorous, and constantly in action. This culture contains a great deal of argument, usually much more rigorous, than literary persons' arguments—even though the scientists do cheerfully use words in senses which literary persons don't recognise, the senses are exact ones, and when they talk about "subjective," "objective," "philosophy" or [14] "progressive," they know what they mean, even though it isn't what one is accustomed to expect.

Remember, these are very intelligent men. Their culture is in many ways an exacting and admirable one. It doesn't contain much art, with the exception, an important exception, of music. Verbal exchange, insistent argument. Long-playing records. Colour-photography. The ear, to some extent the eye. . . .

Of books, though, very little. And of the books which to most literary persons are bread and butter, novels, history, poetry, plays, almost nothing at all. It isn't that they're not interested in the psychological or moral or social life. In the social life, they certainly are, more than most of us. In the moral, they are by and large the soundest group of intellectuals we have; there is a moral component right in the grain of science itself, and almost all scientists form their own judgments of the moral life. In the psychological they have as much interest as most of us, though occasionally I fancy they come to it rather late. It isn't that they lack the [15] interests. It is much more that the whole literature of the traditional culture doesn't seem to them relevant to those interests. They are, of course, dead wrong. As a result, their imaginative understanding is less than it could be. They are self-impoverished.

But what about the other side? They are impoverished too—perhaps more seriously, because they are vainer about it. They still like to pretend that the traditional culture is the whole of "culture," as though the natural order didn't exist. As though the exploration of the natural order was of no interest either in its own value or its consequences. As though the scientific edifice of the physical world was not, in its intellectual depth, complexity and articulation, the most beautiful and wonderful collective work of the mind of man. Yet most non-scientists have no conception of the edifice at all. Even if they want to have it, they can't. It is rather as though, over an immense range of intellectual experience, a whole group was tone-deaf. Except that this tone-deafness doesn't come by nature, but by training, or rather the absence of training.

As with the tone-deaf, they don't know what they miss. They give a pitying chuckle at the news of scientists who have never read a major work

of English literature. They dismiss them as ignorant specialists. Yet their
own ignorance and their own specialisation is just as startling. A good many
[16] times I have been present at gatherings of people who, by the standards of the traditional culture, are thought highly educated and who have
with considerable gusto been expressing their incredulity at the illiteracy of
scientists. Once or twice I have been provoked and have asked the company
how many of them could describe the Second Law of Thermodynamics.[7]
The response was cold: it was also negative. Yet I was asking something
which is about the scientific equivalent of: *Have you read a work of Shakespeare's?*. . .

[19] In fact, the separation between the scientists and non-scientists is
much less bridgeable among the young than it was even thirty years ago.
Thirty years ago the cultures had long ceased to speak to each other; but at
least they managed a kind of frozen smile across the gulf. Now the polite-
ness has gone, and they just make faces. It is not only that the young
scientists now feel that they are part of a culture on the rise while the other
is in retreat. It is also, to be brutal, that the young scientists know that with
an indifferent degree they'll get a comfortable job, while their contemporaries and counterparts in English or History will be lucky to earn 60 per
cent as much. No young scientist of any talent would feel that he isn't
wanted or that his work is ridiculous, as did the hero of *Lucky Jim*,[8] and in
fact, some of the disgruntlement of Amis and his associates is the disgruntlement of the under-employed arts graduate.

There is only one way out of all this: it is, of course, by rethinking our
education. In this country, for the two reasons I have given, that is more
difficult than in any other. Nearly everyone will agree that our school education is too specialised. But nearly everyone feels that it is outside the will
[20] of man to alter it. Other countries are as dissatisfied with their education as we are, but are not so resigned. . . .

[35] That brings me back to education. Why aren't we coping with
the scientific revolution? Why are other countries doing better? How are we
going to meet our future, both our cultural and practical future? It should
be obvious by now that I believe both lines of argument lead to the same
end. If one begins by thinking only of the intellectual life, or only of the
social life, one comes to a point where it becomes manifest that our education has gone wrong, and gone wrong in the same way. . . .

[38] With some qualifications, I believe the Russians have judged the
situation sensibly. They have a deeper insight into the scientific revolution
than we have, or than the Americans have. The gap between the cultures
doesn't seem to be anything like so wide as with us. If one reads contemporary Soviet novels, for example, one finds that their novelists can assume in
their audience—as we cannot—at least a rudimentary acquaintance with
what industry is all about. Pure science doesn't often come in, and they
don't appear much happier with it than literary intellectuals are here. But

[39] engineering does come in. An engineer in a Soviet novel is as acceptable, so it seems, as a psychiatrist in an American one. They are as ready to
cope in art with the process of production as Balzac was with the processes
of craft manufacture. I don't want to overstress this, but it may be significant. It may also be significant that, in these novels, one is constantly coming up against a passionate belief in education. The people in them believe
in education exactly as my grandfather did, and for the same mixture of
idealistic and bread-and-butter reasons.

Anyway, the Russians have judged what kind and number of educated
men and women a country needs to come out top in the scientific revolution. I am going to oversimplify, but their estimate, and I believe it's pretty
near right, is this. First of all, as many alpha plus scientists as the country
can throw up. No country has many of them. Provided the schools and
universities are there, it doesn't matter all that much what you teach them.
They will look after themselves. We probably have at least as many pro-rata
as the Russians and Americans; that is the least of our worries. Second, a
much larger stratum of alpha professionals—these are the people who are
going to do the supporting research, the high class design and development.
In quality, England compares well in this stratum with the U.S.A. or
U.S.S.R.: this is what our education is specially [40] geared to produce. In
quantity, though, we are not discovering (again per head of the population) half as many as the Russians think necessary and are able to find.
Third, another stratum, educated to about the level of Part I of the Natural
Sciences or Mechanical Sciences Tripos,⁹ or perhaps slightly below that.
Some of these will do the secondary technical jobs, but some will take major
responsibility, particularly in the human jobs. The proper use of such men
depends upon a different distribution of ability from the one that has grown
up here. As the scientific revolution goes on, the call for these men will be
something we haven't imagined, though the Russians have. They will be
required in thousands upon thousands, and they will need all the human
development that university education can give them. It is here, perhaps,
most of all that our insight has been fogged. Fourthly and last, politicians,
administrators, an entire community, who know enough science to have a
sense of what the scientists are talking about.

That, or something like that, is the specification for the scientific revolution. I wish I were certain that in this country we were adaptable enough
to meet it. In a moment I want to go on to an issue which will, in the world
view, count more: but perhaps I can be forgiven for taking a sideways look
at our own fate. It happens that of all the advanced countries, our position
is by a long way the most [41] precarious. This is the result of history and
accident, and isn't to be laid to the blame of any Englishman now living. If
our ancestors had invested talent in the industrial revolution instead of the
Indian Empire, we might be more soundly based now. But they didn't.

We were left with a population twice as large as we can grow food for, so that we are always going to be *au fond* more anxious than France or Sweden: and with very little in the way of natural resources—by the standard of the great world powers, with nothing. The only real assets we have, in fact, are our wits. Those have served us pretty well, in two ways. We have a good deal of cunning, native or acquired, in the art of getting on among ourselves: that is a strength. And we have been inventive and creative, possibly out of proportion to our numbers. I don't believe much in national differences in cleverness, but compared with other countries we are certainly no stupider.

Given these two assets, and they are our only ones, it should have been for us to understand the scientific revolution first, to educate ourselves to the limit, and give a lead. Well, we have done something. In some fields, like atomic energy, we have done better than anyone could have predicted. Within the pattern, the rigid and crystallised pattern of our education and of the two cultures, we have been trying moderately hard to adjust ourselves.

[42] . . . To say we have to educate ourselves or perish, is a little more melodramatic than the facts warrant. To say we have to educate ourselves or watch a steep decline in our own lifetime, is about right. We can't do it, I am now convinced, without breaking the existing pattern. I know how difficult this is. It goes against the emotional grain of nearly all of us. In many ways, it goes against my own, standing uneasily with one foot in a dead or dying world and the other in a world that at all costs we must see born. I wish I could be certain that we shall have the courage of what our minds tell us.

More often than I like, I am saddened by a historical myth. Whether the myth is good history or not, doesn't matter; it is pressing enough for me. I can't help thinking of the Venetian Republic in their last half-century. Like us, they had once been fabulously lucky. They had become rich, as we did, by accident. They had acquired immense political skill, just as we have. A good many of them were tough-minded, realistic, patriotic men. They knew, just as clearly as we know, that the current of history had begun to flow against them. Many of them gave their minds to working out ways to keep going. It would have meant breaking the pattern into which they had crystallised. They were fond of the pattern, just as we are fond of ours. They never found the will to break it. . . .

[53] Meanwhile, there are steps to be taken which aren't outside the powers of reflective people. Education isn't the total solution to this problem: but without education the West can't even begin to cope. All the arrows point the same way. Closing the gap between our cultures is a necessity in the most abstract intellectual sense, as well as in the most practical. When those two senses have grown apart, then no society is going to be able to think with wisdom. For the sake of the intellectual life, for the sake of this country's special danger, for the sake of the western society

living precariously rich among the poor, for the sake of the poor who needn't be poor if there is intelligence in the world, it is obligatory for us and the Americans and the whole West to look at our education with [54] fresh eyes. This is one of the cases where we and the Americans have the most to learn from each other. We have each a good deal to learn from the Russians, if we are not too proud. Incidentally, the Russians have a good deal to learn from us, too.

Isn't it time we began? The danger is, we have been brought up to think as though we had all the time in the world. We have very little time. So little that I dare not guess at it.

NOTES

1. polar. "Diametrically opposed in nature, action, etc., as the poles of a magnet" [WID].

2. Kyd. Thomas Kyd (1558-1594), Elizabethan dramatist, specialist in the "tragedy of blood." His *The Spanish Tragedy* (1585) was possibly the most popular play of the period.

3. Greene. Robert Greene (*c.* 1560-1592), Elizabethan dramatist and pamphleteer, remembered for the pamphlet in which he attacked Shakespeare as "an upstart crow."

4. Rutherford. Ernest Rutherford, First Baron (1871-1937), British physicist, famous for his studies in radioactivity, for his discovery of the alpha particle (1904) and the proton (1920). In 1919 Rutherford obtained the first nuclear reaction by bombarding atoms of nitrogen with alpha particles. He was awarded the 1908 Nobel Prize for Chemistry.

5. Dickens. Charles Dickens (1812-1870), English novelist, famous for such works as *David Copperfield* (1849-1850), *Pickwick Papers* (1836-1837), *Great Expectations* (1860-1861), and *A Christmas Carol* (1843).

6. Rilke. Rainer Maria Rilke (1875-1926), sensitive, introspective lyric poet of modern Germany. His works have unusual music, unusual visual imagery, a prophetic tone. *Poems from the Book of House* (English translation 1941) brought him fame; *Duinese Elegies* (English translation 1939), were his own favorites.

7. Second Law of Thermodynamics. "When free exchange of radiant energy or heat conduction takes place between two bodies at different temperatures, it is always the hotter of the two that loses energy and the colder that gains energy" [WID].

8. *Lucky Jim*. A humorous and satiric novel by Kingsley Amis (1922-   ) one of the generation of postwar English novelists. Amis' other works include *That Uncertain Feeling* (1955), *Take a Girl Like You* (1960), and *One Fat Englishman* (1960).

9. Mechanical Science Tripos. An honors examination in mathematical science at Cambridge.

TOPICS FOR DISCUSSION

1. Describe the breakdown in modern communication which Snow deplores. What loss does this failure represent? Do you find evidence of such a breakdown in communication in American life? In your own life? Explain.

2. Discuss Snow's thoughts concerning Russia's structuring of education in the light of the scientific revolution. What warning does he have for England in regard to that country's traditional educational system? How does this warning about the widening gap between scientist and nonscientist compare with those of the other essayists?

3. Identify the familiar attitudes toward science and scientific discipline which Snow displays. What place, if any, does he grant the humanities in modern education? In modern life? How much and what kind of evidence does he present for his generalizations?

4. Snow declares, in a portion of the essay not quoted in this volume, "Intellectuals, in particular literary intellectuals, are natural Luddites." Who were the Luddites? What is Snow implying here by his use of the term?

5. How would you characterize the style of the essay, the tone, the allusions? Compare Snow's style and his treatment of science and the humanities with Huxley's. Would Huxley have considered Sir Charles one of the "scientific Goths and Vandals"? Why or why not?

DOUGLAS BUSH

Science and the Humanities

For the past four decades Douglas Bush (b. 1896), as a teacher and scholar, has defended the humanities. He has taught chiefly at the University of Minnesota and at Harvard. He has been professor of English at Harvard since 1937, and Gurney Professor of English there since 1957. In 1934-1935 he was a Guggenheim fellow and, in 1957, he received an award from the American Council of Learned Societies. His special fields of interest are Milton, the Renaissance, and the seventeenth century. His scholarly works include Myth and Renaissance Tradition in English Poetry *(1932),* Myth and the Romantic Tradition in English Poetry *(1937), and* English Literature in the Earlier Seventeenth Century *(1945).*

This essay, like Professor Nagel's "Science and the Humanities," was given as an address in the Tamiment Institute program in the summer of 1958. Though there are some areas of agreement between the two, on most points Bush's address and Nagel's meet in head-on conflict. For a specific discussion of the influence of science upon literature, see Douglas Bush, Science and English Poetry *(New York: Oxford University Press, 1960). [This selection is taken from Douglas Bush, "Science and the Humanities," in Brand Blanshard (ed.),* Education in the Age of Science *(New York: Basic Books, 1959), pp. 167-87.]*

[167] While other subjects in the curriculum may have their ups and downs, it is always proper to speak of "the plight of the humanities," and in the hushed, melancholy tone of one present at a perpetual deathbed. For something like twenty-five hundred years the humanities have been in more or less of a plight. I should like to give some reasons for the uphill struggle they have always had and always will have. The chief reasons may be grouped under the heading of original sin. Since the humanities are opposed to and opposed by man's animal nature and animal drives, [168] the essential causes of opposition are very old; but they have taken on many new forms and have gained enormously in strength in modern times.

First of all, there is the inspiring and dispiriting fact that, while the goals of science are predictable and attainable, the goal of the humanities is not—unless human nature undergoes a miraculous transformation. It is much easier to make discoveries in the laboratory, to put satellites into the earth's orbit, than it is to achieve humane wisdom, imagination, and insight in thought, feeling, and action. And the latter, the true end of man, is far less compelling than lower ends. The mass of mankind has always been mainly absorbed in the struggle for subsistence or comfort or pleasure or power. To recall a saying of the wise humanist Montaigne,[1] Socrates[2] was a greater man than Alexander[3] because while Alexander conquered cities, Socrates conquered himself. In the Renaissance creed, man was a creature halfway between the beasts and the angels, drawn both downward and upward by elements in his own nature; the aim of education was to make him less like a beast and more like an angel. The aim of the humanities, an aim that can never be fulfilled but can never be abandoned, is to humanize and civilize the aggressive and sensual animal, to lead him to realize his distinctively human endowments, to refine and multiply his moments of vision, to free his better self from bondage of his ordinary self.

SOPHISTICATED VULGARITY

No one would disparage the multiplying benefits that science and technology have supplied, but it cannot be denied that they have also imposed stultifying pressures on man's mind and character and aesthetic sensibility. [169] Whatever may be hoped for from science in the distant future, it would seem that at present we have more to fear from the mass civilization of our Western world than from Russia. The modern rise in the material well-being of the common man—which includes woman and child —of course has been long overdue, but one unhappy result so far has been the debasement of traditional culture. . . . The general diffusion of literacy has enabled millions to consume the husks provided for them and to make more precarious than ever the survival of high standards of enlightenment and taste. . . .

[170] Moreover, the media and standards of mass civilization do not operate merely on the lowest economic and cultural levels; they more or less infect the millions who have attended college and might be thought to have higher interests and better taste. One symptom is the way in which the uneducated misuse of words and idioms becomes, overnight, common usage among the supposedly educated and promptly gets into the dictionaries. It is a painful fact of American life and education that, after leaving college, the majority of people virtually give up serious reading; and that, of the minority who do not, only a fraction pays any attention to literature, new or old. In a survey made in 1956, only 17 per cent of American adults were found to be reading books, as compared with 31 per cent in Canada, 34 per cent in Australia, and 55 per cent in England; 57 per cent of our high-school graduates and 26 per cent of our college graduates had not read a single book during the preceding year; of the college graduates, 9 per cent could not name the author of any one of twelve famous books in English,

and 39 per cent could not name more than three; 45 per cent could not name any recently published book. . . .

THE ASCENDENCY OF SCIENCE

[171] I have spoken of two things that work against the humanities: one negative—the common lack of a desire, capacity, or opportunity for humane self-discipline, for moral and aesthetic cultivation—and one positive—the gross or insidious allurements and pressures of mass civilization. A third is the direct pressure of science and the [172] supreme authority claimed for and given to the scientific method and outlook. Science is of course a large and essential part of a liberal education, and the placing of science in partial opposition to the humanities requires explanation. It is often urged that the scientific imagination and the poetic imagination are very close to each other, if not identical; and doubtless there is a rarefied plane on which that is true—the plane of curiosity, wonder, and the inspired leap of intuition, not to mention fundamental brainwork. But in their normal working these two faculties are very distinct, simply because the natural scientist is largely concerned with physical nature, with things, while the artist is concerned with the nature and behavior of man. Obviously the scientist, *qua* man, shares the general experience of humanity, and, *qua* scientist, he may have not only intellectual but moral and aesthetic experience; but it is no less obvious that science *per se* does not operate in the human realm of moral values and moral choice. Without the humanities and what they represent, science can become merely the instrument of man's aggressive passions.

In the second place, as science and scientific method have more and more come to dominate the modern mind, scientists, philosophers, and laymen more and more have assumed that there is only one kind of truth, one kind of reality—that which is discovered, measured, and verified by science. Viewed in that light, literature sinks to the level of an insignificant reaction or an insidious fantasy of wish-fulfillment. Antagonism or condescension toward literature may not be typical of modern scientists, but such attitudes have many exemplars from Bacon down to Freud[4] and the present moment. A positivist philosopher once put the case to me in a memorable syllogism: The end of life [173] is the contemplation of true propositions; Shakespeare has no true propositions; therefore Shakespeare is not worth reading. So all literature goes into the wastebasket, along with metaphysics and religion.

To register another modern phenomenon from which the humanities especially suffer, it was no doubt inevitable that the immense growth of modern knowledge should lead to subdivision and specialization, but it was no less inevitable that such specialization should be in many ways disastrous. We may remember the old medical doctrine of the four humours: if one of the four grew predominant, the physical and mental constitution became diseased. In the modern world of learning and science such disease is the normal condition. From ancient times up through a good part of the nineteenth century the mass of educated men, including scientists, had a more or less uniform education, a common cultural heritage, a more or less common outlook—however much they might diverge later. But the once seamless robe of Truth has become a thing of holes and lumps and shreds and patches. The fifty departments of a modern university are aggregates of electrons moved by repulsion; and the educated public tends to be an aggregate of heterogeneous groups which do not speak the same language, which share only a minimum of common culture. I am told that mathematicians and physicists, who used to be blood brothers, are now growing apart and unable to communicate with one another. The Modern Language Association meets in a multitude of groups, and the expert in one is an alien in forty others. . . .

[174] But mere knowledge of disciplines other than one's own is less important than a sympathetic understanding, and it may be suggested that many scientists and social scientists are so wedded to scientific method and materials that they do not understand what the humanities are and seek to do. European and English scientists are perhaps less open to this criticism than Americans, since they are more likely to have had a humanistic education and are also more likely to continue general reading through their life. We might recall, though, one who did not have a [175] humanistic education, T. H. Huxley. In his debate with Matthew Arnold over the educational claims of literature and science, while Arnold was appealing to man's profound concern with the power of conduct, of intellect and knowledge, of beauty, of social life and manners, Huxley saw "culture" as only belletristic ornament and diversion.

Further, the humanities by nature and definition embrace all kinds of knowledge and experience over the whole of mankind's history, whereas the natural scientist, as such, is concerned only with the latest developments. The history of science is itself an enlightening and important discipline which may well be included under the humanities, but science *per se* is quite different. The scientific mind instinctively assumes that knowledge means chiefly new knowledge; the humanities, on the other hand, are not measured in terms of novelty and discovery. The humanist's object is to conserve and propagate our cultural heritage, to transmit the wisdom and art of the past to people of the present and future. Naturally there is continual reinterpretation of the great works of literature and art, continual rewriting of the evolution of ideas (and cultural history is a valuable discipline in itself), but considerations of old and new, of time and history, are only secondary to making the assimilation of those great works a richer experience. . . .

WHAT THE HUMANITIES CAN DO FOR MAN

[182] In sketching the multitudinous things that work against the humanities, I have partly indicated what the humanities have always been and what, if given a chance, they can always be, even if they lack the pragmatic or spectacular appeal of the social or the natural sciences. I assume of course that all three branches of study make unique contributions and are essential elements in a liberal education. But, as I have said, it is clear that many people, including not a few scientists, social scientists, and philosophers, look on the humanities as an outmoded luxury. On the contrary, the humanities are a prime and practical necessity if men and women are to be fully human; they are in fact *the* prime necessity, since they are part of our everyday living and being. But it is not front-page news if [183] a rocket goes off in the mind of John or Mary Smith, if he or she, through absorbing a poem, becomes a person of richer imaginative and moral insight, of finer wisdom and discrimination and stability. For the experience of literature and art is an individual experience, and, like all other really important things, it cannot be measured. . . .

The old classical education is usually condemned by its foes because it could suffer at times from low aims and poor teaching and because, so they say, it was narrow and remote. Well, low aims and poor teaching can afflict the most modern studies. As for narrowness, the great virtue of the old classical education was, and is, its combined unity and variety. One body of material, the expression of two great and related civilizations, contained an array of masterpieces in prose and verse which not only gave full play to the imaginative, emotional, aesthetic, and critical [184] faculties, but embraced the first principles of ethics, metaphysics, history, politics, and economics. As everyone knows, this body of material provided in Europe for many centuries—and to some degree still provides—a stable community and continuity of ideas and values. For a long time it governed American education; it nourished the men who wrote the Constitution and the Bill of Rights. The large gap left by the dropping of the classics has been recognized even by education of lukewarm sympathy, and the vacuum has been filled, after a fashion, by courses in "general education" and the like.

It may be said that a sane and rational approach to the problems of man and society can be achieved through means other than the humanities. Doubtless it can, up to a point—though I think natural scientists as well as humanists may feel depressed when they scan many of the courses offered by our departments of sociology; and I myself, I might say, have little faith in the wisdom of much current psychology, which in some forms seems a crude affront to the dignity of man. At any rate, one of the distinctive things about the kind of illumination to be gained from the humanities is that one is never allowed to forget the individual person, to lose sight of oneself and others in a large blur of social and economic forces and formulas. The basic question, which contains and dwarfs all others, is whether John Smith—or Ivan Ivanovitch—feels and thinks and acts rightly or wrongly, whether he loves what the best experience has found lovable and enlightening and sustaining. The materials of the humanities are the products of great individual minds, and they work directly upon individuals. As Whitehead declared, "Moral education is impossible apart from the habitual vision of greatness." I do not know where the habitual vision of greatness is found except in the humanities.

[185] From antiquity until recent times, literature has been the chief medium of education, and in spite of—or because of—the emergence of new kinds of knowledge, its responsibilities have not shrunk. They have indeed grown more important than ever, as many things have combined to lower the dignity, benumb the sensibility, and drown the voice of individual man. The aim of the humanities is not to adjust people to life, to the pressures and low ideals of mass civilization, but to enlighten and disturb them, to inspire and strengthen them to adjust life and themselves to the great traditional ideals of the best minds, the saving remnant of the human race. The subject matter of literature is the whole range and texture of life, the material conditions of existence, all that man does and is and would be as an individual being, his desires and hopes and joys and fears and sufferings and defeats and victories; and, along with that, all that he experiences as one of a family, of a community, of a nation, of the human race. Such headings apply to man and literature in all ages, and literature at once reflects, opposes, and creates the spirit of every particular age. Modern literature, the literature of the age of anxiety, has been preoccupied with man's increasing consciousness of his loss of outward and inward wholeness and order, with his sense of being a fragment in a fragmentary world. And the eternal quest of literature, intensified by the common modern loss of religious assurance, has been the quest of order. From the chaos of life and society the artist seeks a pattern of explanation, a pattern that helps him and his readers to achieve some measure of dominion over experience. The value of the success of such efforts depends upon many things, from his own and his readers' powers of imagination to the feeling for a structure and tone and the texture of word and rhythm. Historical and philosophical and every other kind of knowledge, including that [186] of everyday life, enter into the creation of and the response to the work of art, but the work in itself is unique, and no discursive substitute can take its place. . . .

GREAT WRITERS AS THE CONSCIENCE OF MANKIND

[187] . . . The great artist's vision of life is not dimmed or deadened by time, because it is a distillation of man's finest insights, of his supreme awareness both of what man is and of what man might be. Thus the literature of the centuries of ancient paganism, of the centuries of Christianity, and of our own era, the era that it has become fashionable to call post-

Christian—all this constitutes a simultaneous and living whole. Whatever the vagaries of Homer's gods, his ethics have an unfailing soundness and rightness. So likewise do Shakespeare's, though Shakespeare's religious creed is very different from Homer's. Shakespeare's highroad leading nowhere, as Alfred Harbage[5] has said, is the road home; what he tells us is what we have always known—though he tells us much more too.

When the slayer of Hector and the father of Hector[6] meet, brought together by the command of Zeus, they both learn the meaning of compassion. The same lesson is learned, through suffering, by King Lear, and he dies, like the aged Oedipus, in the knowledge of love given and received. The mind of Hamlet swarms with ideas and feelings unknown to Orestes,[7] but there are affinities between them. And the religious integrity that unites Antigone[8] with Jeanie Deans[9] bridges the gulf between the laws that grow not old and the God of Scottish Calvinism.[10] The shock of a young man's initiation into the adult world of evil links Sophocles' Neoptolemus[11] with the central figure in Hemingway's "The Killers." Thus the great writers—pagan, Christian, agnostic—"are folded in a single party"; they are the imagination and the conscience of mankind. If we have any hope of going forward, or of not slipping further backward, they must be our guides.

NOTES

1. Montaigne Michel Eyquem, Seigneur de Montaigne (1533-1592). French essayist and philosopher. His *Essais*, I, II (1580) illustrate his urbane style and skeptical spirit.

2. Socrates (469-399 B.C.). Greek philosopher whose teachings are available to us chiefly through the writings of his disciple Plato.

3. Alexander. Alexander the Great (356-323 B.C.), King of Macedon 336-323 B.C. Having conquered the known world at the age of thirty-three, he became a legendary hero for later generations.

4. Freud. Sigmund Freud (1856-1939), founder of modern psychoanalysis. His emphasis on the importance of the unconscious and of the role of sex in human life, as well as the development of the psychoanalytic method, are considered his most notable contributions. His influence has extended to art (as in surrealist painting) and literature (with the development of the stream-of-consciousness novel).

5. Alfred Harbage (1901-   ). Shakespearean scholar, general editor of the Pelican edition of Shakespeare.

6. Slayer of Hector and father of Hector. Achilles, the Greek warrior, and Priam, the King of Troy, whose meeting is described in Homer's *Iliad*.

7. Orestes. Son of Agamemnon and Clytemnestra. Agamemnon was murdered by Clytemnestra and her lover Aegisthus; later, the murder was avenged by Orestes, spurred on by his sister Electra. See the *Orestes* of Euripides, or Aeschylus' trilogy *The Agamemnon, The Choephori*, and *The Eumenides*.

8. Antigone. Sophocles, chronologically the second of the great Greek tragedians, created in Antigone a tragic heroine who symbolizes the resistance of the individual conscience to civic tyranny.

9. Jeanie Deans. The heroine of Sir Walter Scott's novel *The Heart of Midlothian* (1818).

10. Scottish Calvinism. The doctrines of the Protestant reformer John Calvin (1500-1564) were established in Scotland by John Knox (1503-1572). Scottish Calvinism is particularly notable for its stern and rigid discipline.

11. Sophocles' Neoptolemus. Sometimes called Pyrrhus; son of Achilles, he was the boy hero in Sophocles' drama *Philoctetes*.

TOPICS FOR DISCUSSION

1. How does Bush justify his thesis that "original sin" accounts for much of the continuing opposition to the humanities?

2. Describe the differences in goals and concepts of knowledge that distinguish the sciences from the humanities and discuss the effect of such differences in furthering the power of contemporary science. Explain why Bush terms these differences both "inspiring and dispiriting."

3. How can Bush's complaints about the effects of science and technology on modern life be reconciled with Glass' view that science has ennobled man by enlarging his freedom of choice?

4. How would you reply to the syllogism of the "positivist philosopher" that concluded "therefore Shakespeare is not worth reading"?

5. "Without the humanities and what they represent, science can become merely the instrument of man's aggressive passions," says Bush. Which of the essayists represented in this volume would agree with him? Which would dissent most sharply? Why?

6. Compare Bush's comments on the breakdown of communication between the disciplines with C. P. Snow's. Compare Bush's comment on the narrowness of Huxley's views of literature with Huxley's statement of his own position.

7. Give some examples of "the pragmatic or spectacular appeal of the social or the natural sciences."

8. Compare the last two paragraphs of this essay with the closing paragraph of Barzun's. How effectively has each author employed allusions to reinforce his argument?

9. Both Barzun and Bush defend the humanities. To what extent does their defense rest on similar grounds? Which author do you feel has made the stronger case? Why?

JACQUES BARZUN

A Truce to the Nonsense
on Both Sides

Jacques Barzun (b. 1907) is Dean of Faculties and Provost of Colum-
bia University. Born in France, he came to America at the age of twelve, in
1919 and became a naturalized citizen in 1933. God's Country and Mine,
published in 1954, presents his reflections on the American scene. He has
written with eloquence, scholarship, and insight on music, teaching, litera-
ture, and intellectual history. His many works include The Teacher in
America (1945), Berlioz and the Romantic Century (1950), The Energies
of Art (1956), The House of Intellect (1959), Classic, Romantic and
Modern (1961), *and* Science: The Glorious Entertainment (1964).
In December 1963, at a convocation at Hofstra University, Professor
Barzun voiced the fear that the liberal arts college in America is gradually
being forced out of existence by pressure from below generated by the tak-
ing over by the secondary schools of courses once reserved for the college,
and by pressure from above in the form of encroachment by graduate and
professional schools. His House of Intellect (New York: Harper & Row,
1959) *further analyzes the effect of the harmful influence of science on*
modern life and learning. [This selection is taken from Jacques Barzun,
"Science vs. the Humanities," Saturday Evening Post, CCXXX (May 3,
1955), 26-28. The subtitle of the article is "A Truce to the Nonsense on
Both Sides."]

[28] The cause of the unending discussion about the humanities is, I suspect, that most of those concerned do not quite know what to believe and
do not quite believe what they know. Whether from fatigue or confusion,
to which we are all increasingly liable, many distrust their ancient convictions and suppose that some new arguments have been found, some clinch-
ing formula which will restore their faith in the humanities and make it
secure in a world of technologists, businessmen, and foundation officials.

It is the search for this formula which produces on this subject the
great "and" literature—the humanities *and* the democratic way of life; the

humanities *and* the well-rounded man; the humanities *and* a creative culture; the humanities *and* the understanding of the self; the humanities *and* leisure in a welfare state; the humanities *and* world peace. The hope implied is that the link between the humanities and things desirable will suggest the relation of cause and effect. The humanities will then be valued, justified, supported as essential to democracy, self-knowledge, world peace, and the rest. This is a deplorable hope. These well-meant attempts at raising price and prestige are not only tedious and vague but contradictory and unconvincing.

No set of matters can by itself secure these desired ends. If they could do so by influencing individual minds, why have they done so little in so long a time? The claim of the humanities to be a remedy is, in fact, absurd. The humanities will not rout the world's evils and were never meant to cure individual troubles; they are entirely compatible with those evils and troubles. Nor are the humanities a substitute for medicine or psychiatry; they will not heal diseased minds or broken hearts any more than they foster political democracy or settle international disputes. All the evidence goes the other way. The so-called humanities have meaning chiefly because of the *in*humanity of life; what they depict and discuss is strife and disaster. The *Iliad* is not about world peace; *King Lear* is not about a well-rounded man; *Madame Bovary*[1] is not about the judicious employment of leisure time.

If it is argued that the contemplation of disaster through art or history serves as a warning and teaches morality by inverse example, I ask what evidence there is that a good book has ever prevented a bad action, or a fine sonata a foolish deed. The addiction to books and music begins in early life, before passion and society pose their problems of conduct; and it is also true that in modern as in ancient times the persons reared in the humanities have been exemplars of individual and social unrest. It is men brought up on art, literature, languages, history and philosophy who have been the ambitious and the intriguers, the rebels and the tyrants, the libertines and the agitators, as well as the great tragic figures of discontent in the biographical history of art.

To this catalogue of misrule you may object that, as the term is used today, the servants of the humanities are found rather among another group of people who seldom riot or transgress, and that it is this group, the students and scholars of the humanities, who require prestige and support for the sake of their law-abiding example and harmless teachings.

True, and this double use of the word *humanities* confuses the argument; we need some definitions. We use the term at times in the loose sense of "the arts," or culture at large; and at other times in the academic sense of the study and teaching of the arts. To the scholar, the humanities are a group of subjects set off from the natural and the social sciences—simply open a college catalogue and you will find that chemistry, sociology and English literature are under different headings, taught by different persons, usually in different buildings, and often in what seems like different languages. The pure sciences teach the behavior of nature; the social sciences, the behavior of men in large groups; the humanities deal with the individual—hence my notion of *mis*behavioral science.

This rough classification is clear enough. What is more doubtful is where certain subjects belong. History and anthropology are sometimes classed with literature and philosophy, sometimes with social science; symbolic logic has close affinities with mathematics and other "natural" sciences, just as these sciences have with philosophy. And where do we put psychology, geography, and the history of the natural sciences? It is soon evident that all subjects are interrelated through the single mind of man, and that we shall never be able to carve up the domain of thought along fixed lines.

The conclusion is of capital importance, for one of the current clichés is that the humanities, as their name suggests, are more human than science and social science—in fact, the only form of thought that remains truly human in a civilization given over to mathematics and machinery. On reflection, these beliefs turn out to be mere verbalisms, the expression of impulses with which one may sympathize, but which must not be allowed to cloud the mind.

In the first place, etymology is a poor guide in this as in other arguments. The term *humanities*, descended from the Renaissance catch phrase *litterae humaniores*, can be appealed to as carrying the suggestion of "peculiarly human," but it is mere suggestion, not proof. If we respect fact and language, we must stop using the word "human" as an honorific term. Everything that men do is human; if an "especially" or "peculiarly" is to be added, it must apply to what men do with deliberation and intelligence. Accordingly, all subjects of research and instruction are human—peculiarly human—and so are a number of activities that the moral sense condemns, such as the deliberate and intelligent preparation of cruelty, criminal violence, and war. Once again, to define the humanities by honorifics is a delusion.

But to understand the cause of that delusion is a step forward in their correct identification. For we have reached the point where the discussion of the humanities as academic subjects leads us to think again of culture at large, and notably of the arts, whose dwelling place is unlimited and whose life dare not be academic. The arts exist in the market place, in Bohemia, in journalism, as well as in the cultivated parts of society, and they belong to none exclusively. In recent years, for various reasons, more and more people have come to regard art as the principal justification of man's existence, the redemption of his follies through perfect and lasting creation. Whereas in religious times man is said to work for the greater glory of God, in the modern secular world he prides himself on being what we call creative; all his efforts are equated with—or at least measured by—the work of the artist. This produces another confusion among related but distinct activities —the arts, the humanities, creation and culture. And we can see why the dedicated students of the arts—particularly those who teach the humanities —claim special regard. Their work brings them in daily touch with what the world considers the highest embodiment of man's spirit.

As an immediate result of this pride, they experience the age-old distress of the priesthood, which is to see that though the world worships the true God, it carries its golden tribute to alien altars. The result, among our humanists, is the putting forth of those utilitarian arguments we noticed before; they promise personal happiness or social harmony as the by-product of studying the imagery of Shakespeare or digging in the midden[2] heaps of Mesopotamia.

Unfortunately the promise, though honestly meant, is false; and what is worse, this missionary role puts the humanities in an untenable position, materially and spiritually, for the missionary must offer the ultimate word on mankind, the secret of salvation, which proves his special insight into the transcendent. What more, then, does he want? The world correctly considers that he has been paid in the coin he values most and that it is only weakness in him to want power and wealth besides.

On top of this, it turns out that his secret is a pious fraud. Experience has shown again and again that the humanities are as powerless as any other branch of learning to solve the riddle of the Sphinx or chart the course for Utopia. If they could, and if this were in fact their utility, their importance would come to an end in the very instance of success. For such is the fate of all mere devices.

But the humanities are not a mere device; they are not agencies for general improvement. The humanities in the broad cultural sense and in the narrow academic one have uses that are much more intimate and permanent. In any generation persons are born who, finding in the world books and music and works of art and theaters, are instinctively drawn to them. These people grow up with an ingrained desire for the objects of their interest [60] and a preference for people of a like taste. A larger group, though less intent, takes from time to time similar pleasure in artistic activities. The two groups together are strong enough to impose on the remainder the daily presence of what delights them.

Thus the art of architecture and its decoration—the post-office mural or the restored Williamsburg—are forced on millions who, left to themselves, might live in a cave or a tent. Thus newspapers and magazines reproduce pictures, retell history, comment on art old and new, criticize music and books, write about the lives and opinions of artists—in short, cater for the minority who sway us all by their peculiar tastes.

Thus again, public libraries and museums and concerts in parks and dinner-hour broadcasts "make available to all" (as we say) the products of these special concerns. Consequently, when we repeat the commonplace that the modern world is ruled by science, we must at once add that that same world is given its shape and color by art, its most pleasing sounds and meanings by music and poetry, its categories, characters, and catchwords by philosophy, fiction, and history. Imagine all the devotees of the humanities suddenly withdrawing to a monastery, taking with them all that belongs to them, and the workaday world we know would turn before our astonished faces into something bleak, dark, soundless, bare of sensuous charm, and empty of any meaning beyond that of immediate needs and their fulfillment by mechanic aids.

A few persons—many fewer than the humanities can count as devotees —might still enjoy intellectual contemplation and mathematical thrills, but even they might miss from the stripped stage of daily life the furniture we call civilization.

This contrast is at once instructive and comforting. It tells us that the arts produce objects for the senses and not only for the mind, which is one reason why the humanities are not interested in proofs or in statistics; in place of proof they give possession, and in place of averages they give uniqueness. And despite fashions in taste, these objects form an ever-enlarging treasury. We speak of 3,000 years of literature, philosophy, and architecture; of a vast collection of objects of art, of an impressive repertory of music—all of it as varied, new, and mysterious as it ever was. This reality points to the true role, the indispensable function, of the *academic* humanities—they are the organizers of our huge inheritance of civilization. Without the continual work of humanistic scholars we should be living not in a culture full of distinct and vigorous traditions—national, religious, artistic, philosophical, scientific, and political; rather, we should be rummaging about in an attic full of incomprehensible relics.

Let us take one or two examples, beginning with the simplest and most obvious, which is to say the commonest and least noticed. Take a man who lives in a small town, a businessman who is not aware of any intellectual interests, though he feels a sturdy patriotism, local and national. Such a man, contrary to all appearances, and whether he knows it or not, is a client of scholarship. With every commemorative stamp that reinforces his pride, he absorbs a product of art and research. Every political speech he hears invoking the memory of Jefferson or Lincoln implies his recognition of ideas and allusions that belong to the domain of the humanities. He need not belong to the county historical society to approve, as bank director, a decision to make the new bank building a replica of Independence Hall; he probably approves out of natural piety.

But this puts him at once in the grip of half a dozen humanities. Questions of art, of taste, of semantics, of period style, of historical accuracy bother his unaccustomed head. He begins to live at once in the present and in the past; his imagination adds to its work on discount rates, visions of pediments, and meditations on cracked bells. This Philistine, whom the learned world looks upon merely as census fodder, invades the library, reads books, and compares old engravings. What is more, he may shortly be seen struggling with his native idiom in the course of preparing a prospectus for future visitors to the bank; he is but a step away from becoming an anti-quarian and a numismatist. Meanwhile he has turned author after having become a consumer of scholarship, a defender of it to his exasperated family —indeed, a scholar in spite of himself.

As for the bank building, however foolishly inappropriate and preten-tious it may be, it stands as a monument to the force of tradition and points to the need for its due ordering.

Next, consider the sophisticated citizen of the metropolis who goes to see an Old Vic production of Shakespeare. He enjoys the performance or he does not, but in either case he takes its availability for granted, like the arrival of his coffee at breakfast. Shakespeare is there, waiting; Shakespeare is always with us. It probably does not occur to this patron of the theater that between the blotted lines as they left Shakespeare's hand and their repetition on Broadway, thousands of minds have toiled to rescue perishable art from neglect and misunderstanding. If you mention to him the lighting effects, our spectator may give a fleeting thought to the scientific effort behind the development of electricity, but as he argues with you about the acting of the play, he has no notion that, like the clarity of the text, the production draws on three hundred years of critical thought, of which his own remarks are but echoes filtered through textbooks and newspapers. Shakespeare, then, exists for him only by the joint effort of many expert hands, which have, as a by-product, fashioned the beholder's mind to per-ceptiveness.

Without this double action of humanistic scholarship repeated every generation, our heritage of art and thought would soon crumble into noth-ingness. All we need in order to be sure of this is to hear a publisher talk about book sales—if school adoption is likely the work is printed and stays in print. This means that in addition to bringing order into the high prod-ucts of civilization, the teaching and scholarship of the humanities keep that civilization in being. Let no word be said in school about Shakespeare and Doctor Johnson,[3] let no pressure be put on youth to learn the familiar dates and names, the terms and meanings of past eras, by oral tradition or with the aid of a few quickly perishable books, and local lore would soon replace what we now call common knowledge. The enterprise of learning would collapse as soon as the assumption of its unity and necessity was removed, leaving the individual at the mercy of chance encounters and without hope of light. The scientist and the [62] statistician would be cut off from the rest of mankind—unless they diverted part of their energies to re-creating a common intellectual world—and those of whom I have spoken as being born with a passion for art and letters would be thrown back entirely on their own resources, like the survivors of a barbarian invasion.

When, therefore, the representative of a foundation expresses official skepticism about the humanities in the modern world (not ever speaking for himself, since he is a humanist at heart, but for his Board of Trustees, whose hardheadedness is reported as granitic), the argument against his skepticism is quite simple: The humanities are of no use in the social worker's sense of "useful." They are of use, unobtrusively, all day and every day, to those who respect and enjoy and require the evidences of civilization.

I have used the board of a foundation only as an example. The conflict between the "practical" sciences and the "superfluous" humanities is not a real conflict to those who know the realities they are talking about. Rather, it is a conflict with the thoughtless about the meaning of utility.

The spokesmen for the "practical" view that only science and social science are worth their cost, because they feed and cure and retrain mankind, have never measured any such costs or verified any results. They act on prejudice, or in fear of a popular opinion which has never been canvassed. They moreover limit the useful to large social necessities, such as national defense or the reduction of juvenile delinquency. But necessity is a strange test to apply in a society with pretensions such as ours, a society which might be described as in flight from necessity. Apply the test to the "practical" spokesman himself and he would soon cry mercy; no necessity exists for him to go fishing, for his wife to wear mink, for his office to be attractively decorated. If he is a man of business, he knows that trade depends on people's desire for products they could easily live without. The desire, the taste, establishes the utility of all man-made things, a fifth of whisky or a Fifth of Beethoven.

The use of the humanities, then, is proved and fixed by the ancient, unshakable, ever-spreading desire for them. On the surface these uses appear more individual than social, more self-indulgent than altruistic. Some men are so selfish that they read a book or go to a concert for their own sinister pleasure, instead of doing it to improve social conditions, as the good citizen does when drinking cocktails or playing bridge. . . .

The fact that the academic humanities provide the intellectual structure of the civilized life in no way guarantees that the humanistic scholar is a model of civilized intelligence and good taste. Any such view of him is an assumption that reality often dispels, which may explain why the public mistrusts the scholar; he does not look like the noble image one forms of *the* humanist, something like Holbein's portrait of Erasmus.[4] The world is better prepared to find the artist an odd fish—in fact, it is disappointed if he isn't. And this expectation suggests to some that perhaps the scholar looks strange because he, too, is a kind of artist; from which it is only a step to saying that humanistic scholarship is creative.

The academic humanities undoubtedly deal with the arts; why, then, doesn't it follow that scholars and teachers in those fields are artists, or at least cultivated men? The fact is that they are not, or need not be. This must be bluntly said, if only to prevent the serious claims of the humanities from being understood as the claims of humanists to wisdom, elegance and glamour. Not long ago a well-known psychiatrist denounced the humanities as a wasteful expense. Put the time and money into mass psychoanalysis, he said, and the sum of individual happiness in this country would be immeasurably increased. This sort of argument is unanswerable. It is also irrelevant. But it shows the danger of perpetuating conventional nonsense about the academic humanists and their work. They can be adequately rewarded and respected only when they appear in their true colors.

The academic humanities, I repeat, are not a form of creation. It is really strange that one should have to say this, when the very definition of the academic humanities is the *study* of art and thought. In a culture with less reverence for art than ours, and freer of social anxiety about proving one's worthiness, no sensible scholar would ever have decorated himself and his fellows with the title of creator. The scholar, to be sure, often possesses the intelligence, imagination, [63] subtlety or other qualities that are found in artists. But a creator—a maker of something new that stands by itself— he is not. Observation shows that the artistic and the scholarly temperaments rarely combine. They are not even well paired within the university, and we have yet to hear of any masterpiece hatched on a campus. I do not mean a work that has been published or produced—I mean a masterpiece.

It is because of this fundamental difference that works of attempted creation ought not to qualify for academic credit. I know such crediting is an accepted practice, and I despair of making clear the reasons why it is unjust and ludicrous, but no matter. The point here is that the public must support the work of the humanistic scholars, teachers and critics, not because they produce art, but because they serve art. They serve art, as I have shown, by introducing the new generations to it, thus keeping alert the eye, ear and mind; they serve art by maintaining order around it, thus preventing its obscuration by error and nonsense; they serve art, finally, by tracing out connections and principles throughout the whole domain, thus satisfying curiosity and enhancing pleasure. That is the practical service rendered in answer to the inborn need of man for art and thought. . . .

Whatever mixture of aims and talents occurs in any individual life, professional obligations are distinct from personal. This is why a scholar need not even be a cultivated man. Many scholars qualify as both, but that remains their privilege, not their duty. This amounts to saying that scholarship, like teaching, is a special gift which does not necessarily imply any other. Richard Bentley, the seventeenth-century scholar, was a genius in his line; he did not merely know, but he felt the classical languages by ear as well as intellectually. Yet his edition of Milton shows that he hardly understood his native English idiom, and that off bounds his common sense completely deserted him.

It is, moreover, a fact that a large part of scholarship is drudgery, from which it follows that many scholars are drudges. Who shall say that they are not necessary, worthy, even admirable? The people who edit letters and annotate classics, who compile bibliographies, catalogues and lexicons, are as indispensable as the laboratory technicians who repeat minute determinations, or the tabulators who turn questionnaires into curves. None of them directly delight the mind; we must have them, nevertheless, and be grateful. It is as unfair to expect that he who compiles a concordance of a poet shall be lyrical as that he who drives fat oxen shall himself be fat.

The humanities, then, are not a Cinderella who goes forth into the world only with the aid of magic and has to scurry home when real life resumes its sway. Quite the contrary, the humanities are permanently abroad and if in their academic setting they are poor, it is because their actual services are taken too much for granted; it is that by dint of living on their intellectual capital they look rich—rich in students, rich in enthusiasm, rich in intangible rewards. They are poor in means because they have not known how to make out their case on their own grounds. They have claimed powers that belong either to no man or to other men, and at the same time they have been culpably modest and retiring.

They have heard sanctimonious voices repeated *ad nauseam* that "man does live by bread alone," and they have never interrupted to say, "bakers and butchers, be quiet—and discharge your debt to us for the alchemy which makes your life behind the counter bearable."

That rejoinder, to be sure, is neither gracious nor ennobling, but it is at least honest and, when competition is the order of the day, it is appropriate. In more contemplative moments, the humanities can find other words to represent them, and it is with an approximation of such words that I want to close.

The humanities are a form of knowledge. Like other knowledge, this deals with man's life in nature and society, but it is acquired through the study of man's spiritual creations—language, art, history, philosophy, and religion. This filtering of the subject, man, through the medium of mind has the effect of keeping always in the foreground the element of novelty, of uniqueness, of astonishing unpredictability. Whereas the study of nature assumes and finds its uniformities, and whereas the scientific study of society tries also to grasp what is regular and inevitable, the study of nature and man through the humanities dwells on what is individual and unlike and archaic. It finds what does *not* conform to rule, what has no counterpart, what does not "behave," but simply is or acts—this is the splendid and refreshing spectacle of the humanities. It is the Antigone of Sophocles, who is like no other woman—which is like no other drama; the Athenian plague in Thucydides, which is at once unknown, vividly present and forever the

past; the old woman painted by Rembrandt,[5] whose like we shall never see
again, but in that record; the adagio of Beethoven's[6] Fourth Symphony,
which rose from no formula and yields none; the Zarathustra of Nietzsche,[7]
which is an impossibility and a revelation; the lyrics of Thomas Hardy,[8]
which defy all the canons of diction and sentiment and prove them wrong;
the languages of a thousand peoples, which are each more illogical and
more subtle than the next. These are the substance which the humanities
present to us in the order of logic and veracity, combining thereby fixed
reason with wayward spirit, and thus alone deserving the name of Misbehavioral Science.

NOTES

1. *Madame Bovary*. Emma Bovary is the passion-driven heroine of the novel
by Gustav Flaubert (1857).

2. Midden. "An accumulation of refuse about a dwelling place" [WID].

3. Dr. Johnson. Samuel Johnson (1709-1784), English critic and lexicogra-
pher. His notable works include his *Dictionary* (1765) and *Lives of the Poets*
(1781).

4. Erasmus. Desiderius Erasmus (1467-1536). Dutch humanist; his satire
Praise of Folly (1501) is a famous indictment of the weaknesses of his age.

5. Rembrandt. Rembrandt van Ryn (1660-1669), greatest master of the
Dutch school of painting and etching.

6. Beethoven. Ludwig van Beethoven (1770-1827), "the Shakespeare of music"; among his scores of masterpieces are the *"Eroica" Symphony*, the *Fifth
Symphony*, the *Pastoral Symphony*, the *Ninth Symphony*, the *Kreutzer Sonata*,
the last *Quartets* (op. 130-135).

7. Zarathustra of Nietzsche. Fredrich Wilhelm Nietzsche (1844-1900), a
German philosopher, expounded his doctrine of the Superman in *Thus Spake
Zarathustra* (1883-1884).

8. Thomas Hardy (1840-1928). English novelist and poet. Among his novels
are *Tess of the D'Urbervilles* (1891) and *Jude the Obscure* (1895). His poetry
includes *Poems of the Past and Present* (1892) and *The Dynasts* (1904-1908).

TOPICS FOR DISCUSSION

1. What is the author's opinion of the "humanities-and" line of defense? Of
the argument that the humanities teach a moral lesson to man? Of the "peculiarly
human" quality of the humanities? How would his position on these points compare with those of Bush, Nagle, Krutch, and C. P. Snow?

2. What term does Barzun prefer to the traditional term "humanities" and
what are his reasons for this preference?

3. Discuss the nature of the weakness Barzun discerns in "the missionary role
of the humanities." Would Douglas Bush agree?

4. If the academic humanities are not in themselves creative, how do they
serve art? Compare Barzun's views on this point with Professor Jones' discussion of
the relationship of scholarship to art in "A Joy Forever."

5. Explain the statement ". . . in place of proof [the humanities] give possession, and in place of averages they give uniqueness." Compare this with Joseph Krutch's ". . . [the humanities] are that branch of inquiry concerned with the unmeasurable and dealing with it in such a way that although nothing is proved, something is, nevertheless, believed."

6. What is "the meaning of utility," a key point in the argument about the "practical" sciences and the "superfluous" humanities? What other essays in the collection make much of this point?

7. What, finally, is the nature of the contribution of the humanities and humanistic scholarship to the modern world?

8. How do the examples cited in the last paragraph justify Barzun's classification of the humanities as "the misbehavioral science"? What paradox underlies the term?

9. In developing his theme, what use does Barzun make of suspense, provocative statements, homely images, irony, allusion? Is his long introductory destruction of familiar defenses of the humanities effective, and, if so, why?

THE NATURE OF
A LIBERAL
EDUCATION

A Study in Contrasts

JOHN HENRY NEWMAN

Knowledge Its Own End

John Henry Newman (1801-1890), English churchman and author. A tutor at Oriel College, Oxford, and later vicar of St. Mary's, Oxford. Newman was one of the leaders of the Oxford Movement, devoted to the reform of the Church of England. In 1845 Newman became a convert to Roman Catholicism and in 1847 was ordained a Catholic priest. In 1879 he was created a cardinal. His Idea of a University, nine discourses, set forth his ideal of liberal education at a time when he was engaged in helping to found the Catholic University in Dublin. Originally published in 1852, the work was revised and reprinted later in the century; the definitive edition is that of 1873. Though all of Newman's prose (e.g., the "Grammar of Assent" [1870]) has a classic beauty of style matched with intellectual acuteness and subtlety, his masterpiece is his Apologia pro Vita Sua, his defense of his spiritual integrity against the insinuations of Charles Kingsley that priests of the Roman faith are inclined to be careless of truth. The Apologia, which gives an account of Newman's conversion, is a great spiritual autobiography. Together with The Idea of a University it remains Newman's most lasting work.

The three discources which follow "Knowledge Its Own End" are recommended to the student who wishes to gain a more thorough understanding of Newman's conception of liberal education. These are Discourse VI, "Knowledge Viewed in Relation to Learning," Discourse VII, "Knowledge Viewed in Relation to Professional Skill," and Discourse VIII, "Knowledge Viewed in Relation to Religion." [This selection is taken from John Henry Newman, "Knowledge Its Own End," The Idea of a University, Edited with an Introduction and Notes by Martin J. Svaglie (New York: Rinehart & Co., Inc., 1960), pp. 74-93.]

[76] It is a great point then to enlarge the range of studies which a University professes, even for the sake of the students; and, though they cannot pursue every subject which is open to them, they will be the gainers by living among those and under those who represent the whole circle. This I conceive to be the advantage of a seat of universal learning, considered as a place of education. An assemblage of learned men, zealous for their own

sciences, and rivals of each other, are brought, by familiar intercourse and for the sake of intellectual peace, to adjust together the claims and relations of their respective subjects of investigation. They learn to respect, to consult, to aid each other. Thus is created a pure and clear atmosphere of thought, which the student also breathes, though in his own case he only pursues a few sciences out of the multitude. He profits by an intellectual tradition, which is independent of particular teachers, which guides him in his choice of subjects, and duly interprets for him those which he chooses. He apprehends the great outlines of knowledge, the principles on which it rests, the scale of its parts, its lights and its shades, its great points and its little, as he otherwise cannot apprehend them. Hence it is that his education is called "Liberal." A habit of mind is formed which lasts through life, of which the attributes are freedom, equitableness, calmness, moderation, and wisdom; or what in a former Discourse I have ventured to call a philosophical habit. . . .

[77] And now the question is asked me, What is the *use* of it? and my answer will constitute the main subject of the Discourses which are to follow. . . .

I am asked what is the end of University Education, and of the Liberal or Philosophical Knowledge which I conceive it to impart: I answer, that what I have already said has been sufficient to show that it has a very tangible, real, and sufficient end, though the end cannot be divided from the knowledge itself. Knowledge is capable of being its own end. Such is the constitution of the human mind, that any kind of knowledge, if it be really such, is its own reward. And if this is true of all knowledge, it is true also of that special Philosophy, which I have made to consist in a comprehensive view of truth in all its branches, of the relations of science to science, of their mutual bearings, and their respective values. What the worth of such an acquirement is, compared with [78] other objects which we seek,— wealth or power or honour or the conveniences and comforts of life, I do not profess here to discuss; but I would maintain, and mean to show, that it is an object, in its own nature so really and undeniably good, as to be the compensation of a great deal of thought in the compassing, and a great deal of trouble in the attaining. . . .

Hence it is that Cicero,[1] in enumerating the various heads of mental excellence, lays down the pursuit of Knowledge for its own sake, as the first of them. "This pertains most of all to human nature," he says, "for we are all of us drawn to the pursuit of [79] Knowledge; in which to excel we consider excellent, whereas to mistake, to err, to be ignorant, to be deceived, is both an evil and a disgrace."* And he considers Knowledge the very first object to which we are attracted, after the supply of our physical wants. After the calls and duties of our animal existence, as they may be termed, as

---

* Cicer. Offic. init.

regards ourselves, our family, and our neighbours, follows, he tells us, "the search after truth. Accordingly, as soon as we escape from the pressure of necessary cares, forthwith we desire to see, to hear, and to learn; and consider the knowledge of what is hidden or is wonderful a condition of our happiness."

This passage, though it is but one of many similar passages in a multitude of authors, I take for the very reason that it is so familiarly known to us; and I wish you to observe, Gentlemen, how distinctly it separates the pursuit of Knowledge from those ulterior objects to which certainly it can be made to conduce, and which are, I suppose, solely contemplated by the persons who would ask of me the use of a University or Liberal Education. So far from dreaming of the cultivation of Knowledge directly and mainly in order to our physical comfort and enjoyment, for the sake of life and person, of health, of the conjugal and family union, of the social tie and civil security, the great Orator implies, that it is only after our physical and political needs are supplied, and when we are "free from necessary duties and cares," that we are in a condition for "desiring to see, to hear, and to learn." Nor does he contemplate in the least degree the reflex or subsequent action of Knowledge, when acquired, upon those material goods which we set out by securing before we seek it; on the contrary, he expressly denies its bearing upon social life altogether, strange as such a procedure is to those who live after the rise of the Baconian philosophy, and he cautions us against such a cultivation of it as will interfere with our duties to our fellow-creatures. "All these methods," he says, "are engaged in the investigation of truth; by the pursuit of which to be carried off from public occupations is a transgression of duty. For the praise of virtue lies altogether in action; yet intermissions often occur, and then we recur to such pursuits; not to say that the incessant activity of the mind is vigorous enough to carry us on in the pursuit of knowledge, even without any exertion of our own." [80] The idea of benefiting society by means of "the pursuit of science and knowledge" did not enter at all into the motives which he would assign for their cultivation. . . .

Things, which can bear to be cut off from everything else and yet persist in living, must have life in themselves; pursuits, which issue in nothing, and still maintain their ground for ages, which are regarded as admirable, though they have not as yet proved themselves to be useful, must have their sufficient end in themselves, whatever it turn out to be. And we are brought to the same conclusion by considering the force of the epithet, by which the knowledge under consideration is popularly designated. It is common to speak of "*liberal* knowledge," of the "*liberal* arts and studies," and of a "*liberal* education," as the especial characteristic or property of a University and of a gentleman; what is really meant by the word? Now, first, in its grammatical sense it is opposed to *servile*; and by "servile work" is understood, as our catechisms inform us, bodily labour, mechanical employment, and the like, in which the mind has little or no part. Parallel to such servile works are those arts, if they deserve the name, of which the poet speaks,* which owe their origin and their method to hazard, not to skill; as, for instance, the practice and operations of an empiric. As far as this contrast may be considered as a guide into the meaning of the world, liberal education and liberal pursuits are exercises of mind, of reason, of reflection.

But we want something more for its explanation, for there are [81] bodily exercises which are liberal, and mental exercises which are not so. For instance, in ancient times the practitioners in medicine were commonly slaves; yet it was an art as intellectual in its nature, in spite of the pretence, fraud, and quackery with which it might then, as now, be debased, as it was heavenly in its aim. And so in like manner, we contrast a liberal education with a commercial education or a professional; yet no one can deny that commerce and the professions afford scope for the highest and most diversified powers of mind. There is then a great variety of intellectual exercises, which are not technically called "liberal"; on the other hand, I say, there are exercises of the body which do receive that appellation. Such, for instance, was the palaestra,[2] in ancient times; such the Olympic games, in which strength and dexterity of body as well as of mind gained the prize. In Xenophon[3] we read of the young Persian nobility being taught to ride on horseback and to speak the truth; both being among the accomplishments of a gentleman. War, too, however rough a profession, has ever been accounted liberal, unless in cases when it becomes heroic, which would introduce us to another subject.

Now comparing these instances together, we shall have no difficulty in determining the principle of this apparent variation in the application of the term which I am examining. Manly games, or games of skill, or military prowess, though bodily, are, it seems, accounted liberal; on the other hand, what is merely professional, though highly intellectual, nay, though liberal in comparison of trade and manual labor, is not simply called liberal, and mercantile occupations are not liberal at all. Why this distinction? Because that alone is liberal knowledge, which stands on its own pretensions, which is independent of sequel, expects no complement, refuses to be *informed* (as it is called) by any end, or absorbed into any art, in order duly to present itself to our contemplation. The most ordinary pursuits have this specific character, if they are self-sufficient and complete; the highest lose it, when they minister to something beyond them. It is absurd to balance, in point of worth and importance, a treatise on reducing fractures with a game of cricket or a fox-chase; yet of the two the bodily exercise has that quality which we call "liberal," and the intellectual has it not. And so of the

---

*Τέχνη τύχην ἔστερξε καὶ τύχη τέχνην. Vid. Aris. Nic. Ethic. vi. (Art is in love with chance, and chance with art.) *Rhetoric*, 1390a30-1390b11, trans. Rhys Roberts, in Vol. XI of *The Works of Aristotle*, ed. W. D. Ross (Oxford: The Clarendon Press). Quoted with permission of the publisher.

learned professions altogether, considered merely as professions; although [82] one of them be the most popularly beneficial, and another the most politically important, and the third the most intimately divine of all human pursuits, yet the very greatness of their end, the health of the body, or of the commonwealth, or of the soul, diminishes, not increases, their claim to the appellation "liberal," and that still more, if they are cut down to the strict exigencies of that end. If, for instance, Theology, instead of being cultivated as a contemplation, be limited to the purposes of the pulpit or be represented by the catechism, it loses,—not its usefulness, not its divine character, not its meritoriousness (rather it gains a claim upon these titles by such charitable condescension),—but it does lose the particular attribute which I am illustrating; just as a face worn by tears and fasting loses its beauty, or a labourer's hand loses its delicateness;—for Theology thus exercised is not simple knowledge, but rather is an art or a business making use of Theology. And thus it appears that even what is supernatural need not be liberal, nor need a hero be a gentleman, for the plain reason that one idea is not another idea. And in like manner the Baconian Philosophy, by using its physical sciences in the service of man, does thereby transfer them from the order of Liberal Pursuits to, I do not say the inferior, but the distinct class of the Useful. And, to take a different instance, hence again, as is evident, whenever personal gain is the motive, still more distinctive an effect has it upon the character of a given pursuit; thus racing, which was a liberal exercise in Greece, forfeits its rank in times like these, so far as it is made the occasion of gambling.

All that I have been now saying is summed up in a few characteristic words of the great Philosopher. "Of possessions," he says, "those rather are useful, which bear fruit; those *liberal, which tend to enjoyment*. By fruitful, I mean, which yield revenue; by enjoyable, where *nothing accrues* of consequence beyond the using."*

Do you suppose, that in thus appealing to the ancients, I am throwing back the world two thousand years, and fettering Philosophy with the reasonings of paganism. While the world lasts, [83] will Aristotle's doctrine on these matters last, for he is the oracle of nature and of truth. While we are men, we cannot help, to a great extent, being Aristotelians, for the great Master does but analyze the thoughts, feelings, views, and opinion of human kind. He has told us the meaning of our own words and ideas, before we were born. In many subject-matters, to think correctly, is to think like Aristotle; and we are his disciples whether we will or no, though we may not know it. Now, as to the particular instance before us, the word "liberal" as applied to Knowledge and Education, expresses a specific idea, which ever has been, and ever will be, while the nature of man is the same, just as the idea of the Beautiful is specific, or of the Sublime, or of the Ridiculous, or

---

* Aristot. *Rhet.* i.5.

of the Sordid. It is in the world now, it was in the world then; and, as in the case of the dogmas of faith, it is illustrated by a continuous historical tradition, and never was out of the world, from the time it came into it. There have indeed been differences of opinion from time to time, as to what pursuits and what arts came under that idea, but such differences are but an additional evidence of its reality. That idea must have a substance in it, which has maintained its ground amid these conflicts and changes, which has ever served as a standard to measure things withal, which has passed from mind to mind unchanged, when there was so much to colour, so much to influence any notion or thought whatever, which was not founded in our very nature. Were it a mere generalization, it would have varied with the subjects from which it was generalized; but though its subjects vary with the age, it varies not itself. The palaestra may seem a liberal exercise to Lycurgus,[4] and illiberal to Seneca;[5] coach-driving and prize-fighting may be recognized in Elis,[6] and be condemned in England; music may be despicable in the eyes of certain moderns, and be in the highest place with Aristotle and Plato,—(and the case is the same in the particular application of the idea of Beauty, or of Goodness, or of Moral Virtue, there is a difference of tastes, a difference of judgments)—still these variations imply, instead of discrediting, the archetypal idea, which is but a previous hypothesis or condition, by means of which issue is joined between contending opinions, and without which there would be nothing to dispute about.

I consider, then, that I am chargeable with no paradox, when [84] I speak of a Knowledge which is its own end, when I call it liberal knowledge, or a gentleman's knowledge, when I educate for it, and make it the scope of a University. And still less am I incurring such a charge, when I make this acquisition consist, not in Knowledge in a vague and ordinary sense, but in that Knowledge which I have especially called Philosophy, or, in an extended sense of the word, Science; for whatever claims Knowledge has to be considered as a good, these it has in a higher degree when it is viewed not vaguely, not popularly, but precisely and transcendently as Philosophy. Knowledge, I say, is then especially liberal, or sufficient for itself, apart from every external and ulterior object, when and so far as it is philosophical, and this I proceed to show.

Now bear with me, Gentlemen, if what I am about to say, has at first sight a fanciful appearance. Philosophy, then, or Science, is related to Knowledge in this way: —Knowledge is called by the name of Science or Philosophy, when it is acted upon, informed, or if I may use a strong figure, impregnated by Reason. Reason is the principle of that intrinsic fecundity of Knowledge, which, to those who possess it, is its especial value, and which dispenses with the necessity of their looking abroad for any end to rest upon external to itself. Knowledge, indeed, when thus exalted into a scientific form is also power; not only is it excellent in itself, but whatever such excellence may be, it is something more, it has a result beyond itself.

Doubtless; but that is a further consideration, with which I am not concerned. I only say that, prior to its being a power, it is a good; that it is, not only an instrument, but an end. I know well it may resolve itself into an art, and terminate in a mechanical process, and in tangible fruit; but it also may fall back upon that Reason which informs it, and resolve itself into Philosophy. In one case it is called Useful Knowledge, in the other Liberal. The same person may cultivate it in both ways at once; but this again is a matter foreign to my subject; here I do but say that there are two ways of using Knowledge, and in matter of fact those who use it in one way are not likely to use it in the other, or at least in a very limited [85] measure. You see, then, here are two methods of Education; the end of the one is to be philosophical, of the other to be mechanical; the one rises towards general ideas, the other is exhausted upon what is particular and external. Let me not be thought to deny the necessity, or to decry the benefit, of such attention to what is particular and practical, as belongs to the useful or mechanical arts; life could not go on without them; we owe our daily welfare to them; their exercise is the duty of the many, and we owe to the many a debt of gratitude for fulfilling that duty. I only say that Knowledge, in proportion as it tends more and more to be particular, ceases to be Knowledge. It is a question whether Knowledge can in any proper sense be predicted of the brute creation; without pretending to metaphysical exactness of phraseology, which would be unsuitable to an occasion like this, I say, it seems to be improper to call that passive sensation, or perception of things, which brutes seem to possess, by the name of Knowledge. When I speak of Knowledge, I mean something intellectual, something which grasps what it perceives through the senses; something which takes a view of things; which sees more than the senses convey; which reasons upon what it sees, and while it sees; which invests it with an idea. It expresses itself, not in a mere enunciation, but by an enthymeme:[7] it is of the nature of science from the first, and in this consists of dignity. The principle of real dignity of Knowledge, its worth, its desirableness, considered irrespectively of its result, is this germ within it of a scientific or a philosophical process. This is how it comes to be an end in itself; this is why it admits of being called Liberal. Not to know the relative disposition of things is the state of slaves or children; to have mapped out the Universe is the boast, or at least the ambition, of Philosophy.

Moreover, such knowledge is not a mere extrinsic or accidental advantage, which is ours to-day and another's to-morrow, which may be got up from a book, and easily forgotten again, which we can command or communicate at our pleasure, which we can borrow for the occasion, carry about in our hand, and take into the market; it is an acquired illumination, it is a habit, a personal possession, and an inward endowment. And this is the reason, why it is more correct, as well as more usual, to speak of a University as a place of education, than of instruction, though, when [86] knowledge

is concerned, instruction would at first sight have seemed the more appropriate word. We are instructed, for instance, in manual exercises, in the fine
and useful arts, in trades, and in ways of business; for these are methods,
which have little or no effect upon the mind itself, are contained in rules
committed to memory, to tradition, or to use, and bear upon an end external to themselves. But education is a higher word; it implies an action upon
our mental nature, and the formation of a character; it is something individual and permanent, and is commonly spoken of in connexion with religion and virtue. When, then, we speak of the communication of Knowledge as being Education, we thereby really imply that that Knowledge is a
state or condition of mind; and since cultivation of mind is surely worth
seeking for its own sake, we are thus brought once more to the conclusion,
which the word "Liberal" and the word "Philosophy" have already suggested, that there is a Knowledge, which is desirable, though nothing come
of it, as being of itself a treasure, and a sufficient remuneration of years of
labour. . . .

It may be objected then, that, when we profess to seek Knowledge for
some end or other beyond itself, whatever it be, we speak intelligibly; but
that, whatever men may have said, however obstinately the idea may have
kept its ground from age to age, still it is simply unmeaning to say that we
seek Knowledge for its own sake, and for nothing else; for that it ever leads
to something beyond itself, which therefore is its end, and the cause why it
is desirable;—moreover, that this end is twofold, either of this world [87]
or of the next; that all knowledge is cultivated either for secular objects
or for eternal; that if it is directed to secular objects, it is called Useful
Knowledge, if to eternal, Religious or Christian Knowledge;—in consequence, that if, as I have allowed, this Liberal Knowledge does not benefit
the body or estate, it ought to benefit the soul; but if the fact be really so,
that it is neither a physical or a secular good on the one hand, nor a moral
good on the other, it cannot be a good at all, and is not worth the trouble
which is necessary for its acquisition.

And then I may be reminded that the professors of this Liberal or
Philosophical Knowledge have themselves, in every age, recognized this exposition of the matter, and have submitted to the issue in which it termi-
nates; for they have ever been attempting to make men virtuous; or, if not,
at least have assumed that refinement of mind was virtue, and that they
themselves were the virtuous portion of mankind. This they have professed
on the one hand; and on the other, they have utterly failed in their professions, so as ever to make themselves a proverb among men, and a laughing-
stock both to the grave and the dissipated portion of mankind, in consequence of them. Thus they have furnished against themselves both the
ground and the means of their own exposure, without any trouble at all to
any one else. In a word, from the time that Athens was the University of
the world, what has Philosophy taught men, but to promise without practis-

ing, and to aspire without attaining? What has the deep and lofty thought of its disciples ended in but eloquent words? Nay, what has its teaching ever meditated, when it was boldest in its remedies for human ill, beyong charming us to sleep by its lessons that we might feel nothing at all? like some melodious air, or rather like those strong and transporting perfumes, which at first spread their sweetness over every thing they touch, but in a little while do but offend in proportion as they once pleased us. Did Philosophy support Cicero under the disfavour of the fickle populace, or nerve Seneca to oppose an imperial tyrant? It abandoned Brutus,[8] as he sorrowfully confessed, in his greatest need, and it forced Cato,[9] as his panegyrist strangely boasts, into the false position of defying heaven. How few can be counted among its professors, who, like Polemo,[10] were thereby converted from a profligate course, or like Anaxagoras,[11] thought the world well lost in [88] exchange for its possession? The philosopher in Rasselas[12] taught a superhuman doctrine, and then succumbed without an effort to a trial of human affection.

"He discoursed," we are told, "with great energy on the government of the passions. His look was venerable, his action graceful, his pronunciation clear, and his diction elegant. He showed, with great strength of sentiment and variety of illustration, that human nature is degraded and debased, when the lower faculties predominate over the higher. He communicated the various precepts given, from time to time, for the conquest of passion, and displayed the happiness of those who had obtained the important victory, after which man is no longer the slave of fear, nor the fool of hope. . . . He enumerated many examples of heroes immoveable by pain or pleasure, who looked with indifference on those modes or accidents to which the vulgar give the names of good and evil."

Rasselas in a few days found the philosopher in a room half darkened, with his eyes misty, and his face pale. "Sir," said he, "you have come at a time when all human friendship is useless; what I suffer cannot be remedied, what I have lost cannot be supplied. My daughter, my only daughter, from whose tenderness I expected all the comforts of my age, died last night of a fever." "Sir," said the prince, "mortality is an event by which a wise man can never be surprised; we know that death is always near, and it should therefore always be expected." "Young man," answered the philosopher, "you speak like one who has never felt the pangs of separation." "Have you, then, forgot the precept," said Rasselas, "which you so powerfully enforced? . . . consider that external things are naturally variable, but truth and reason are always the same." "What comfort," said the mourner, "can truth and reason afford me? Of what effect are they now, but to tell me that my daughter will not be restored?" . . .

[90] Useful Knowledge then, I grant, has done its work; and Liberal Knowledge as certainly has not done its work,—that is, supposing, as the objectors assume, its direct end, like Religious Knowledge, is to make men

better; but this I will not for an instant allow, and, unless I allow it, those objectors have said nothing to the purpose. I admit, rather I maintain, what they have been urging, for I consider Knowledge to have its end in itself. For all its friends, or its enemies, may say, I insist upon it, that it is as real a mistake to burden it with virtue or religion as with the [91] mechanical arts. Its direct business is not to steel the soul against temptation or to console it in affliction, any more than to set the loom in motion, or to direct the steam carriage; be it ever so much the means or the condition of both material and moral advancement, still, taken by and in itself, it as little mends our hearts as it improves our temporal circumstances. And if its eulogists claim for it such a power, they commit the very same kind of encroachment on a province not their own as the political economist who should maintain that his science educated him for casuistry or diplomacy. Knowledge is one thing, virtue is another; good sense is not conscience, refinement is not humility, nor is largeness and justness of view faith. Philosophy, however enlightened, however profound, gives no command over the passions, no influential motives, no vivifying principles. Liberal Education makes not the Christian, not the Catholic, but the gentleman. It is well to be a gentleman, it is well to have a cultivated intellect, a delicate taste, a candid, equitable, dispassionate mind, a noble and courteous bearing in the conduct of life;—these are the connatural qualities of a large knowledge; they are the objects of a University; I am advocating, I shall illustrate and insist upon them; but still, I repeat, they are no guarantee for sanctity or even for conscientiousness, they may attach to the man of the world, to the profligate, to the heartless,—pleasant, alas, and attractive as he shows when decked out in them. Taken by themselves, they do but seem to be what they are not; they look like virtue at a distance, but they are detected by close observers, and on the long run; and hence it is that they are popularly accused of pretence and hypocrisy, not, I repeat, from their own fault, but because their professors and their admirers persist in taking them for what they are not, and are officious in arrogating for them a praise to which they have no claim. Quarry the granite rock with razors, or moor the vessel with a thread of silk; then may you hope with such keen and delicate instruments as human knowledge and human reason to contend against those giants, the passion and the pride of man.

Surely we are not driven to theories of this kind, in order to vindicate the value and dignity of Liberal Knowledge. Surely the real grounds on which its pretensions rest are not so very subtle or abstruse, so very strange or improbable. Surely it is very [92] intelligible to say, and that is what I say here, that Liberal Education, viewed in itself, is simply the cultivation of the intellect, as such, and its object is nothing more or less than intellectual excellence. Every thing has its own perfection, be it higher or lower in the scale of things; and the perfection of one is not the perfection of another. . . . . The artist puts before him beauty of feature and form; the poet, beauty of mind; the preacher, the beauty of grace: then intellect too, I repeat, has its beauty, and it has those who aim at it. To open the mind, to correct it, to refine it, to enable it to know, and to digest, master, rule, and use its knowledge, to give it power over its own faculties, application, flexibility, method, critical exactness, sagacity, resource, address, eloquent expression, is an object as intelligible (for here we are inquiring, not what the object is of a Liberal Education is worth, nor what use the Church makes of it, but what it [93] is in itself), I say, an object as intelligible as the cultivation of virtue, while, at the same time, it is absolutely distinct from it.

NOTES

1. Cicero. Marcus Tullius Cicero (109-43 B.C.), Roman statesman and philosopher, and Rome's greatest orator. His works include essays, such as *On Friendship* and *On Duty*; orations, for example, *Orations against Cataline* and the *Philippics* (against Antony); treatises, such as his *On the Nature of the Gods*.

2. palaestra. "A wrestling school; hence a gymnasium or place for athletic exercise in general" [WID].

3. Xenophon (c. 434-355 B.C.). An Athenian historian and general. His most famous work is the *Anabasis*, which has a vivid account of the march of 10,000 Greek troops from the Euphrates to the Black Sea.

4. Lycurgus. The legendary ruler of Sparta, possibly belonging to the ninth century B.C., credited with the reform of Sparta's laws.

5. Seneca. Lucius Annaeus Seneca (3 B.C.-A.D. 65), Stoic philosopher, orator, dramatist, senator, tutor to Nero. By A.D. 62 enemies at the court forced his retirement. In A.D. 65 Nero accused him of treason and ordered him to commit suicide.

6. Elis. An ancient country in southern Greece. It included the plain of Olympia, site of the Olympic games.

7. enthymeme. An argument in which one of the premises is understood rather than stated, e.g., he has high blood pressure and therefore should avoid excitement. Implied is the premise that excitement is bad for high blood pressure.

8. Brutus. Marcus Junius Brutus (85-42 B.C.), co-conspirator with Cassius and others in the assassination of Julius Caesar. Defeated by Antony in the second Battle of Philippi, Brutus committed suicide by falling on his sword.

9. Cato. Marcus Polcius Cato (Cato the Younger) (95-46 B.C.), a stoic statesman honored for the strict integrity of his public and private life. Devoted to the ideal of the early Republic, he opposed Caesar and finally, hearing of Caesar's victory at Thapsus, killed himself rather than live under the power of the new dictator.

10. Polemo. Polemon (d. 273 B.C.), Athenian philosopher, a Platonist. A profligate as a youth, he changed his course of life overnight after hearing the philosopher Xenocrates lecture on temperance.

11. Anaxagoras (500-428 B.C.). An Ionian philosopher and scientist, he taught Euripides and Pericles, possibly Socrates. At twenty he gave away his possessions and traveled to Athens, where he remained as a teacher for thirty years, until Athenian resentment of the "impiety" of his doctrines forced him into exile.

12. Rasselas. *Rasselas*, by Samuel Johnson (1709-1784), is an allegory, pub-

lished in 1759, that recounts the wanderings of Rasselas, Prince of Abyssinia, in search of happiness.

TOPICS FOR DISCUSSION

1. A comparison of the title of Newman's essay with that of Jensen's indicates the basic difference between the approach of the two writers to the question of liberal education; explain this essential difference.

2. How does Newman's concept of liberal knowledge differ from the views of such of his contemporaries as Arnold and Huxley?

3. In what sense does this author use the words *science* and *sciences*? How does his use of these terms differ from that of most of the other essayists represented?

4. According to Newman, what is the use of liberal knowledge? Identify the arguments of the ancients which he uses to support this concept. Discuss the line of reasoning which he draws from the nature of knowledge itself to support his theory of knowledge.

5. What sets liberal knowledge apart from other kinds of activity? What are Newman's reasons for claiming that, under certain conditions, war is liberal and theology is not?

6. Discuss the two methods of education which Newman describes. Under what labels would we identify them today? How can one distinguish between education and instruction?

7. Comment on the following image as an illustration of Newman's view of the relationship of liberal knowledge and virtue: "Quarry the granite rock with razors, or moor the vessel with a thread of silk; then may you hope with such keen and delicate instruments as human knowledge and human reason to contend against those giants, the passion and the pride of man." Which of the other essayists would be nearest agreement with him on this point? Which would most strongly disagree? Why?

8. What sort of person can liberal knowledge create? What is its effect on the individual mind?

9. Describe the tone of Newman's essay and its method of development. From the content and style, what would you deduce about the author's own temperament and training?

10. "Not to know the relative disposition of things is the state of slaves or children. . . ." How do these words of Newman compare with the statements of others on the effects of liberal education?

ARTHUR E. JENSEN

Leadership Through
the Liberal Arts

Arthur E. Jensen, educator (b. 1903), studied at Brown, the University of Edinburgh, and Dartmouth. A professor of English at Dartmouth since 1937, he is currently Chairman of the English Department there and Dean of Faculty. Between 1949 and 1952 he directed the Great Issues Course at Dartmouth. Since 1960 he has been a consultant in management training for International Business Machines Corporation.

This address was given at a celebration in honor of the fiftieth anniversary of The Northwestern University School of Business. The subhead of the speech is "The Executive deals with People, not only with figures and balance sheets." [This selection is taken from Dr. Arthur E. Jensen, "Leadership Through the Liberal Arts," Vital Speeches, XXIV (July 15, 1958), 601-3.]

[601] . . . There has been a dramatic change in men's thinking about the development of executive leadership. It may be that for many years we were on the wrong track. Certainly, during the early part of this century we were bemused into talking about the businessman, or the banker, or the lawyer, or the professor. In any civilized society there must, of course, be a division of labor. In our recognition of that fact, however, we came to accept not only the division of labor but unfortunately also the division of individual men.

Over a hundred years ago Ralph Waldo Emerson[1] pointed out in a speech given just a few miles from here that one is not a businessman, a banker, or a lawyer, but one is a man who is in business, a man who runs a bank, or a man who practices law. Two years ago, also at Harvard, Clarence Randall, retired Chairman of Inland Steel, said that the great discovery of our time was people. The man of business deals with people, not only with figures and balance sheets. And people are complete entities, not segments.

It is interesting and I think significant that in a generation when corporations have become larger, when automation and IBM machines have seemed to take over much of the routine work of industry, we have witnessed two major developments in business. One is the growing realization of the interdependence of our economy, and the other is that our executives are men first, and that their caliber as men ultimately determines their caliber as executives.

Particularly since World War II we have witnessed the growth of a new climate in American business. We have come increasingly to recognize that an individual business does not and cannot exist in isolation. . . .

The demand for executives who can survey this new economy steadily, and survey it whole, and can consequently take part in responsible policy decisions affecting not only an individual business but a whole community has called forth a fresh approach to management development. A creative modern manager must have a complex of diverse qualities, but foremost among them is a perspective on the contemporary economic and political scene and the ability to ask searching questions about the whole social matrix of his own business. Only then can he insure its long-run survival and growth. That ability is unfortunately rare. . . .

The kind of educated man in business that is called for was described very well by Harry A. Bullis, Chairman of the Board of General Mills, in an article in the *Saturday Review* in which he said:

> A highly educated man has been educated at two levels: first, he has a practical understanding of modern technology, is able to foresee its developments and their economic and sociological impact on modern society. Second, he has been tutored in humanistic values. His knowledge of history, economics, religions, sociology, and psychology must be so thorough that he can evaluate [602] change in terms of continuing human progress rather than as a threat to human stability.
>
> At the same time he must be so mentally flexible that he can avoid at all times the psychic shock that too often comes with changes. He must be able to accept new techniques and precedent-destroying discoveries without discarding the valid experiences of the past. Rather he must be able to re-examine historic contributions to human progress and relate them to current thinking and technological advance. The ability constantly to reappraise the factors of civilization in terms of progress is the mark of the intellectually and emotionally mature man.

No man is this paragon when he graduates from college. He can approach this ideal only by a long and sustained program of self-development. But as we must know, we are all extremely busy and we all have our human weaknesses. Moreover, men at certain periods of their lives need a fresh start toward this goal. They need a real punctuation mark in their careers. They need for a period of weeks to be released or to release themselves from the conventional routine to take stock by taking a long look at themselves and their business in the light of the changing values and changing issues in our society.

American business has increasingly recognized this approach to executive development. As a result, there has grown up in this country a wide variety of programs, conferences, and courses for business leaders. They have had one common purpose: to make the executive an abler person on his job and more valuable to his company, and at the same time a man who, when promoted to a policy-making position, has a greater breadth of view and a sounder perspective than he would otherwise have. . . .

The purpose of management development is, I think I have made clear, not the training of skills. We have to make a sharp distinction between the concept of training and that of management development. Training has for its purpose the reproduction of its own image. It is the means by which an accepted pattern of behavior is transferred from one individual to another. Education, on the other hand, has for its purpose the giving to the individual a larger capacity for a creative relationship to his life and work. It induces men to re-examine the premises and judgments they had come to accept, and to gain fresh perspectives and insights that will make for more creative work and life. It aims to free men from patterns of behavior. . . .

Who is the effective executive, the man for whom every company is looking? We can be reasonably sure that he is not one of that species that has been given so much publicity lately: the organization man. The organization man is completely loyal to his company; he is usually fairly intelligent. Then why does he not have the requirements of a good manager? To begin with, he is too often an affable cog, a man who has rubbed off his own corners until he is indeed the well-rounded man—within a very short radius. He fears uniqueness, individuality. He fears the responsibility and loneliness of real decision. He is fairly easy to live with. He is not really to be as easily condemned as has become fashionable. After all, the real fulfillment of many an individual is to become part of a larger unit, to be able to merge the self in a larger whole. It is the ultimate value of this larger whole that gives the measure of the organization man, and usually he falls short. There is really nothing wrong with a man who conforms. He may still be using his full abilities. The real tragedy comes when he does not know he is conforming, when he does so without making a conscious choice.

At the other end of the spectrum from the organization man we may place the complete individualist, the maverick. His discrete individuality is very precious to him, and rightly so. Out of his urge to safeguard his own personality he refuses to commit himself to either his business or his profession. He really dreads the thought of becoming a team player. Because he does not submit himself to team play, the maverick is of limited use to any large organization, although I must add hastily that he is sometimes its only articulate, and consequently very useful, conscience.

The modern corporation is perhaps not so receptive to the maverick as it should be. It is probably too receptive to the organization man.

But neither is the successful executive. The man who can serve his individual business best and, I submit, also serve society, is neither the organization man nor the maverick. Like the organization man he has the quality of loyalty to his company and willingness to subordinate at least part of himself for the good of the business. Like the maverick he insists on saving a large and precious part of his own individuality for himself. He is a man in business, not a mere businessman. His fertile creativity comes to a large extent from the tension that exists within him between himself as a private individual and himself as a company man. He is both, and in struggling to realize two goals he not only acquires a fresh perspective on both but he is able to see both himself and his company as part of an even larger whole.

The aim of management development through liberal arts is to create and to capitalize on that fertile tension. When a man has a richer understanding of himself and his relationship to the world about him, his judgments are surer and wiser. A program for executive development based on the liberal arts will have for its purpose the development of the man, rather than the manager. It will aim to extend intellectual horizons, deepen understanding, and quicken insights. The faith of those of us who have been working in this area of the development of leadership in business has been steadily strengthened by experience. We are convinced that if we stimulate the man we make him a more valuable executive. Furthermore, the stimulation can last, because it whets the appetite for more.

Let us take a man in his 30's or 40's who is looking forward to steady promotion in his company. He has been about fifteen or twenty years out of college, and a good many of his fine resolutions for continued self-development have been lost in the rush of day-to-day living. He reads his paper, or selected parts of it, a magazine or two, and sometimes a book. He needs to be refueled intellectually before he goes into a position [603] of business leadership. That is where further training in liberal arts comes in.

Moreover, it comes at the right time. The mature man exposed to fresh facts and ideas can immediately square them with his own experience, not merely with his previous reading. The new ideas are much more meaningful and more immediately relevant to him than they are to the college student. At this stage of a man's career the right sort of exposure to liberal arts really takes hold.

The selection of areas of study in such a program should be determined by its broad purposes. These three purposes are:

1. To broaden interests and extend habits of inquiry and reflection;
2. To sharpen awareness of the social, political, and economic climate of today and the role of the businessman in it;

3. To stimulate the executive to undertake a sustained program of self-development.

By what sort of specific program can such aims be realized? It was with those objectives that several educational institutions have been sponsoring conferences for executives. These conferences have been of various lengths but have usually been for eight weeks. Some are four weeks, and one extends for nine months. Aims as far-reaching as these certainly can't be achieved in a week-end retreat. The executive must be released long enough from his daily tensions to regenerate his perspectives on values in the modern world. If he is to make his way to a new equilibrium within the tensions that are inevitably his, he must have a decent interval in which to do it. At Williams College, where the American Telephone and Telegraph Company has sent a group for two summers, the program has been based on issues in American history. At Dartmouth College, where for a period of eight weeks we have had Bell executives as well as executives from savings banks, we have tried to build a program around the great issues of our time. The men sent to us took three basic courses. The first was *Religion, Science and Man*, which explored the dramatic changes that have been forced on men's religious and philosophic thinking by a century of scientific achievement. The second was *The Individual and the State*, which considered the relations of individual men, and such organized groups as business corporations, to a state which is assuming a larger and larger role in individual lives. The third course for one summer was *Traditional and Modern Values*, in which we examined the values of various civilizations of the past and compared them with those of the present. For the most recent summer instead of this last course we substituted one called *The Individual and Society in Literature*, which had the same purpose but used a different approach. We had other lectures, designed to open windows in various directions. We also had the men engage in a practical study of modern journalism by having them read, over a period of time, several diverse newspapers and magazines in order that they might form comparative judgments.

I outline this program as an example, not as a model. There is no one path to the goals I have outlined. We found this approach extremely effective. Other approaches might be even better. They all point to the liberally educated man. That term comes, as you realize, from the Latin *libertas* meaning *free*. The Romans gave training to their servants, but the liberated or freeman was worthy of an education that would give him understanding and insights that would enable him to remain free, both politically and, more importantly, intellectually, and thus better serve the state.

In our civilization we are fighting for the survival of freedom. Both because of self-interest and national interest, we as businessmen and as citizens have to make sure we are able to take the larger view and the longer view. American business seems to be responding to that challenge. They are beginning to insure that their executives remain intellectually alive, that they are men before they are managers. The day of the anti-intellectual, the man with a mucker pose of contempt for what he calls the eggheads, is over although there remain a few who do not yet recognize that fact.

We are coming into a period in which both business decisions and individual decisions have to be made in a matrix of increasing complexity. It will also be a period of greatly increased leisure. That leisure that our economy creates can, if properly used, serve to nourish the economy still further by developing the new executive who is first of all a broad-gauge man.

Some years ago when the philosopher Bergson[2] was an old man, he felt himself too feeble to attend a philosophic meeting. He was then asked to send a message, which would sum up his years of study of the human scene and give younger men some guide. He wrote only this: "Think as men of action; act as men of thought." For too long we have separated the doer and the thinker. One of the significant facts of our generation is that the man of thought and the man of action are increasingly one. To help achieve that synthesis in their executives, American business is calling on liberal arts colleges for assistance. Out of a reawakened realization of what the colleges can do in this field has come increased support to them from business. In our generation we have seen how the American college and American business can join their strengths to the great advantage of each and to the benefit of society.

NOTES

1. Emerson. Ralph Waldo Emerson (1803-1882), American philosopher, essayist, poet; his *Journals, Essays,* and *Poems* mark him as the leading spokesman for American transcendentalism in the nineteenth century. "The American Scholar," his Phi Beta Kappa address at Harvard (1837), challenged American intellectuals to declare their cultural independence of Europe.

2. Bergson. Henri Bergson (1859-1941), French philosopher, proponent of intuition and the "vital impulse" (*élan vital*).

TOPICS FOR DISCUSSION

1. Identify and describe the special qualities which are essential to the modern executive.

2. Discuss the ways in which skill training differs from management development.

3. What are the strengths and weaknesses of the organization man, the maverick? Identify the qualities of each which are needed by the successful executive.

4. What is the aim of management development through the liberal arts? What connection is there between the liberal arts in their historic sense and the interest of modern business in these studies?

5. The themes of specialization, the fragmentation of modern man, the arts versus vocational training, and education as a lifelong process occur repeatedly in

the essays in this collection; which of these themes does Jensen touch on? On which does he seem most distant from the views of the other essayists?

6. According to Jensen, do the liberal arts retain their traditional function, or have they become a kind of vocational training? Explain.

7. Jensen states that "The day of the anti-intellectual, the man with a mucker pose of contempt for what he calls the eggheads, is over. . . ." Do you agree? Why or why not? Does Jensen's essay offer support for this statement? If so, in what way?

ROBERT M. HUTCHINS

A Letter to the Reader

Robert M. Hutchins, educator, university president, and fund executive, was born in 1899. He served as acting dean, dean, and professor of law at Yale, leaving there in 1929 to become the country's youngest university president. In that year he headed the University of Chicago, where he remained as president and later as Chancellor until 1954. Since 1954 he has been President of the Fund for the Republic. He has pleaded the cause of the "Great Books" approach to liberal education in his writings and has repeatedly challenged American higher education to reappraise its standards, its methods, and its goals. His works include Learning in America *(1938),* Education for Freedom *(1943,)* The Great Conversation *(1951),* The Conflict in Education *(1953),* The University of Utopia *(1953), and* The Foundation of a Liberal Education *(1954).*

The Great Books theory of liberal education, associated with Professor Hutchins and the University of Chicago and later adopted by St. John's University, Annapolis, seeks to give the college student a firsthand knowledge of the classics of the Western world. Further details of the "Great Books" plan may be found in Hutchins' Education for Freedom *(Baton Rouge: Louisiana State University Press, 1947) and in* The Conflict in Education *(New York: Harper & Row, 1953). Stringfellow Barr's article "Liberal Education: A Common Adventure,"* Antioch Review, *XV (September 1955), 300-12, gives an enthusiastic defense of the Great Books approach by a teacher and administrator who helped to set up the great books curriculum at St. John's, Annapolis. [This selection and "The Tradition of the West" are taken from Robert M. Hutchins,* Great Books: The Foundation of a Liberal Education *(New York: Simon & Schuster, 1954), pp. 12-32.]*

[22] . . . Do you need a liberal education? I say that it is unpatriotic not to read great books. You may reply that you are patriotic enough without them. I say that you are gravely cramping your human possibilities if you do not read these books. You may answer that you have troubles enough already.

This answer is the one that Ortega attacks in *The Revolt of the*

Masses. It assumes that we can leave all intellectual activity, and all political responsibility, to somebody else and live our lives as vegetable beneficiaries of the moral and intellectual virtue of other men. The trouble with this assumption is that, whereas it was once possible, and even compulsory, for the bulk of mankind, such indulgence now, on the part of anybody, endangers the whole community. It is now necessary for everybody [23] to try to live, as Ortega says, "at the height of his times." The democratic enterprise is imperiled if any one of us says, "I do not have to try to think for myself, or make the most of myself, or become a citizen of the world republic of learning." The death of democracy is not likely to be an assassination from ambush. It will be a slow extinction from apathy, indifference, and undernourishment. . . .

THE TRADITION OF THE WEST

[26] The tradition of the West is embodied in the Great Conversation that began in the dawn of history and that continues to the present day. Whatever the merits of other civilizations in other respects, no civilization is like that of the West in this respect. No other civilization can claim that its defining characteristic is a dialogue of this sort. No dialogue in any other civilization can compare with that of the West in the number of great works of the mind that have contributed to this dialogue. The goal toward which Western society moves is the Civilization of the Dialogue. The spirit of Western civilization is the spirit of inquiry. Its dominant element is the *Logos*.[1] Nothing is to remain undiscussed. Everybody is to speak his mind. No proposition is to be left unexamined. The [27] exchange of ideas is held to be the path to the realization of the potentialities of the race.

At a time when the West is most often represented by its friends as the source of that technology for which the whole world yearns and by its enemies as the fountainhead of selfishness and greed, it is worth remarking that, though both elements can be found in the Great Conversation, the Western ideal is not one or the other strand in the Conversation, but the Conversation itself. It would be an exaggeration to say that Western civilization means great books. The exaggeration would lie in the omission of the plastic arts and music, which have quite as important a part in Western civilization as the great productions included in this set. But to the extent to which books can present the idea of a civilization, the idea of Western civilization is presented in great books.

These books are the means of understanding our society and ourselves. They contain the great ideas that dominate us without our knowing it. There is no comparable repository of our tradition.

To put an end to the spirit of inquiry that has characterized the West, it is not necessary to burn the books. All we have to do is to leave them unread for a few generations. On the other hand, the revival of interest in these books from time to time throughout history has provided the West with new drive and creativeness. Great books have salvaged, preserved, and transmitted the tradition on many occasions similar to our own.

[28] The books contain not merely the tradition, but also the great exponents of the tradition. Their writings are models of the fine and liberal arts. They hold before us what Whitehead called "the habitual vision of greatness." These books have endured because men in every era have been lifted beyond themselves by the inspiration of their example. Sir Richard Livingstone said: "We are tied down, all our days and for the greater part of our days, to the commonplace. That is where contact with great thinkers, great literature helps. In their company we are still in the ordinary world, but it is the ordinary world transfigured and seen through the eyes of wisdom and genius. And some of their vision becomes our own."

Until very recently these books have been central in education in the West. They were the principal instrument of liberal education, the education that men acquired as an end in itself, for no other purpose than that it would help them to be men, to lead human lives, and better lives than they would otherwise be able to lead.

The aim of liberal education is human excellence, both private and public (for man is a political animal). Its object is the excellence of man as man and man as citizen. It regards man as an end, not as a means; and it regards the ends of life, and not the means of it. For this reason it is the education of free men. Other types of education or training treat men as means to some other end, or are at best concerned with the means of life, with earning a living, and not with its ends.

[29] The substance of liberal education appears to consist in the recognition of basic problems, in knowledge of distinctions and interrelations in subject matter, and in the comprehension of ideas.

Liberal education seeks to clarify the basic problems and to understand the way in which one problem bears upon another. It strives for a grasp of the methods by which solutions can be reached and the formulation of standards for testing solutions proposed. The liberally educated man understands, for example, the relation between the problem of the immortality of the soul and the problem of the best form of government; he understands that the one problem cannot be solved by the same method as the other, and that the test that he will have to bring to bear upon solutions proposed differs from one problem to the other.

The liberally educated man understands, by understanding the distinctions and interrelations of the basic fields of subject matter, the differences and connections between poetry and history, science and philosophy, theoretical and practical science; he understands that the same methods cannot be applied in all these fields; he knows the methods appropriate to each.

The liberally educated man comprehends the ideas that are relevant to the basic problems and that operate in the basic fields of subject matter. He knows what is meant by soul, state, God, beauty, and by the other terms that are basic to the discussion of fundamental issues. He has some [30] notion of the insights that these ideas, singly or in combination, provide concerning human experience.

The liberally educated man has a mind that can operate well in all fields. He may be a specialist in one field. But he can understand anything important that is said in any field and can see and use the light that it sheds upon his own. The liberally educated man is at home in the world of ideas and in the world of practical affairs, too, because he understands the relation of the two. He may not be at home in the world of practical affairs in the sense of liking the life he finds about him; but he will be at home in that world in the sense that he understands it. He may even derive from his liberal education some conception of the difference between a bad world and a good one and some notion of the ways in which one might be turned into the other.

The method of liberal education is the liberal arts, and the result of liberal education is discipline in those areas. The liberal artist learns to read, write, speak, listen, understand, and think. He learns to reckon, measure, and manipulate matter, quantity, and motion in order to predict, produce, and exchange. As we live in the tradition, whether we know it or not, so we are all liberal artists, whether we know it or not. We all practice the liberal arts, well or badly, all the time every day. As we should understand the tradition as well as we can in order to understand ourselves, so we should be as good liberal artists as we can in order to become as fully human as we can.

[31] The liberal arts are not merely indispensable; they are unavoidable. Nobody can decide for himself whether he is going to be a human being. The only question open to him is whether he will be an ignorant, undeveloped one or one who has sought to reach the highest point he is capable of attaining. The question, in short, is whether he will be a poor liberal artist or a good one.

The tradition of the West in education is the tradition of the liberal arts. Until very recently nobody took seriously the suggestion that there could be any other ideal. The educational ideas of John Locke, for example, which were directed to the preparation of the pupil to fit conveniently into the social and economic environment in which he found himself, made no impression on Locke's contemporaries. And so it will be found that other voices raised in criticism of liberal education fell upon deaf ears until about a half-century ago.

This Western devotion to the liberal arts and liberal education must have been largely responsible for the emergence of democracy as an ideal. The democratic ideal is equal opportunity for full human development, and, since the liberal arts are the basic means of such development, devotion to democracy naturally results from devotion to them. On the other hand, if acquisition of the liberal arts is an intrinsic part of human dignity, then the democratic ideal demands that we should strive to see to it that all have the opportunity to attain to the fullest measure of the liberal arts that is possible to each.

[32]   The present crisis in the world has been precipitated by the vision of the range of practical and productive art offered by the West. All over the world men are on the move, expressing their determination to share in the technology in which the West has excelled. The movement is one of the most spectacular in history, and everybody is agreed upon one thing about it: we do not know how to deal with it. It would be tragic if in our preoccupation with the crisis we failed to hold up as a thing of value for the world, even as that which might show us a way in which to deal with the crisis, our vision of the best that the West has to offer. That vision is the range of the liberal arts and liberal education. Our determination about the distribution of the fullest measure of these arts and this education will measure our loyalty to the best in our own past and our total service to the future of the world.

The great books were written by the greatest liberal artists. They exhibit the range of the liberal arts. The authors were also the greatest teachers. They taught one another. They taught all previous generations, up to a few years ago. The question is whether they can teach us. . . .

NOTE

1. the *Logos*. Literally, "the Word"; philosophically, "the rational principle in the universe" [*WID*].

TOPICS FOR DISCUSSION

1. Why should one bother with the "Great Books"? What is the meaning of Hutchins' statement "The death of democracy is not likely to be an assassination from ambush. It will be a slow extinction from apathy, indifference, and undernourishment"? Do you agree? Support your answer with illustrations from contemporary life.

2. What is the unique mark of the tradition of the West? What do the Great Books of this tradition offer mankind? How does Hutchins' explanation of the relation of the Great Books to the tradition of the West compare with Hook's contention that Hutchins makes the study of books alone the source of that tradition?

3. According to Hutchins, what should be the aim of liberal education? Explain the relation of liberal education to vocational training and to the problem of overspecialization. Do you agree that "We all practice the liberal arts, well or badly, all the time every day"? Why or why not?

4. Explain the connection which Hutchins sees between the liberal arts and the emergence of democracy. How does this compare with the familiar view that the liberal arts are citadels of intellectual snobbery, or dusty repositories of inane

social graces? What is there in the history of these arts that might account for the variety of opinions that exist about their merits?

5. Hook insists that Hutchins is absorbed in the past to the exclusion of the present. Do you agree? Why or why not?

6. What does Hutchins mean when he says that liberal education "regards man as an end, not as a means"? Explain the significance of this view of man.

SIDNEY HOOK

The Content of Education

Sidney Hook (b. 1902) has been Chairman of the Division of Philosophy and Psychology of the graduate school of New York University since 1959. His earliest teaching was done in the New York City public schools; since 1927 he has taught philosophy at New York University. In 1928-1929 he was a Guggenheim fellow, and in 1961-1962 a fellow of the Center for Advanced Studies in the Behaviorial Sciences. He was the organizer of the Conference on Science, Spirit and the Democratic Faith, and of the Congress of Cultural Freedom. His abiding concern with the problem of individual freedom within the social framework is evident in his Education for Modern Man *(1946),* Heresy, Yes—Conspiracy, No *(1953),* Common Sense and the Fifth Amendment *(1957),* Political Power and Personal Freedom *(1959),* The Paradoxes of Freedom *(1962).*

These excerpts from Chapter 5 of Education for Modern Man *highlight certain differences of viewpoint between Professors Hook and Hutchins. The earlier part of the chapter, not given here, indicates other points of disagreement, and the later portion contains Professor Hook's suggestions for a course of study which, in his opinion, would constitute a liberal education for man today, a curriculum which would include the physical, biological, and social sciences, social and political philosophies, inference and argument, composition and literature, a foreign language, art, and music. [This selection is taken from Sidney Hook, "The Content of Education,"* Education for Modern Man *(New York: The Dial Press, Inc., 1946), pp. 68-111.]*

ETERNAL AND TEMPORAL

[79] There is a kind of hypnotic quality about words like "eternal," "absolute" and "permanent." It prevents many who employ them from designating the specific features within experience to which they refer, and from seeing that because these are worthy of study it does not therefore follow that the "temporal," "relational" and "historical" are unworthy of study. Sometimes failure to see this takes bizarre forms. True liberal education, Mr. Hutchins informs us, concerns itself with *"the abiding and the permanent."* Its first requirement is that it must be intellectual; its second,

that it hold up what Whitehead calls "the habitual vision of greatness"; its third, that it [80] must deal with "permanent and not shifting conditions, with ultimate and not relative ends."[1] Do any of these requirements necessitate that the content of education be constructed primarily around the materials of the past?

That education should be intellectual is indisputable; that it should be only that is highly disputable. The Greek ideal included the education of the intellect as part of the harmonious development of all human faculties. For the Greeks the life of reason was not the reasoning life, any more than the joy of life was a life of joy. The medieval ideal included the education of the intellect as part of the preparation of man for true spirituality. The ideal of *purely* intellectual education, if it has any historical root at all, is an outgrowth of our modern—nay, our contemporary—world of overspecialization. It expresses perhaps what an advanced research scientist might believe the goal of education to be. It is a little ironical that none of the ages glorified in the classical curriculums stressed the ideal of intellectual education or even made it the supreme virtue. This does not thereby invalidate it as an ideal of education. But for present purposes it is enough to point out that no matter how rigorously intellectual education be conceived, there is nothing in the vast collection of modern disciplines which prevents them from becoming the medium of such education.

To hold up before students the "habitual vision of greatness" is excellent. But as Whitehead himself emphasizes, this does not mean that the heroes of action and the titans of thought inhabit only the realms of the past. Nor does it mean that the study of *books*, or the study of great books, or the study *only* of great books, or the study of great books only of the *past*—to rise in the scale of absurdity—must be central [81] to a liberal education. Great books by all means; but why not also great pictures and symphonies, great plays and cinemas, great social changes and mass movements, as well as the great Armageddons of our own time? We can learn at least as much from the heroic tragedy of Warsaw as from the last stand at Thermopylae. The habitual vision of greatness is important not only because it delights us to lift up our eyes on high but because it gives us working standards of comparative judgment. It enables us to distinguish between the authentic and spurious. It teaches us not to be impatient with what is struggling to be born, to respond to the new and inchoate in the light of its own potentialities of greatness. It helps us to accept the responsibility of making our judgment of greatness here and now, and not timidly playing it safe by deferring to the judgment of the next hundred or thousand years. Absorption in study of the greatness of the past which does not quicken our sense for greatness in the present is a preparation for a life of intellectual snobbery. In face of the emergence of the new, it often leads to a kind of cultural philistinism. "To have spent one's youth at college," writes William James, "in contact with the choice and rare and precious, and yet still to be a blind prig or vulgarian, unable to scent out human excellence or to divine it amid its accidents, to know it only when ticketed and labelled and forced on us by others, this indeed should be accounted the very calamity and shipwreck of a higher education."*

Even more grandiose is Mr. Hutchins' demand that liberal education deal "with permanent and not shifting conditions, with ultimate and not relative ends." But not very sensible! Slavery, feudalism, capitalism, the rise and decline of great empires, colonial and revolutionary America, the migrations [82] of peoples and the patterns of technological change—all would have to be excluded from a liberal education. For they certainly are not permanent. Indeed, everything historical would evaporate from the course of study. But if so, then why study Greek culture? And if Greek culture, why not American? And if there is something permanent in historical change, why is it privileged over what is not permanent? How can we distinguish which is which, without studying *both?* The same argument applies to "ultimate" and "relative" ends. This is a distinction in a certain theory of value. But values as given are not labeled "ultimate" or "relative." Under either label they may be equally valid in their respective contexts. Is it true, as a matter of fact or analysis, that what are called "ultimate" values have the same meaning, as distinct from their formal verbal expression, in all times, places and cultures? How can we tell without examining the values of at least some different cultures? But this is an argument for comparative culture study and critical anthropology which, though it tames the fanaticism of virtue, need not lead, as Mr. Hutchins fears, to the identification of custom and morality.

Grant for the moment all of Mr. Hutchins' dubious premises. Grant that there are eternal problems and eternal truths. Why cannot they emerge from a consideration of the important issues of *our* age? *What is eternally true must be true at any time, including the present.* The half-unconscious identification of the eternal with the ancient, of the permanent with the past, has continuously been drawn in history. It is not for nothing that governments are always on the side of the eternal. But metaphysical and political issues aside, a program like the one Mr. Hutchins advocates is educationally unsound. For whatever the alleged advantages of a curriculum [83] organized around the materials of the past—and all curriculums have some advantages—they can also be won by an intelligent analysis of modern culture. The enormous differential gain in the modern approach is that the knowledge and values which emerge from inquiries into the massive and dramatic problems of our times have a definite relevance to the perennial task of making life better here and now. On the other hand, if we assume that we already are in possession of eternal truths that need only be applied to the present, we are likely to overlook what is distinctive in our own times.

---

* "Value of the College Bred," reprinted in *Essays for College Men*, edited by Foerster, Manchester, and Young, New York, 1913, p. 167.

There is a natural bias to discount the evidence showing that propositions believed eternally true are actually false or have only a *limited historical validity*. The creative sterility of modern adherents of great systems of past thought is in part due to their failure to dip into the fresh seas of contemporary experience in order to test and amplify their stock of "eternal truths."

The whole notion that the past is to be ransacked only to discover the "truths" it can bequeath to the present is parochial. Its more fruitful use, as in literature and art, where the past is not directly relevant to present-day social problems or programs of action, is the ever-present occasion it offers for the enlargement of meanings and the cultivation of the imagination.

TRADITION

It is often alleged that a modern curriculum sins against tradition, and thus violates one of the deepest hungers of man—continuity with the past. But as important as tradition is, reflection makes clear that by itself it cannot determine the content of instruction. No matter what turning in the road we [84] take, it is continuous with the road by which we have come. And there are few things we can do today for which some warrant in past traditions cannot be found. Those who defend tradition in education would be the first to deny that the traditional is synonymous with the dead or obsolete. How, then, do we distinguish between obsolete and living traditions? When traditions are invoked to settle issues, they are always *selections* from the heritage of the past—judgments of comparative worth or value testifying to needs in the present—and are justified by their consequences.

The deepest traditions of a community are those that are so completely taken for granted that they rarely emerge on the level of critical awareness, and still more rarely become subjects of debate—like our language and folkways. But let an issue once force itself on the attention of a community to the point of arousing discussion, then it becomes obvious that what the tradition *has* been of itself does not decide. It is we who decide what our tradition *should* be. The past is so rich that we can always find an historical paternity to legitimize our current offspring.

Those who appeal to tradition as a bulwark against change are curiously unaware of its actual content. For most traditions represent departures from earlier traditions, and their subsequent history is full of further departures from their original purposes and beginnings. No one can survey the history of American religious practice, for example, without realizing that tolerance to dissenters marked a break with earlier traditions, and that the recognition of equal rights for all religions marked a departure from the tradition of mere tolerance. How much truer is this for the history of Western culture. Those who speak of the great tradition of the Western world, and charge [85] "decadent" liberals with attempting to ignore it, betray an insensitiveness to the richness, complexity and contradictory features of what is summed up by the phrase. The dominant features of Greek culture are at least as fundamentally different from those of medieval Christendom as the latter are from the traditions of the Renaissance, the Reformation, and the American, the French, and the Industrial Revolutions. In different respects, we are the inheritors of them all. Our indiscriminate allegiance to them testifies to a basic confusion in our purposes and values. It is an evasion of the challenge of our own time and culture.

The function of a liberal education in the modern world is to bring some degree of order to minds that have inherited conflicting traditions. It must weave the problems and materials of the modern world into a recognizable pattern by which individuals may take their bearings for a full and responsible life. In liberating individuals from confusion, such education liberates within them fresh energies to redirect and remake, separately and together, the worlds they live in. If their action is enlightened, it will increase human freedom by extending control of nature; if it is mature, it will enhance the quality of freedom by bringing the control of nature under wise human control.

NOTE

1. Robert Hutchins, *Education for Freedom* (Baton Rouge: Louisiana State University Press, 1943), p. 57. See also the second broadcast of the series of thirteen broadcasts under the auspices of Education for Freedom, Inc.; "a digest of these addresses and a commentary on them" was given in "Thirteen Arrows Against Liberal Education," *The Humanist* (Spring 1944). (This information is condensed from Professor Hook's notes to the chapter.)

TOPICS FOR DISCUSSION

1. Cite two points of immediate disagreement between Hook and Hutchins. Would the latter agree that his system of education precluded study of such movements as feudalism, slavery, capitalism? If not, can you identify the permanent conditions, underlying issues, and ultimate ends which he might discern beneath the changing historical conditions?

2. Describe the strategy of diction, tone, and argument which Hook uses to discredit Hutchins' theories of education. How do you think Livingstone would reply to Hook's claim that the study of modern culture can give at least as valuable intellectual insights as can the study of the past? What do you think?

3. Does Hook find any value in the study of the past? Would Arnold agree that the literature and art of the past are not "directly relevant to present-day social problems or programs of action"? Would Leavis? Krutch? Do you? In the phrase quoted, what question does the qualifying adjective "directly" raise?

4. Other writers have expressed concern over the breakdown of communication in modern times, the uniquely modern break with the tradition of the past, and consequently the uniquely modern sense of alienation. Yet Sidney Hook says

of mankind: "No matter what turning in the road we take, it is continuous with the road we have come." What do you think? (In this connection you may find interesting "How Human Is Man?" by Loren Eiseley in his *The Firmament of Time* [New York: Atheneum, 1960], pp. 117-49.)

5. Describe the nature of the goal which this essay proposes for modern liberal education. To what extent is this aim echoed by other authors in this book?

III

EDUCATION IN THE MODERN WORLD

A Further Commentary

III

ARTHUR E. BESTOR

Training for a Livelihood

Arthur E. Bestor, American historian (b. 1908), is Professor of History at the University of Washington, Seattle. Educated at Lincoln University, Pennsylvania, at Oxford, and at Yale, he has taught at Columbia, Stanford, Wisconsin, and the University of Illinois. During 1956-1957 he was Harmsworth Professor of American History at Oxford. His works include studies in American history, among them David Jacks of Monterey *(1945),* Education and Reform at New Harmony *(1948),* The Heritage of the Middle West *(1958), and analyses of the needs of contemporary education—*Educational Wastelands *(1953),* The Restoration of Learning *(1955).*

In this particular excerpt Bestor is concerned with the problem of vocational education as contrasted with liberal training. His other writings contain detailed discussion of the values of a liberal education and the shortcomings of the contemporary American curriculum in this respect. See, for example, the chapters "Is a Good Education Undemocratic?" and "The Structure of a Liberal Education" in Educational Wastelands *(Urbana: University of Illinois Press, 1953) and "The Ideal of Disciplined Intelligence," in Bestor's* The Restoration of Learning. *[This selection is taken from Arthur E. Bestor, "Training for a Livelihood," in* The Restoration of Learning *(New York: Alfred A. Knopf, 1955), pp. 79-83.]*

[79] . . . One perfectly good reason for refusing to devote an extensive amount of time to instruction of this kind [a purely vocational approach to education] is its relative ineffectiveness. The popular sneers at book-learning are not really directed at learning in the liberal sense. They arise because of the bumbling inefficiency shown in real life by students who have learned so-called "practical" subjects from a book, under an instructor who perhaps never practiced the trade he purports to teach. It is not the liberally educated man who becomes a laughing stock. It is the journalism major whose sentences no editor would print, the speech major whom no one would hear with patience in a public hall, the home-economics major who knows less about the subject she teaches than the parents of her own pupils, the commerce major who cannot carry on a business as successfully as the man who

never took a commercial course in his life. The school makes itself ridiculous whenever it undertakes to deal *directly* with "real-life" problems, instead of *indirectly* through the development of generalized intellectual powers.

Besides being ineffective, formal instruction in trivial problems of vocational or personal life is dangerously *mis*educative in its effect. It generates in the student the belief that he cannot deal with any matter until he has taken a course in it. Timidity, self-distrust, and conformity are pathetically evident among the graduates of American teacher-training curricula (the most blatantly vocational and anti-intellectual of all programs), for many of these poor souls seem to doubt their ability even to open a schoolroom window until they have been told in a textbook or by a professor of education how high it should be raised. But the decline of resourcefulness, imagination, and independence of mind is alarmingly apparent in the entire mass of present-day students. Alma mater has become a typically overprotective mother, and her children have been spoonfed so long that they dare not begin to live until they have received detailed instructions from her on all their most personal affairs.

Liberal education is designed to produce self-reliance. It expects a man to use his general intelligence to solve particular problems. Vocational and "life-adjustment" programs, on the other hand, breed servile dependence. Originality, reason, and common sense are at a discount; maxims, formulas, and rules (the most degraded kinds of book-learning) are at a premium. The nation should view with grave alarm the undermining of that self-reliance upon which its greatness was based. One can search history and biography in [80] vain for evidence that men or women have ever accomplished anything original, creative, or significant by virtue of narrowly conceived vocational training or of educational programs that aimed merely at "life adjustment." The West was not settled by men and women who had taken courses in "How to be a pioneer." The mechanical ingenuity that is the proverbial characteristic of the American people owes nothing whatever to schoolroom manipulation of gadgets. To transfer to the classroom the kinds of learning that occur naturally in real life is evidence not merely of a disbelief in intellectual training. It reveals also a contemptuous lack of faith in the native good sense of the common man.

A few basic principles emerge from what has just been said, principles according to which vocational training can be integrated with liberal education without destroying the values of either.

If vocational training is to be soundly conducted in our schools, the beginning of each program should be set as late in a student's educational career as possible, so that he may bring the broadest background of liberal education to his task. The beginning point should be set late for another important reason. No training is so worthless as specialized training for an occupation that a man finally decides not to pursue. By beginning vocational training too early a student runs the risk that he may change his mind and thus find all his effort wasted. Liberal education is training in intellectual disciplines of general applicability. The man who possesses it has an automobile that can travel freely over every public highway, not a switch-engine that can run only on a standard-gauge track owned and controlled by somebody else.

To begin with, the specialized training required for any given profession or vocation should be determined by those who know at first hand its real requirements, not by those who have an interest in expanding the number of courses offered. Classwork of a purely vocational sort (as distinguished from general intellectual studies that are likewise requisite) should be formulated as a specialized vocational program, designed to be completed in a few months, a year, or a period of years, as the case may be—the rule being, of course, that no more time is allotted than is absolutely required to assure the necessary technical proficiency. Once such programs have been agreed upon, students should be fully informed of their character and especially of their duration, and should not be permitted to embark upon them at an earlier stage of their [81] education than their situations and their academic prospects warrant.

The prerequisites, as well as the content, of such specialized programs should be clearly set forth. By "prerequisites" I mean simply the basic intellectual disciplines that ought to be mastered before professional or vocational training begins. There is need to specify what mathematics and physics a future engineer should learn before he begins to specialize in engineering, what history a future attorney should know before he enters law school, what languages a future research worker should master before he starts graduate study, or (to take an instance of a different sort) what proficiency in reading and spelling and what acquaintance with literature a future printer should possess before he commences to learn the trade. These prerequisites should be known to the student so that he may wisely choose among the options open to him in a flexible program of liberal education. But the prerequisites should be met as a *part* of his liberal education; they should not be offered as special pre-vocational courses, taught from the vocational point of view.

Finally, vocational programs must be thorough and systematic, and the achievement of each student must be rigorously tested. Genuine vocational training is a vital part of our educational enterprise. It must not be weakened by being confused with pseudo-vocational programs that consist merely of haphazard assortments of courses designed to look relevant on an application for a job. It must not be weakened by being confused with "life-adjustment" programs that merely encourage a little puttering about in a workshop or a little half-hearted clerking in a store. Professional or vocational training, like every other form of education, is a serious business. To trifle with standards, to dilute content, and to accept any other test for graduation than the demonstrable competence of the student are as dangerous to genuine vocational training as to liberal education.

Besides vocational training in the specialized sense, there are many kinds of practical training, non-intellectual in character, which a school or college may nevertheless properly offer as complements to its central program of liberal education. Home economics, shopwork, typewriting, and bookkeeping represent skills of such general value that no student is likely to find them inapplicable to the life he eventually leads. They remain technical skills, not intellectual disciplines, but if they are clearly recognized as such [82] and are not permitted to become substitutes for training in the ability to think, no valid reason can be given why the school or college should not offer supplementary instruction in them.

Such arrangements as these can give reality to the concept of a "single educational ladder," which educators so frequently (and so properly) eulogize. Schools are not making this concept a reality merely by housing all sorts of classrooms in the same building. A single educational ladder is one that all children climb together, pursuing the same basic studies until they reach the point, near the very end of each one's educational career, when each must commence highly specialized, and hence divergent, technical training.

Let me not be misunderstood. I am not asserting that a lawyer is a better man than a truck-driver. I am not asserting that lawsuits are more important to the nation than truck transportation. I am not asserting that a man who is a lawyer is entitled to a better education than a man who drives a truck. I am simply asserting that specialized training for the law requires more time than specialized training for truck-driving. I believe that, as citizens, both men are in need of, and both are entitled to, the broadest and most liberal education that can be provided. As a matter of fact, if both can spend and are willing to spend the same amount of time in study, the truck-driver is actually the better off, educationally speaking, for he needs to divert less time from the studies that are of most general worth.

Society needs thoughtful citizens and cultivated men, whether by profession they be butchers or television announcers or civil engineers. They ought to receive sound and extensive education, regardless of their profession. The point is that the schooling which will make them intelligent men is liberal education, not courses in meat-handling or script-writing or strength of materials. There ought to be no limit on the education offered to any man. But the segment of this education that is devoted to mere vocational training should be strictly limited by the actual requirements of the occupation itself. To spend more time in specialized training than is absolutely essential for the practice of the trade or profession means the diversion of time from liberal education. What counts in making an intelligent and reflective man is the effort he expends on the generalized intellectual and cultural disciplines. A rough measure is the total time he has spent in study, *minus* the time that has had to be diverted to vocational training and the time that has [83] been wasted on trivialities. This invaluable residue in many educational programs of the present day is precariously small.

A citizen today needs an *education*, not a headful of helpful hints. The problems of modern life are so complicated that a vast fund of knowledge and a developed skill in the use of intellectual processes are required to handle them. Engineering and medicine, for example, rest upon formal education—not, however, the kind that purports to satisfy immediate "real-life" needs, but the kind that consists in prolonged and systematic study of the basic disciplines of mathematics, chemistry, and biology. Statesmanship, which we need even more desperately, calls for education, and for something more substantial than high-school civics. The men who drafted our Constitution were not trained for the task by "field trips" to the mayor's office and the county jail. They were endowed with the wisdom requisite for founding a new nation by *liberal* education—that is to say, by an education that was general rather than specific, intellectual rather than "practical," indirect rather than (in the vocational sense) direct. Through study of the classics they came to the study of history and political philosophy and jurisprudence. And through these great disciplines they reached an understanding of the general problems of government. This understanding they applied, with attention both to ultimate principles and to local peculiarities, in the creation of the greatest single constitutional document in the history of mankind.

To deny that liberal education in the basic disciplines is a preparation for life is to deny the testimony of those who have accomplished the most in life, practical as well as intellectual. That liberal education must often be supplemented by specialized professional or vocational training is obvious. Equally obvious is the fact that the fields in which such training may appropriately be offered grow more numerous with the passage of time. But the notion that vocational training can take the place of thorough study of the fundamental intellectual disciplines as a preparation for successful accomplishment and for mature citizenship is a fallacy so thoroughly exploded that anyone who propounds it thereby confesses his invincible ignorance of human experience.

TOPIC FOR DISCUSSION

1. What fault does Bestor find with vocational training as currently given? Would he approve of vocational training in any form? If so, what kind? Why does he feel that certain kinds of vocational training and life-adjustment courses are actually dangerous to the student?

2. What would he list as the "prerequisites" for any sound vocational training? What does Bestor mean by a "single educational ladder" and how do his proposals for education provide for it?

3. Where in the essays of other authors do you find views similar to Bestor's statement that "Society needs thoughtful citizens and cultivated men, whether by profession they be butchers or television announcers or civil engineers"?

4. Compare Bestor's "Training for a Livelihood" with Fadiman's "The Case for Basic Education." What points have they in common? Where does their emphasis differ?

ALFRED NORTH WHITEHEAD

Technical Education and Its Relation to Science and Literature

Alfred North Whitehead (1861-1947), Cambridge-educated English mathematician and philosopher, is notable for his contributions to mathematics, logic, the philosophy of science, and metaphysics. Central to his metaphysics is the "philosophy of organism" which, he felt, was better suited than traditional philosophical categories to convey the interrelation of matter, space, and time. Professor Whitehead lectured and taught at the University of London and at Edinburgh; from 1924 to 1937 he was professor of mathematics at Harvard. In 1925 he received the Sylvester Medal from the Royal Society of London, in 1930 the Butler Medal from Columbia University. From 1915 to 1919 he was president of the Mathematical Association. His Principia Mathematica *(3 volumes, 1910-1913) is a major contribution to the study of logic. His many other works include* The Principle of Relativity (1922), Science and the Modern World (1925), The Aims of Education and Other Essays (1929), Adventures of Ideas (1933), *and* Essays in Science and Philosophy (1947).

The reader interested in discovering what place, if any, Professor Whitehead assigns to the classics in modern education should read his chapter "The Place of the Classics in Education" in The Aims of Education and Other Essays *and compare it with essays on the same topic by Matthew Arnold, Sir Richard Livingstone, and Edith Hamilton. [This selection is taken from A. N. Whitehead, LLD., Sc.D., F.R.S., "Technical Education and Its Relation to Science and Literature,"* The Aims of Education and Other Essays *(New York: The Macmillan Company, 1959), pp. 66-92.]*

[74] Disinterested scientific curiosity is a passion for an ordered intellectual vision of the connection of events. But the goal of such curiosity is the marriage of action to thought. This essential intervention of action even in abstract science is often overlooked. No man of science wants merely to know. He acquires knowledge to appease his passion for discovery. He does

not discover in order to know, he knows in order to discover. The pleasure which art and science can give to toil is the enjoyment which arises from successfully directed attention. Also it is the same pleasure which is yielded to the scientist and to the artist.

The antithesis between a technical and a liberal education is fallacious. There can be no adequate technical education which is not liberal, and no liberal education which is not technical: that is, no education which does not impart both technique and intellectual vision. In simpler language, education should turn out the pupil with something he knows well and something he can do well. The intimate union of practice and theory aids both. The intellect does not work best in a vacuum. The stimulation of creative impulse requires, especially in the case of a child, the quick transition to practice. Geometry and mechanics, followed by workshop practice, gain that reality without which mathematics is verbiage.

[75] There are three main methods which are required in a national system of education, namely, the literary curriculum, the scientific curriculum, the technical curriculum. But each of these curricula should include the other two. What I mean is, that every form of education should give the pupil a technique, a science, an assortment of general ideas, and aesthetic appreciation, and that each of these sides of his training should be illuminated by the others. Lack of time, even for the most favoured pupil, makes it impossible to develop fully each curriculum. Always there must be a dominant emphasis. The most direct aesthetic training naturally falls in the technical curriculum in those cases when the training is that requisite for some art or artistic craft. But it is of high importance in both a literary and a scientific education.

The educational method of the literary curriculum is the study of language, that is, the study of our most habitual method of conveying to others our states of mind. The technique which should be acquired is this technique of verbal expression, the science is the study of the structure of language and the analysis of the relations of language to the states of mind conveyed. Furthermore, the subtle relations of language to feeling, and the high development of the sense organs to which written and spoken words appeal, lead to keen aesthetic appreciations being aroused by the successful employment of language. Finally, the wisdom of the world is [76] preserved in the masterpieces of linguistic composition.

This curriculum has the merit of homogeneity. All its various parts are co-ordinated and play into each other's hands. We can hardly be surprised that such a curriculum, when once broadly established, should have claimed the position of the sole perfect type of education. Its defect is unduly to emphasize the importance of language. Indeed the varied importance of verbal expression is so overwhelming that its sober estimation is difficult. Recent generations have been witnessing the retreat of literature, and of literary forms of expression, from their position of unique importance in intellectual life. In order truly to become a servant and a minister of nature something more is required than literary aptitudes.

A scientific education is primarily a training in the art of observing natural phenomena, and in the knowledge and deduction of laws concerning the sequence of such phenomena. But here, as in the case of a liberal education, we are met by the limitations imposed by shortness of time. There are many types of natural phenomena, and to each type there corresponds a science with its peculiar modes of observation, and its peculiar types of thought employed in the deduction of laws. A study of science in general is impossible in education, all that can be achieved is the study of two or three allied sciences. Hence the charge of narrow specialism [77] urged against any education which is primarily scientific. It is obvious that the charge is apt to be well-founded; and it is worth considering how, within the limits of a scientific education and to the advantage of such an education, the danger can be avoided.

Such a discussion requires the consideration of technical education. A technical education is in the main a training in the art of utilizing knowledge for the manufacture of material products. Such a training emphasizes manual skill, and the co-ordinated action of hand and eye, and judgment in the control of the process of construction. But judgment necessitates knowledge of those natural processes of which the manufacture is the utilization. Thus somewhere in technical training an education in scientific knowledge is required. If you minimize the scientific side, you will confine it to the scientific experts; if you maximize it, you will impart it in some measure to the men, and—what is of no less importance—to the directors and managers of the businesses.

Technical education is not necessarily allied exclusively to science on its mental side. It may be an education for an artist or for apprentices to an artistic craft. In that case aesthetic appreciation will have to be cultivated in connection with it.

An evil side of the Platonic culture has been its total neglect of technical education as an ingredient in the complete development of ideal human beings. This neglect has arisen from two disastrous [78] antitheses, namely, that between mind and body, and that between thought and action. I will here interject, solely to avoid criticism, that I am well aware that the Greeks highly valued physical beauty and physical activity. They had, however, that perverted sense of values which is the nemesis of slave-owning.

I lay it down as an educational axiom that in teaching you will come to grief as soon as you forget that your pupils have bodies. This is exactly the mistake of the post-renaissance Platonic curriculum. But nature can be kept at bay by no pitchfork; so in English education, being expelled from the classroom, she returned with a cap and bells in the form of all-conquering athleticism.

The connections between intellectual activity and the body, though diffused in every bodily feeling, are focused in the eyes, the ears, the voice, and the hands. There is a co-ordination of senses and thought, and also a reciprocal influence between brain activity and material creative activity. In this reaction the hands are peculiarly important. It is a moot point whether the human hand created the human brain, or the brain created the hand. Certainly the connection is intimate and reciprocal. Such deep-seated relations are not widely atrophied by a few hundred years of disuse in exceptional families.

The disuse of hand-craft is a contributory cause to the brain-lethargy of aristocracies, which is only [79] mitigated by sport where the concurrent brain-activity is reduced to a minimum and the hand-craft lacks subtlety. The necessity for constant writing and vocal exposition is some slight stimulus to the thought-power of the professional classes. Great readers, who exclude other activities, are not distinguished by subtlety of brain. They tend to be timid conventional thinkers. No doubt this is partly due to their excessive knowledge outrunning their powers of thought; but it is partly due to the lack of brain-stimulus from the productive activities of hand or voice.

In estimating the importance of technical education we must rise above the exclusive association of learning with book-learning. First-hand knowledge is the ultimate basis of intellectual life. To a large extent book-learning conveys second-hand information, and as such can never rise to the importance of immediate practice. Our goal is to see the immediate events of our lives as instances of our general ideas. What the learned world tends to offer is one second-hand scrap of information illustrating ideas derived from another second-hand scrap of information. The second-handedness of the learned world is the secret of its mediocrity. It is tame because it has never been scared by facts. The main importance of Francis Bacon's influence does not lie in any peculiar theory of inductive reasoning which he happened to express, but in the revolt against second-hand information of which he was a leader.

[80] The peculiar merit of a scientific education should be, that it bases thought upon first-hand observation; and the corresponding merit of a technical education is, that it follows our deep natural instinct to translate thought into manual skill, and manual activity into thought.

The logic of discovery consists in the weighing of probabilities, in discarding details deemed to be irrelevant, in divining the general rules according to which events occur, and in testing hypotheses by devising suitable experiments. This is inductive logic.

The logic of the discovered is the deduction of the special events which, under certain circumstances, would happen in obedience to the assumed laws of nature. Thus when the laws are discovered or assumed, their utilization entirely depends on deductive logic. Without deductive logic science would be entirely useless. It is merely a barren game to ascend from the particular to the general, unless afterwards we can reverse the process and descend from the general to the particular, ascending and descending like the angels on Jacob's ladder.[1] When Newton had divined the law of gravitation he at once proceeded to calculate the earth's attractions on an apple at its surface and on the moon. We may note in passing that inductive logic would be [81] impossible without deductive logic. Thus Newton's calculations were an essential step in his inductive verification of the great law.

Now mathematics is nothing else than the more complicated parts of the art of deductive reasoning, especially where it concerns number, quantity, and space.

In the teaching of science, the art of thought should be taught: namely, the art of forming clear conceptions applying to first-hand experience, the art of divining the general truths which apply, the art of testing divinations, and the art of utilizing general truths by reasoning to more particular cases of some peculiar importance. Furthermore, a power of scientific exposition is necessary, so that the relevant issues from a confused mass of ideas can be stated clearly, with due emphasis on important points.

By the time a science, or a small group of sciences, has been taught thus amply, with due regard to the general art of thought, we have gone a long way towards correcting the specialism of science. The worst of a scientific education based, as necessarily must be the case, on one or two particular branches of science, is that the teachers under the influence of the examination system are apt merely to stuff their pupils with the narrow results of these special sciences. It is essential that the generality of the method be continually brought to light and contrasted with the specialty of the particular [82] application. A man who only knows his own science, as a routine peculiar to that science, does not even know that. He has no fertility of thought, no power of quickly seizing the bearing of alien ideas. He will discover nothing, and be stupid in practical applications.

This exhibition of the general in the particular is extremely difficult to effect, especially in the case of younger pupils. The art of education is never easy. To surmount its difficulties, especially those of elementary education, is a task worthy of the highest genius. It is the training of human souls.

Mathematics, well taught, should be the most powerful instrument in gradually implanting this generality of idea. The essence of mathematics is perpetually to be discarding more special ideas in favour of more general ideas, and special methods in favour of general methods. We express the conditions of a special problem in the form of an equation, but that equation will serve for a hundred other problems, scattered through diverse sciences. The general reasoning is always the powerful reasoning, because deductive cogency is the property of abstract form.

Here, again, we must be careful. We shall ruin mathematical education if we use it merely to impress general truths. The general ideas are the means of connecting particular results. After all, it is the concrete special cases which are important. Thus in the handling of mathematics in your results you [83] cannot be too concrete, and in your methods you cannot be too general. The essential course of reasoning is to generalise what is particular, and then to particularise what is general. Without generality there is no reasoning, without concreteness there is no importance.

Concreteness is the strength of technical education. I would remind you that truths which lack the highest generality are not necessarily concrete facts. For example, $x + y = y + x$ is an algebraic truth more general than $2 + 2 = 4$. But "two and two make four" is itself a highly general proposition lacking any element of concreteness. To obtain a concrete proposition immediate intuition of a truth concerning particular objects is requisite; for example, "these two apples and those apples together make four apples" is a concrete proposition, if you have direct perception of immediate memory of the apples.

In order to obtain the full realisation of truths as applying, and not as empty formulae, there is no alternative to technical education. Mere passive observation is not sufficient. In creation only is there vivid insight into the properties of the object thereby produced. If you want to understand anything, make it yourself, is a sound rule. Your faculties will be alive, your thoughts gain vividness by an immediate translation into acts. Your ideas gain that reality which comes from seeing the limits of their application. . . .

[88] It is unfortunate that the literary element in education has rarely been considered apart from grammatical study. The historical reason is, that when the modern Platonic curriculum was being formed Latin and Greek were the sole keys which rendered great literature accessible. But there is no necessary connection between literature and grammar. The great age of Greek literature was already past before the arrival of Alexandria.[2] Of all types of men to-day existing, classical scholars are the most remote from the Greeks of the Periclean times.

Mere literary knowledge is of slight importance. The only thing that matters is, how it is known. The facts related are nothing. Literature only exists to express and develop that imaginative world which is our life, the kingdom which is within us. It follows that the literary side of a technical [89] education should consist in an effort to make the pupils enjoy literature. It does not matter what they know, but the enjoyment is vital. The great English universities, under whose direct authority school-children are examined in the plays of Shakespeare, to the certain destruction of their enjoyment, should be prosecuted for soul murder.

Now there are two kinds of intellectual enjoyment: the enjoyment of creation, and the enjoyment of relaxation. They are not necessarily separated. A change of occupation may give the full tide of happiness which comes from the concurrence of both forms of pleasure. The appreciation of literature is really creation. The written word, its music, and its associations, are only the stimuli. The vision which they evoke is our own doing. No one, no genius other than our own, can make our own life live. But except for those engaged in literary occupations, literature is also a relaxation. It gives exercise to that other side which any occupation must suppress during the working hours. Art also has the same function in life as has literature.

NOTES

1. Jacob's ladder. On his way to Bethel, the patriarch Jacob saw in a vision angels ascending and descending a ladder that stretched between earth and heaven.

2. Alexandria. Classical Greek literature ended in the fourth century B.C. with Aristotle and Demosthenes. The Alexandrian period of Greek literature covered the last centuries B.C. and the first centuries of the Christian era.

TOPICS FOR DISCUSSION

1. What are Whitehead's reasons for stating that the artist and the scientist feel the same kind of pleasure in their work? What does he mean by "there can be no adequate technical education which is not liberal, and no liberal education which does not impart both technique and intellectual vision"? Would Bestor agree with him? Would Newman? Would you?

2. Describe the three curricula which make up or should make up a system of education. Why should each division of such a curriculum include the other two?

3. Compare Whitehead's comment on intellectual activity and bodily activity as necessary components of a valid curriculum with Hook's remarks on the subject.

4. How should science be taught? What is the importance of technical education? Do you think that the other advocates of the liberal arts would agree with Whitehead on this point? Would they be interested in it?

5. How would you describe the pleasure which can be derived from art and literature? Discuss the relationship between this pleasure element and the teaching of literature. Compare Whitehead's remarks on the inept teaching of literature with criticisms offered by other essayists on the poor teaching of classical literature in the traditional liberal arts curriculum. Have you found pleasure in the study of literature? If not, do you think it was the way literature was taught which destroyed the enjoyment? If so, what suggestions would you make for improving the presentation of literary works in the classroom?

CLIFTON FADIMAN

The Case for Basic Education

Clifton Fadiman, editor, author, radio and television entertainer. A graduate of Columbia, Mr. Fadiman served as an editor for Simon & Schuster 1936-1945 and as an editor for The New Yorker *from 1933 to 1943. As the urbane and witty moderator of* Information Please *he delighted radio audiences during the decade 1938-1948. The same urbanity and wit mark his writing. His books include* Party of One *(1955),* Any Number Can Play *(1957), and* Enter Conversing *(1962).*

The book which the following essay introduces was sponsored by a "non-profit, lay-oriented" organization called The Council for Basic Education. The Council's original statement of purpose, issued in 1956, reads in part: "The Council for Basic Education was established in the belief that the purpose of education is the harmonious development of the mind, the will, and the conscience of each individual so that he may use to the full his intrinsic powers and shoulder the responsibilities of citizenship. It believes in the principle of universal education and in the tax-supported public school system. It insists that only by the maintenance of high academic standards can the ideal of democratic education be realized. . . ." Note how Fadiman's description of his own early education gives concrete illustration of the goals with which the Council is concerned. [This selection is taken from Clifton Fadiman, "The Case for Basic Education" in James D. Koerner (ed.), The Case for Basic Education *(Boston: Little, Brown & Company, 1959) pp. 3-14.]*

[3] The present educational controversy, like all crucial controversies, has its roots in philosophy. One's attitude toward the proposals advanced in this book depends on one's nature, his powers, and his reason for existence.

If, consciously or unconsciously, one takes the position that his nature is essentially animal; that his powers lie largely in the area of social and biological adaptation; and thus his reason for existence is either unknowable or (should he advance one) a form of self-delusion—then the case for basic education, and consequently for education itself, falls to the ground. By the same token the case for physical, social, and vocational training becomes irrefutable.

On the other hand, if one takes the position that man's nature is both animal *and* rational; that his powers lie not only in the area of adaptation but also in that of creation; and that his reason for existence is somehow bound up with the fullest possible evolution of his mental and spiritual capacities—then the case for basic education, and consequently for education itself, is established; and further discussion becomes a matter, however interesting and important, of detail.

[4] A crisis period is not necessarily marked by disaster or violence or even revolutionary change. It is marked by the absence of any general, tacit adherence to an agreed-upon system of values. It is in such a crisis period that we live. Of the two positions briefly outlined above, a minority adheres to the first. Another minority adheres to the second. But most of us waver between the two or have never reflected on either. Our present educational system quite properly mirrors this uncertainty of the majority. It mirrors our own mental chaos. There is nothing else it *can* do, for ours is a democratic society, and all our institutions are representative.

Now neither of the positions is logically demonstrable, though some have tried to bend them to logic, as well as to propaganda. They are faiths. The scholars whose essays comprise this book deal explicitly with questions of curriculum. Implicitly, however, they are proclaiming the faith by which they live. Furthermore they are proclaiming that this is the faith by which Western civilization lives.

Because all faiths are attackable, everything they say can be attacked. Indeed everything they say may be wrong. But the attack can only be sustained by the proclamation of an opposing faith. And if they are wrong, they are wrong only in the sense that no faith can be "proved" right.

Thus the *Metaphysics* of Aristotle opens with the well-known statement: "All men by nature desire to know." This is not a statement of fact in the sense that "All men are born with lungs" is a statement of fact. It is not statistically checkable. It is not a self-evident truth. Cursory observation of many men seems to give it the lie. Depending on whether we prefer the language of logic or the language of emotion we may call it either an assumption or a declaration of faith. If the assumption is denied, or the declaration countered by an opposing declaration, this book, as well as education itself, becomes [5] an irrelevancy. But in that case the cultural fruits of civilization also become an irrelevancy, because they would appear to flow, not from some blind process of unending adaptation, but from Aristotle's proposition. Any doubt cast on that proposition also casts doubt on the permanent value of culture.

It may be that the proposition *is* untenable. Perhaps all men do not by nature desire to know. We can then fall back on a second line of defense. We can say that at least men have acted *as if* they did so desire. Aristotle's dictum may be an illusion. But it looks like a creative illusion.

He has another dictum. He tells us that man is a social animal. Put the two statements together. Were man not a social animal but an anarchic animal, his desire to know would have both its origin and its terminus located in himself. But, as he is a social and not an anarchic animal, he socializes and finally systematizes his desire to know. This socialization and systematization are what we mean by education. The main, though not the only, instrument of education is an odd invention, only three thousand years old, called the school. The primary job of the school is the efficient transmission and continual reappraisal of what we call tradition. Tradition is the mechanism by which all past men teach all future men.

Now arises the question: If all men by nature desire to know, and if that desire is best gratified by education and the transmission of tradition, what should be the character of that education and the content of that tradition? At once a vast, teeming chaos faces us: apparently men desire to know and transmit all kinds of matters, from how to tie a four-in-hand to the attributes of the Godhead.

Obviously this chaos cannot be taught. Hence in the past men have imposed upon it form, order, and hierarchy.[1] They have selected certain areas of knowledge as the ones that, to the exclusion of others, both *can* and *should* be taught.

[6] The structure of this hierarchy is not a matter of accident. Nor is it a matter of preference. The teacher may not teach only what happens to interest him. Nor may the student choose to be taught only what happens to interest him. The criteria of choice are many and far from immutable. But there is an essential one. Basic education concerns itself with those matters which, once learned, enable the student to learn all the other matters, whether trivial or complex, that cannot properly be the subjects of elementary and secondary schooling. In other words, both logic and experience suggest that certain subjects have generative power and others do not have generative power. When we have learned to tie a four-in-hand, the subject is exhausted. It is self-terminating. Our knowledge is of no value for the acquisition of further knowledge. But once we have learned to read we can decipher instructions for the tieing of a four-in-hand. Once we have learned to listen and observe, we can learn from someone else how to tie a four-in-hand.

It has, up to our time, been the general experience of men that certain subjects and not others possess this generative power. Among these subjects are those that deal with language, whether or not one's own; forms, figures and numbers; the laws of nature; the past, and the shape and behavior of our common home, the earth. Apparently these master or generative subjects endow one with the ability to learn the minor or self-terminating subjects. They also endow one, of course, with the ability to learn the higher, more complex developments of the master subjects themselves.

To the question, "Just what are these master subjects?" the contributors to this book supply a specific answer. It happens to be a traditional answer. That is, these are, more or less, with modifications in each epoch, the subjects that Western civilization has up to very recent times considered basic. That they [7] are traditional is not an argument in their favor. The contributors believe that they are sanctioned not only by use and wont but by their intrinsic value.

The word *intrinsic* is troublesome. Is it possible that, as the environment changes, the number and names of the basic subjects must also change? At a certain time, our own for example, is it possible that driver-education is more basic than history? Many of us think so, or act as if we thought so. Again I would suggest that if we do think so, or act as if we thought so, it is not because we wish to lower the accident rate (though that is what we say) but because we unconsciously conceive of man primarily as an adaptive animal and not as a rational soul. For if he is primarily the first, then at the present moment in our human career driver-education *is* basic; but if he is primarily the second it is, though desirable, not basic.

I think the authors of this book would concede that with environmental changes the relative importance of the basic subjects will also change. It is obvious that a post-Newtonian world must accord more attention to the mathematical and physical sciences than did the pre-Newtonian world. But *some* science has at all times been taught. Similarly in a hundred years the American high school student may be universally offered Russian rather than French or German. But this does not affect the principle that *some* systematic instruction in *some* leading foreign language will remain a basic necessity.

In other words, however their forms may be modified, a core of basic or generative subjects exists. This core is not lightly to be abandoned, for once it is abandoned we have lost the primary tools which enable us to make any kind of machine we wish. Other subjects may seem transiently attractive or of obvious utility. It is pleasant to square-dance, for instance, and it is useful to know how to cook. Yet we cannot afford to be seduced by such "subjects." Hard though it may be, we must [8] jettison them in favor of the basic subject matters. And there is no time for an eclectic mixture: only a few years are available in which educe [*sic*], to educate the rational soul. We cannot afford bypaths. We cannot afford pleasure. All education, Aristotle tells us, is accompanied by pain. Basic education is inescapably so accompanied, as well as by that magnificent pleasure that comes of stretching rather than tickling, the mind.

I have briefly outlined the standard case for basic education insofar as it rests on an unchanging philosophic faith or view of human nature. But there is a more urgent, though less fundamental, argument still to be advanced. In sum it is this: while basic education is *always* a necessity, it is peculiarly so in our own time.

Perhaps I can best make this clear by a personal reference which I hope the reader will forgive.

I am a very lucky man, for I believe that my generation was just about the last one to receive an undiluted basic education. As this is written, I am fifty-four years old. Thus I received my secondary school education from 1916 to 1920. Though I was not well educated by European standards, I was very well educated by present-day American ones. For this I am grateful to my country, my city, and my teachers. Of personal credit I can claim little.

My high school was part of the New York City system. It had no amenities. Its playground was asphalt and about the size of two large drawing rooms. It looked like a barracks. It made no provision for dramatics or square dancing. It didn't even have a psychiatrist—perhaps because we didn't need one. The students were all from what is known as the "underprivileged"—or what we used to call poor—class. Today this class is depended on to provide the largest quota of juvenile delinquents. During my four years in high school there was [9] one scandalous case in which a student stole a pair of rubbers.

Academically my school was neither very good nor very bad. The same was true of me. As the area of elective subjects was strictly limited, I received approximately the same education my fellows did. (Unfortunately Latin was not compulsory: I had to learn it—badly—by myself later on.) Here is what—in addition to the standard minors of drawing, music, art and gym—I was taught some forty years ago:

Four years of English, including rigorous drill in composition, formal grammar and public speaking.

Four years of German.

Three years of French.

Three or four years (I am not sure which) of history, including classical, European and American, plus a no-nonsense factual course in civics, which was dull but at least didn't pretend to be a "social science."

One year of physics.

One year of biology.

Three years of mathematics, through trigonometry.

That, or its near equivalent, was the standard high school curriculum in New York forty years ago. That was all I learned, all any of us learned, all all of us learned. All these subjects can be, and often are, better taught today—when they are taught at all on this scale. However, I was taught French and German well enough so that in later years I made part of my living as a translator. I was taught rhetoric and composition well enough to make it possible for me to become a practicing journalist. I was taught public speaking well enough to enable me to replace my lower-class accent with at least a passable one; and I learned also the rudiments of enunciation, placing, pitch, and proper breathing so that in after years I found it not too difficult to get odd jobs as a public lecturer and radio-and-television handyman.

[10] I adduce these practical arguments only to explode them. They may seem important to the life-adjuster. They are not important to me. One can make a living without French. One can even make a living without a knowledge of spelling. And it is perfectly possible to rise to high estate without any control whatsoever over the English language.

What *is* important about this old-fashioned basic education (itself merely a continuation and sophistication of the basic education then taught in the primary schools) is not that it prepared me for life or showed me how to get along with my fellow men. Its importance to me and, I believe, to most of my fellow students, irrespective of their later careers, is twofold:

1. It furnished me with a foundation on which later on, within the limits of my abilities, I could erect any intellectual structure I fancied. It gave me the wherewithal for the self-education that should be every man's concern to the hour of his death.

2. It precluded my ever becoming Lost.

In drawing the distinction between generative and self-terminating subjects we have already discussed (1).

I want now to explain (2) because the explanation should help to make clear why in our time basic education is needed not only in principle but as a kind of emergency measure.

Again I hope the reader will forgive the intrusion of the autobiographical note.

Considered as a well-rounded American I am an extremely inferior product. I am a poor mechanic. I play no games beyond a little poorish tennis and I haven't played that for five years. I swim, type, dance and drive raggedly, though, with respect to the last, I hope non-dangerously. I have had to learn about sex and marriage without benefit of classroom instruction. I would like to be well-rounded and I admire those who are. But it is too late. I take no pleasure in my [11] inferiorities but I accept the fact that I must live with them.

I feel inferior. Well and good. It seems to hurt nobody. But, though I feel inferior, I do not feel Lost. I have not felt lost since being graduated from high school. I do not expect ever to feel lost. This is not because I am wise, for I am not. It is not because I am learned, for I am not. It is not because I have mastered the art of getting along with my peers, for I do not know the first thing about it. I am often terrified by the world I live in, often horrified, usually unequal to its challenges. But I am not lost in it.

I know how I came to be an American citizen in 1959; what large general movements in history produced me; what my capacities and limitations are; what truly interests me; and how valuable or valueless these interests are. My tastes are fallible but not so fallible that I am easily seduced by the vulgar and transitory—though often enough I am unequal to a proper appreciation of the noble and the permanent. In a word, like tens of millions of others in this regard, I feel at home in the world. I am at times scared but I can truthfully say that I am not bewildered.

I do not owe this to any superiority of nature. I owe it, I sincerely believe, to the conventional basic education I received beginning about a century ago. It taught me how to read, write, speak, calculate, and listen. It taught me the elements of reasoning and it put me on to the necessary business of drawing abstract conclusions from particular instances. It taught me how to locate myself in time and space and to survey the present in the light of an imperfect but ever-functioning knowledge of the past. It provided me with great models by which to judge my own lesser performances. And it gave me the ability to investigate for myself anything that interested me, provided my mind was equal to it.

I admit this is not much. But it is something, and that a [12] vital something. And that something—here we touch the heart of our discussion —is becoming ever rarer among the products of our present educational system.

The average high school graduate today is just as intelligent as my fellow students were. He is just as educable. But he is Lost, in greater or less degree.

By that I mean he feels little relation to the whole world in time and space, and only the most formal relation to his own country. He may "succeed," he may become a good, law-abiding citizen, he may produce other good, law-abiding citizens, and on the whole he may live a pleasant—that is, not painful—life. Yet during most of that life, and particularly after his fortieth year or so, he will feel vaguely disconnected, rootless, purposeless. Like the very plague he will shun any searching questions as to his own worth, his own identity. He will die after having lived a fractional life.

Is this what he really wants? Perhaps it is. It all comes round again to what was said at the opening of these remarks. Again it depends on one's particular vision of man. If we see our youngster as an animal whose main function is biological and social adaptation on virtually a day-to-day basis, then his fractional life is not fractional at all. It is total. But in that case our school curriculum should reflect our viewpoint. It should include the rudiments of reading so that our high school graduate may deciper highway markers, lavatory signs, and perhaps the headlines of some undemanding newspaper. It should include a large number of electives, changing every year, that may be of use to him in job hunting. And primarily it should include as much play and sport as possible, for these are the proper activities of animals, and our boy is an animal.

Yet the doubt persists. *Is* this really what he wants? And once again the answer depends on our faith. For example, the [13] "Rockefeller Report" on Education (published in 1958 and called *The Pursuit of Excellence*) did not issue, except indirectly, from surveys, analyses, polls or statistical abstracts. It issued from faith. The following sentences do not comprise a scientific conclusion. They are an expression of faith, like the Lord's Prayer:

"What most people, young or old, want is not merely security or comfort or luxury—although they are glad enough to have these. They want meaning in their lives. If their era and their culture and their leaders do not or cannot offer them great meanings, great objectives, great convictions, then they will settle for shallow and trivial meanings."

There is no compulsion to believe this. If we do not believe it, and unqualifiedly, there is no case for basic education. Which means that, except for the superior intellect, there is no case for traditional education at all. In that event we should at once start to overhaul our school system in the light of a conception of man that sees him as a continually adjusting, pleasure-seeking, pain-avoiding animal.

But if we do believe it, and unqualifiedly, then the proposals contained in this book might at least be considered as guide-lines, subject to discussion and modification.

The root of our trouble does not lie in an unbalanced curriculum, or in an inadequate emphasis on any one subject, or in poor teaching methods, or in insufficient facilities, or in under-paid instructors. It lies in the circumstance that somehow the average high school graduate does not know who he is, where he is, or how he got there. It lies in the fact that naturally enough he "will settle for shallow and trivial meanings." If nothing in his early education has convinced him that Newton, Shakespeare and Lincoln are both more interesting and more admirable than Frank Sinatra, Jerry Lewis and Pat Boone, he will find answers to his questions in Sinatra, Lewis and Boone, [14] and not in Newton, Shakespeare and Lincoln. If he has learned little or no history, geography, science, mathematics, foreign languages, or English he will, naturally enough, learn (for even if all men do not desire to know, in Aristotle's sense, surely they desire to know *something*) golf, quail-shooting, barbecuing, and some specialized technique of buying and selling.

In accordance with his luck and his temperament, he may become happily lost, or unhappily lost. But lost he will become. Lost he will remain. Lost he will die.

And if we allow these lost ones to multiply indefinitely, they will see to it that our country is lost also.

NOTE

1. hierarchy. A series of items or persons arranged in ranks according to their importance.

TOPICS FOR DISCUSSION

1. Fadiman claims that varying concepts of human nature underlie the controversy about the proper education for man. Describe the view of man implied in his essay. Identify the concepts of man's nature which are stated or implied in other essays in this collection.

2. What, according to Fadiman, constitutes the crisis of the present age? To what extent is his view of the nature of the crisis echoed by other essayists?

3. What is basic education concerned with? How does it decide on "master subjects" and what allowance does it make for changing times and conditions?

4. "We cannot afford pleasure [in education]", says Fadiman. Do you think he means that education must necessarily be a disagreeable experience, a sort of torture test for man?

5. Describe the content of Fadiman's own basic education. How does it compare with the education you received in high school? Do you feel that his course of study was about the same as yours? Was it inferior? Superior? Why?

6. What lifelong values did Fadiman derive from this basic education? How does his reaction to his education compare with your educational experience so far? What does he mean when he says "I do not feel lost"? In what ways can education save man from a "lost" feeling? Do other essayists touch on this point at all? Do you think they should?

7. Fadiman's essay is structured so that the end brings the reader back to the basic assumption put forth in the beginning. What is this assumption? Have you found it stated or implied in other discussions of education? Do you find that it is basic to your own ideas of what the school can or should do?

JOSÉ ORTEGA Y GASSET

The Fundamental Question

José Ortega y Gasset (1883-1955), Spanish essayist and philosopher, studied in Germany, where he was influenced by the neo-Kantian system of thought. In 1910 he became professor of metaphysics at the University of Madrid. He helped found the liberal newspaper El Sol, and from 1923 to 1935 he edited and directed the review La Revista de Occidente. A supporter of the republic at the time of the overthrow of the monarchy, he later considered the regime too far to the left and went into exile, first in France and then in Argentina. In 1945 he returned to Spain. Among his many works are The Modern Theme (1931), The Revolt of the Masses (1932), Toward a Philosophy of History (1941), The Mission of a University (1944), The Dehumanization of Art (1948), and Man and People (1957). Of these, perhaps The Revolt of the Masses and The Dehumanization of Art are the best known in this country.

In connection with the general question of the nature of education for contemporary man, the student should find several other chapters in Sr. Ortega y Gasset's the Mission of a University to be of particular interest. These are "Culture and Science," "What the University Must Be Primarily . . . ," and "The Principle of Economy in Education." He will, no doubt, especially approve of the author's insistence upon the university's revising its offerings so as to no longer overwhelm the student with much more material than it is possible for him to absorb. [This selection is taken from José Ortega y Gasset, "The Fundamental Question," Mission of a University, translated, with an Introduction by Howard Lee Nostrand (Princeton: Princeton University Press, 1944), pp. 46-65.]

[55] . . . "General culture." The absurdity of the term, its Philistinism, betrays its insincerity. "Culture," referring to the human mind and not to stock or crops, cannot be anything else but general. There is no being "cultured" in physics or mathematics. That would mean simply to be *learned* in a particular subject. The usage of the expression "general culture" shows an underlying notion that the student ought to be given some ornamental knowledge, which in some way is to educate his moral character or his intellect. For so vague a purpose, one discipline is as good as another,

among those that are more or less indefinite and not so technical—like philosophy, or history, or sociology!

But the fact is that if we go back to the medieval epoch in which the university was created, we see clearly that the relic before us is the humble remains of what then constituted higher education, proper and entire.

[56] The medieval university does no research.* It is very little concerned with professions. All is *"general culture"*—theology, philosophy, "arts." †

But what is called "general culture" today was something very different for the Middle Ages. It was not an ornament for the mind or a training of the character. It was, on the contrary, the system of ideas, concerning the world and humanity, which the man of that time possessed. It was, consequently, the repertory of convictions which became the effective guide of his existence.

Life is a chaos, a tangled and confused jungle in which man is lost. But his mind reacts against the sensation of bewilderment: he labors to find "roads," "ways" through the woods,‡ in the form of clear, firm ideas concerning the universe, positive convictions about the nature of things. The ensemble, or system, of these ideas, is culture in the true sense of the term; it is precisely the opposite of external ornament. Culture is what saves human life from being a mere disaster; it is what enables men to live a life which is something above meaningless tragedy or inward disgrace.

We cannot live on the human level without ideas. Upon them depends what we do. Living is nothing more nor less than doing one thing instead of another. Hence the oldest book of India: "Our acts follow our thoughts as the wheel of the cart follows the hoof of the ox." In this sense—which by itelf implies no intellectualistic doctrine§—we *are* our ideas.

[57] Gideon, in this case exceptionally profound, would make it clear that man is always born into a specific period. That is, he is called to live his life at some definite stage in the unfolding of human destinies. A man belongs to a generation; he is of one substance with it. And each generation takes its place not in some chance location, but directly and squarely upon the preceding one. This comes to mean that man lives, perforce, at *the level of his time,*** and more particularly, at *the level of the ideas of his time*.

Culture is the *vital* system of ideas of a period. It makes not a particle

---

* Which does not mean that no research was done in the Middle Ages.

† [Editor Nostrand's Note.] The exaggeration here does not essentially damage Sr. Ortega's thesis that the modern university should teach a kind of "culture" which this reference to the Middle Ages helps to describe.

‡ Whence there arises at the beginning of all cultures a term explaining "road" in this sense: the *odos* and *methodos* of the Greeks, the *tao* and *te* of the Chinese, the *path* and *vehicle* of India.

§ Our ideas or convictions may well be called unintellectualistic, as mine are, and in general, the ideas of our age.

** For the concept of "the height of the times," see *The Revolt of the Masses*.

of difference whether these ideas, or convictions, lie partly or wholly in the province of science. Culture is not science. It is characteristic of our present culture that a great part of its content proceeds out of science; but in other cultures this has not been the case, nor is it decreed anywhere that in ours it will always be so to the same degree as at present.

Compared with the medieval university, the contemporary university has developed the mere seed of professional instruction into an enormous activity; it has added the function of research; and it has abandoned almost entirely the teaching of transmission of culture.

It is evident that the change has been pernicious. Europe today is taking its sinister consequences. The convulsive situation in Europe at the present moment is due to the fact that the average Englishman, the average Frenchman, the average German are *uncultured*: they are ignorant of the essential system of ideas concerning the world and man, which belong to our time. This average person is the new barbarian, a laggard behind the contemporary civilization, archaic and primitive in contrast with his problems, which are grimly, relentlessly modern.* This new barbarian is [58] above all the professional man, more learned than ever before, but at the same time more uncultured—the engineer, the physician, the lawyer, the scientist.

The blame for this unpredicted barbarity, this radical and tragic anachronism, rests primarily with the pretentious nineteenth-century university of all countries. If this institution should by chance be torn to bits in the frenzy of a barbarous revolution, it would not have the feeblest reason to complain. When one has examined the matter, he must needs come to the conclusion that the guilt of the universities is not compensated for by the prodigious and brilliant service which they have undeniably rendered to science. Let us not be the dupes of science. For if science is the grandest creation of man, it is made possible, after all, by human life. A crime perpetrated against the fundamental conditions of human life cannot be atoned for through science.

The harm is so ingrained that I shall barely be understood by the generation anterior to the one I am addressing.

In the book of a Chinese thinker who lived in the fourth century B.C., Chuang-tsu, certain symbolic characters are conversing together, and one of them, called the God of the Northern Sea, asks, "How shall I talk of the sea to the frog, if he has never left his pond? How shall I talk of the frost to the bird in the summer land, if it has never left the land of its birth? How shall I talk of life with the sage, if he is the prisoner of his doctrine?"

Society needs good professional men—judges, doctors, engineers—and therefore the university is prepared to furnish professional training. But

---

* The analysis of this serious situation is presented in *The Revolt of the Masses*.

society needs before this, and more than this, to be assured that the capacity is developed for another kind of profession, the profession of governing. In every society someone governs, whether a group or a class, few people or many. By "governing" I mean not so much the legal exercise of
authority as a diffuse pressure, or [59] influence, exerted upon the body
politic. Today, the societies in Europe are governed by the bourgeois classes,
whose majority is composed of professional men. It is of the first importance to these societies, therefore, that these professional people, aside from
their several professions, possess the power to make their lives a vital influence, in harmony with the height of their times. Hence it is imperative to
set up once more, in the university, the teaching of the culture, the system
of vital ideas, which the age has attained. This is the basic function of the
university. This is what the university must be, above all else.

If the working man should become the governing man tomorrow, the
problem remains the same: he must govern in accordance with the height
of the times—otherwise his regime will be supplanted.*

When one considers that the European countries have deemed it admissible to grant professional titles and prestige to magistrates and doctors
without making sure that these men have a clear idea, for example, of the
physical conception we now have of the world, and an equally clear idea of
the character and limitations of the marvelous science by which that concept has been attained—we need not be surprised that affairs have come to
such a pass in Europe. At a juncture like this, let us not bandy about fine
phrases. The vague desire for a vague culture, I repeat, will lead us nowhere.
Physics, and its method, is one of the great essential instruments of the
modern mind. Into that science have gone four centuries of intellectual
discipline, and its doctrine is intimately connected with the cultured man's
concept of God and society, of matter and that which is not matter, together with all the other essentials for an enlightened life. Of course, one
can do without that science and be neither [60] disgraced nor condemned
—in certain situations: if one is a humble shepherd in the hills, or a serf
attached to the soil, or a manual laborer enslaved to the machine. But the
gentleman who professes to be a doctor, or magistrate, or general, or philologist, or bishop—that is, a person who belongs to the directive class of
society—if he is ignorant of what the physical cosmos is today for the European man, is a perfect barbarian, however well he may know his laws, or his
medicines, or his Holy Fathers. And I should say the same of the person
who has not a decently coherent picture of the great movements of history
which have brought Humanity to its present parting of ways (for ours is a
day of crucial situations). And I should say the same again of the person
who has no definite idea of how speculative philosophy conceives today its

---

* Since in actual practice the working man does govern, sharing that function with
the middle class, it is urgent that the university education be extended to him.

perpetual essay to formulate a plan of the universe, or how biology endeavors to interpret the fundamental facts of organic life.

For the moment, let us not obscure this simple, evident proposition, by raising the question of how a lawyer, without preparation in higher mathematics, can understand the idea of twentieth-century physics. We shall deal with that question later. For now, let us simply admit into our minds, as we must, the light which proceeds from this observation. The man who does not possess the concept of physics (not the science of physics proper, but the vital idea of the world which it has created), and the concept afforded by history and by biology, and the scheme of speculative philosophy, is not an educated man. Unless he should happen to be endowed with exceptional qualities, it is extremely unlikely that such a man will be, in the fullest sense, a good doctor, a good judge, or a good technical expert. But it is certain that all the other things he does in life, including part of his profession itself which transcends its proper academic boundaries, will turn out unfortunately. His political ideas and actions will be inept; his affairs of the heart, beginning with [61] the type of woman he will prefer, will be crude and ridiculous; he will bring to his family life an atmosphere of unreality and cramped narrowness, which will warp the upbringing of his children; and outside, with his friends, he will emit thoughts that are monstrosities, and opinions that are a torrent of drivel and bluff.

There is no other way: to move with assurance in the tangle of life, one must be cultivated, one must know the topography—the "ways" and "methods." One must have an idea of the time and place in which he lives: in a word, the "culture" of the age. Now then, this culture is either received, or else it is invented. He who exposes himself to the labor of inventing it for himself, accomplishing alone what thirty centuries of humanity have already accomplished, is the only man who has the right to deny the proposition that the university must undertake to impart culture. But the unfortunate truth is that this lone person, who could oppose my thesis, would have to be a madman!

Civilization has had to await the beginning of the twentieth century, to see the astounding spectacle of how brutal, how stupid, and yet how aggressive is the man learned in one thing and fundamentally ignorant of all else.* Professionalism and specialism, through insufficient counterbalancing, have smashed the European man in pieces; and he is consequently missing at all the points where he claims to be, and is badly needed. The engineer possesses engineering; but that is just one piece, one dimension of the European man: the whole man is not to be found in this fragment called "engineer." And so in the rest of the cases. When one says that

---

* See the chapter entitled "The Barbarism of Specialization" in *The Revolt of the Masses.*

"Europe is broken in pieces," thinking to use a baroque and exaggerated expression, he says more truth than he suspects. Indeed, the crumbling away of Europe which we are witnessing is the result of the invisible [62] fragmentation that the European man has progressively undergone.*

The great task immediately before us is something like a jigsaw puzzle: we have to reassemble out of scattered pieces—*disiecta membra*—a complete living organism, the European man. What we must achieve is that every individual, or (not to be Utopian) many individuals, should each succeed in constituting the type of the whole man in its entirety. What force can bring this about, if it is not the university?

Then there are no two ways about it. The university must add this other function, huge as it is, to the list of those it already attempts to accomplish.

For that matter, outside Spain a movement is making itself felt with great vigor, to orient higher education toward the teaching of culture, or the transmission to the newer generation of the system of ideas concerning the world and man which has reached its maturity with the passing generation.

We come to the conclusion therefore that the university's teaching comprises these three functions:

I. The transmission of culture.

II. The teaching of the professions.

III. Scientific research and the training of new scientists.

Have we thus answered our question, What is the mission of the university? By no means: we have only massed together what the university of today believes to be its business, and one thing which, in our judgment, it is not doing but must do. We have prepared the question; no more than that.

TOPICS FOR DISCUSSION

1. Why does Ortega y Gasset despise the term "general culture"? What does he mean when he speaks of its "philistinism"?

2. How would he define "culture in the true sense of the term"? Compare this use of the term culture with Fadiman's "basic education."

3. What fault does the author find with the modern university as contrasted with the medieval? Why does he refer to the professional man of the twentieth century as "the new barbarian"? Do you agree with him? Why or why not?

4. According to "The Fundamental Question," what connection is there between the education of a people and the governing class of a society? Discuss the ways in which some of the other essayists deal with the relationship of education to the well-being of the state.

---

* The statement is true to such a point that it cannot only be made thus vaguely, but it can be developed by enumerating the precise phases of the progressive fragmentation, in three generations of the past century and the first generation of the twentieth.

5. To what extent is a knowledge of science necessary to the cultured man? How does the kind of knowledge of science which Ortega y Gasset describes compare with similar recommendations made by Huxley and Arnold?

6. How does this essay deal with the problem of the development of the whole man as opposed to the training of the specialist?

7. How would you describe the distinctive tone of the essay—personal? Provocative? Lively? Explain.

JACQUES MARITAIN

Liberal Education for All

Jacques Maritain (b. 1882). The leading Neo-Thomist philosopher of our time, M. Maritain has been professor emeritus at Princeton since 1952. He was professor of philosophy there from 1948 until 1952; earlier he had taught at the Institut Catholique de Paris, at the Institute of Medieval Studies, Toronto, and at Columbia University. For the years 1945-1948, the French government appointed him ambassador to the Holy See. During his long and active career M. Maritain has written more than a score of books on philosophy and education including: Art and Scholasticism *(1930),* An Introduction to Philosophy *(1930),* True Humanism *(1938),* Education at the Crossroads *(1943),* The Education of Man *(1962),* Existence and the Existent *(1949),* The Responsibility of the Artist *(1960). His* Reflections on America *(1958) offers perceptive and affectionate observations on American life.*

In the chapter following that from which the essay reprinted below is taken, Maritain further elaborates his view of the humanities as truly humanizing influences on man. He is amused at the idea that some consider these studies mere intellectual pastimes, suitable only for the affluent and leisured. [This selection is taken from Jacques Maritain, "Liberal Education for All," Chapter III, "Thomist Views on Education," in Nelson B. Henry (ed.), Modern Philosophies and Education, *(Chicago: The National Society for the Study of Education, 1955), pp. 77-83.]*

[77] *Concerning Philosophical Principles.* Education directed toward wisdom, centered on the humanities, aiming to develop in people the capacity to think correctly and to enjoy truth and beauty, is education for freedom, or liberal education. Whatever his particular vocation may be, and whatever special training his vocation may require, every human being is entitled to receive such a properly human and humanistic education.

[78] Liberal education was restricted in the past to the children of the upper classes. This very fact reacted on the way in which it was itself conceived. Liberal education for all obliges us, I believe, to undertake a double reconsideration.

In the first place, a serious recasting of the very concept of the humanities and the liberal arts has been made necessary by the development of human knowledge in modern centuries. The notion of the humanistic disciplines and the field of liberal arts must be enlarged so as to comprise physics and the natural sciences, the history of sciences, anthropology and the other human sciences, with the history of cultures and civilizations, even technology (insofar as the activity of the spirit is involved), and the history of manual work and the arts, both mechanical and fine arts.

I would like to insist, in particular, that physics and the natural sciences must be considered one of the chief branches of the liberal arts. They are mainly concerned with the mathematical reading of natural phenomena, and they insure in this way the domination of the human spirit over the world of matter, not in terms of ontological causes but rather in terms of number and measurement. Thus they appear, so to speak, as a final realization of the Pythagorean[1] and Platonist[2] trends of thought in the very field of that world of *experience* and *becoming* which Plato looked upon as a shadow on the wall of the cave. Physics and the natural sciences, if they are taught not only for the sake of practical applications but essentially for the sake of knowledge, provide man with a vision of the universe and a sense of the sacred, exacting, unbending objectivity of the humblest truth, which play an essential part in the liberation of the mind and in liberal education. Physics, like mathematics, if it is viewed as the creative power from which great discoveries proceed, is close to poetry. If it were taught as it demands to be in the light of the spiritual workings of man, it should be revered as a liberal art of the first rank and an integral part of the humanities.

As to the human sciences, the positivistic[3] bias with which, as a rule, they are cultivated today makes their humanistic value rather questionable indeed. Yet this is an abnormal situation, for which they themselves are not responsible. It would be a great misfortune, and a blunder, to exclude from the realm of the humanities the sciences of man, even though developed at the level of empirical[4] [79] knowledge. The problem for them, as for physics and the other sciences of phenomena, is to be set free, in the minds of scientists, from the pseudo-philosophical prejudices which have preyed upon them as parasites. They should be taught, insofar as they are a part of a program in the humanities, from a philosophical point of view, with reference to the particular epistemological[5] approach they involve, and with a constant concern either for the understanding of human nature and the development of its potentialities, or for the understanding of the ways in which the human mind functions.

We have also to stress the crucial importance of the history of sciences with respect to humanistic education. In the perspective of the humanities, the genesis of science in the human mind and its progress, adventures, and vicissitudes in the course of history have as much illuminating power as the results that science attains and the changing disclosures on the universe of nature that it offers us in various periods of its development. Knowledge of the succession of scientific theories, of the inner logic, and also of the part of chance and contingency that can be observed in their evolution, and of the actual ways through which scientific imagination proceeds from discovery to discovery can alone give the student a real understanding of scientific truth and its authentic range. The history of sciences is the genuine instrument through which the physical sciences can be integrated in the humanities and their humanistic value brought out in full light.

In the second place, it has become indispensable to give full recognition to the concept of basic liberal education and to the typical requirements it involves. I have just indicated the necessary *broadening* of the *matters* comprised within the scope of the liberal arts and the humanities. What I am now emphasizing is the necessary *restriction* of the burden imposed on the student, and of the curriculum, as concerns the very *ways and perspective* in which the matters in question have to be taught.

Let us refer to the considerations laid down in a previous section on natural intelligence and basic liberal education. On the one hand, the objective of basic liberal education is not the acquisition of science itself or of art itself, along with the intellectual virtues [80] involved, but rather the grasp of their *meaning* and the comprehension of the truth and beauty they yield. We grasp the meaning of a science or an art when we understand its object, nature, and scope, and the particular species of truth or beauty it discloses to us. The objective of basic liberal education is to see to it that the young person grasps this truth or beauty through the natural powers and gifts of his mind and the natural intuitive energy of his reason backed up by his whole sensuous, imaginative, and emotional dynamism.

On the other hand, as concerns the content of knowledge, of the *things* that the young person has to learn, this content is to be determined by the very requirements of the grasp in question. Many things which were taught in the past in liberal education are useless; many things which were not taught in the past in liberal education are necessary in this regard. But in any case, the subjects and methods which are proper to graduate studies have no place at this level. In short, the guiding principle is less factual information and more intellectual enjoyment. The teaching should be concentrated on awakening the minds to a few basic intuitions or intellectual perceptions in each particular discipline, through which what is essentially illuminating as to the truth of things learned is definitely and unmistakably possessed. The result would be both a rise in quality of the teaching received and an alleviation of the material burden imposed by the curriculum.

Concerning Practical Application. If all the preceding remarks are true, we see that the distinction between basic liberal education and higher learning or graduate studies should be emphasized: because the first deals with a world of knowledge appropriate to natural intelligence, the second with a world of knowledge appropriate to intellectual virtues.

When he enters this world of knowledge proper to higher learning, or the world of technical and professional studies, or the world of practical activity in a given job—the youth will specialize in a particular field. At the same time he will have the opportunity, either by means of the university or the technological institutions, or by his own initiative, to pursue and improve his humanistic education. This would be simply impossible if he were not previously equipped with an adequate basic liberal education.

[81] Basic liberal education should cover both high school and college. During high-school years, the mode of teaching would be adapted to the freshness and spontaneous curiosity of budding reason, stirred and nourished by the life of the imagination. When it comes to college years, we would have to do with natural intelligence in a state of growth, with its full natural aspirations to universal knowledge—and, at the same time, with its normal tendency to develop some more perfect *habitus* or disposition relating to preparation for a particular field of activity. So the college would have to insure both basic liberal education in its final stages and the development of a particular state of capacity. The best arrangement for this purpose would be to have the college divided into a number of fields of concentration or fields of primary interest, each one represented by a given school (or *institut*, in the French sense of the word). In effect, this would be to have the college divided into a number of *schools of oriented humanities*, all of which would be dedicated to basic liberal education, but each of which would be concerned with the preparatory study in a particular field of activity, thus dealing with the beginnings and first development of a given intellectual virtue or a given intellectual skill. And basic liberal education rather than this preparatory study would be the primary aim. But precisely in order to make basic liberal education fully efficacious, the manner in which it would be given, and the teaching organized, would take into consideration the particular intellectual virtue, or the particular intellectual skill, to be developed in the future scientist or businessman, artist, doctor, newspaperman, teacher, lawyer, or specialist in government.

I mean that all the students would have to attend courses in all the matters of the curriculum in basic liberal education; but, on the one hand, the apportionment of the hours given to certain of these courses might be different for the students in the various schools of oriented humanities; and, on the other hand, special courses in each of these schools would enlighten the student on the vital relationship between the particular discipline being taught and the chief disciplines of the common curriculum.

Thus, the essential hierarchy of values inherent in liberal education would be preserved, with the main emphasis, as to the disciplines, on philosophy; and, as to the ways and methods, on the [82] reading of great books. But the practical arrangement of the curriculum would be attuned, in the manner I just indicated, to what will be later on, in actual fact, the principal activity of the person who is now a student. In this way it would be easier to insure the unity and integration of the teaching, especially if the teachers of each school of oriented humanities co-operated in a close and constant manner so as to elaborate and enforce a common educational policy. And the students would receive a kind of pre-professional training (unavoidable as it is in actual existence) which, instead of impairing liberal education and worming its way into it like a parasite, would serve to make the young person more vitally interested in liberal education and more deeply penetrated by it.

The notion of basic liberal education, with the kind of recasting of the list of liberal arts and the method of teaching the humanities we have considered, is of a nature, it seems to me, to give practical and existential value to the concept of *liberal education for all*. On the one hand, basic liberal education, dealing only with the sphere of knowledge and the educational approach appropriate to natural intelligence and respecting the need of natural intelligence for unity and integration, avoids any burden of pseudo-science to be imposed on the student and feeds on the spontaneous, natural interests of his mind. On the other hand, given the broadening of the field of liberal arts and humanities, on the necessity of which I have laid stress, liberal education would cease being considered an almost exclusively literary education. Since the humanities in our age of culture require articulate knowledge of the achievements of the human mind in science as well as in literature and art, and since it is normal to attune, during college years, the common teaching of the humanities, essential for all, to a particular preparatory training diversified according to the various prospective vocations of the students, basic liberal education is adapted to all the real needs which the liberal education of the past was reproached with being unable to satisfy.

Basic liberal education does not look upon students as future professors or specialists in all the branches of knowledge and the liberal arts taught in the curriculum. It does not look upon them as future gentlemen or members of the privileged class. It looks upon them as future citizens, who must act as free men and who are able to make sound and independent judgments in new and changing [83] situations, either with respect to the body politic or to their own particular task. It is also to be expected that these future citizens would educate their children and discuss with them competently the matters taught in school. Moreover, it is assumed that they would dedicate their own leisure time to those activities of rest through which man enjoys the common heritage of knowledge and beauty, or those activities of super-abundance through which he helps his fellow-men with generosity.

NOTES

1. Pythagorean. Pertaining to the philosophy of Pythagoras (*c.* 582 B.C. to *c.* 507 B.C.), founder of mathematical science; credited with the theory of numbers and the mathematical study of music; he conceived of the earth as a sphere and of incommensurable quantities (i.e., quantities that have no common measure between them).

2. Platonist. Pertaining to the philosophy of Plato.

3. Positivist. One who, like Comte, holds that the only data which constitute a valid basis for knowledge is that obtained through the methods and experiments of the "positive" sciences. The purely speculative and metaphysical methods are consequently to be rejected.

4. empirical. Depending solely on experiment and observation.

5. epistemological. Pertaining to that branch of philosophy concerned with the origin and nature of knowledge.

TOPICS FOR DISCUSSION

1. How does Maritain define liberal education? In such an education what role does he assign physics, the natural sciences, and the human sciences? How would Glass and Nagel differ from him on this subject of the teaching of the sciences? On what points do you think they would agree with his view of science? Discuss the basic differences in concepts of man and his education that you would find in, say, Maritain and Nagel.

2. "We grasp the meaning of a science or an art when we understand its object, nature, and scope, and the particular species of truth or beauty it discloses to us." Using *meaning* as Maritain uses it here, explain the *meaning* of a science or an art you have studied.

3. How does Maritain's concept of the objective of a liberal education compare with Newman's description of the goal of liberal knowledge? What distinction does Maritain draw between liberal education and higher learning (graduate studies)? Why?

4. How does this author deal with the problem of overspecialization? The preparation of students for their respective vocations?

5. Compare the benefits of this "basic liberal education" as Maritain describes them with Fadiman's praise of his own "basic education."

JOHN W. GARDNER

The Ideal of Individual Fulfillment

Since 1955 John W. Gardner (b. 1912) has been president of the Carnegie Foundation for the Advancement of Teaching. A graduate of Stanford and the University of California, he has taught philosophy at the University of California, Connecticut College, and Mt. Holyoke. He joined the Carnegie Corporation of New York in 1946. Since 1955 he has been its president. He has also been an advisor to the United States delegation at the U.N. From 1959 to 1962 he was a member of the Advisory Commission for the Social Sciences of the National Science Foundation; from 1960 to 1963 he was a Director of the Woodrow Wilson Foundation. He is currently a trustee of the Metropolitan Museum of Art. As chairman of the Rockefeller Brothers fund panel on Education, he was chief drafter of the group's report, "The Pursuit of Excellence."

Two other chapters in Gardner's Excellence *are of particular interest: "College and the Alternative" and "The Pursuit of Excellence." The question contained in the full title of the book,* Can We Be Equal and Excellent Too?, *voices a problem of increasing concern to contemporary American education. [This selection is taken from John W. Gardner, "The Ideal of Individual Fulfillment,"* Excellence *(New York: Harper & Brothers, 1961), pp. 135-44.]*

[136] . . . Education in the formal sense is only a part of the society's larger task of abetting the individual's intellectual, emotional and moral growth. *What we must reach for is a conception of perpetual self-discovery, perpetual reshaping to realize one's best self, to be the person one could be.*

This is a conception which far exceeds formal education in scope. It includes not only the intellect but the emotions, character, and personality. It involves not only the surface, but deeper layers of thought and action. It involves adaptability, creativeness and vitality.

And it involves moral and spiritual growth. We say that we wish the individual to fulfill his potentialities, but obviously we do not wish to develop great criminals or great rascals. Learning for learning's sake isn't enough. Thieves learn cunning, and slaves learn submissiveness. We may learn things that constrict our vision and warp our judgment. We wish to foster fulfillment within the framework of rational and moral strivings which have characterized man at his best. In a world of huge organizations and vast social forces that dwarf and threaten the individual, we must range ourselves whenever possible on the side of individuality; but we [137] cannot applaud an irresponsible, amoral or wholly self-gratifying individuality.

America's greatness has been the greatness of a free people who shared certain moral commitments. Freedom without moral commitment is aimless and promptly self-destructive. It is an ironic fact that as individuals in our society have moved toward conformity in their outward behavior, they have moved away from any sense of deeply-shared purposes. We must restore *both* a vigorous sense of individuality *and* a sense of shared purposes. Either without the other leads to consequences abhorrent to us.

To win our deepest respect the individual must both find himself and lose himself. This is not so contradictory as it sounds. We respect the man who places himself at the service of values which transcend his own individuality—the values of his profession, his people, his heritage, and above all the religious and moral values which nourished the ideal of individual fulfillment in the first place. But this "gift of himself" only wins our admiration if the giver has achieved a mature individuality and if the act of giving does not involve an irreparable crippling of that individuality. We cannot admire faceless, mindless servants of The State or The Cause or The Organization who were never mature individuals and who have sacrificed all individuality to the Corporate Good.

WASTE ON A MASSIVE SCALE

In our society today, large numbers of young people never fulfill their potentialities. Their environment may not be such as to stimulate such fulfillment, or it may actually be such as to stunt growth. The family trapped in poverty and ignorance can rarely provide the stimulus so necessary to [138] individual growth. The neighborhood in which delinquency and social disintegration are universal conditions cannot create an atmosphere in which educational values hold a commanding place. In such surroundings, the process by which talents are blighted begins long before kindergarten, and survives long afterward.

The fact that large numbers of American boys and girls fail to attain their full development must weigh heavily on our national conscience. And it is not simply a loss to the individual. At a time when the nation must make the most of its human resources, it is unthinkable that we should resign ourselves to this waste of potentialities. Recent events have taught us with a sledge hammer effectiveness the lesson we should have learned from our own tradition—that our strength, creativity and further growth as a society depend upon our capacity to develop the talents and potentialities of our people.

Any adequate attack on this problem will reach far beyond formal educational institutions. It will involve not only the school but the home, the church, the playground, and all other institutions which shape the individual. The child welfare society, the adoption service, the foundlings' home, the hospital and clinic—all play their part. And so do slum clearance projects and social welfare programs that seek to create the kind of family and neighborhood environment which fosters normal growth.

But it is not only in childhood that we face obstacles to individual fulfillment. Problems of another sort emerge at a later stage in the life span.

Commencement speakers are fond of saying that education is a lifelong process. And yet that is something that no young person with a grain of sense needs to be told. Why do the [139] speakers go on saying it? It isn't that they love sentiments that are well worn with reverent handling (though they do). It isn't that they underestimate their audience. The truth is that they know something their young listeners do not know— something that can never be fully communicated. No matter how firm an intellectual grasp the young person may have on the idea that education is a lifelong process, he can never know it with the poignancy, with the deeply etched clarity, with the overtones of satisfaction and regret that an older person knows it. The young person has not yet made enough mistakes that cannot be repaired. He has not yet passed enough forks in the road that cannot be retraced.

The commencement speaker may give in to the temptation to make it sound as though the learning experiences of the older generation were all deliberate and a triumph of character—character that the younger generation somehow lacks. We can forgive him that. It is not easy to tell young people how unpurposefully we learn, how life tosses us head over heels into our most vivid learning experiences, how intensely we resist many of the increments in our own growth.

But we cannot forgive him as readily if he leaves out another part of the story. And that part of the story is that the process of learning through life is by no means continuous and by no means universal. If it were, age and wisdom would be perfectly correlated, and there would be no such thing as an old fool—a proposition sharply at odds with common experience. The sad truth is that for many of us the learning process comes to an end very early indeed. And others learn the wrong things.

The differences among people in their capacity for continued growth are so widely recognized that we need not dwell on them. They must not be confused with differences [140] in the degree of success—as the world measures success—which individuals achieve. Many whom the world counts as unsuccessful have continued learning and growing throughout their lives; and some of our most prominent people stopped learning literally decades ago. . . .

Of course, people are never quite as buffeted by circumstance as they appear to be. The man who experiences great personal growth as a result of some accidental circumstance may have been ready to grow in any case. Pasteur[1] said that chance favors the prepared mind. The man defeated by circumstance might have triumphed had he been made of other stuff. We all know individuals whose growth and learning can only be explained in terms of an inner drive, a curiosity, a seeking and exploring element in their personalities. Captain Cook[2] said, "I . . . had ambition not only to go farther than any man had ever been before, but as far as it was possible for a man to go."* Just as Cook's restless seeking led him over the face of the earth, so other men embark on Odysseys of the mind and spirit. . . .

Unfortunately, the conception of individual fulfillment and lifelong learning which animates the commencement [141] speaker finds no adequate reflection in our social institutions. For too long we have paid pious lip service to the idea and trifled with it in practice. Like those who confine their religion to Sunday and forget it the rest of the week, we have segregated the idea of individual fulfillment into one compartment of our national life, and neglect it elsewhere. We have set "education" off in a separate category from the main business of life. It is something that happens in schools and colleges. It happens to young people between the ages of six and twenty-one. It is not something—we seem to believe—that need concern the rest of us in our own lives. . . .

[142] What we are suggesting is that every institution in our society should contribute to the fulfillment of the individual. Every institution must, of course, have its own purposes and preoccupations, but over and above everything else that it does, it should be prepared to answer this question posed by society: "What is the institution doing to foster the development of the individuals within it?"

Now what does all of this mean? It means that we should very greatly enlarge our ways of thinking about education. We should be painting a vastly greater mural on a vastly more spacious wall. What we are trying to do is nothing less than to build a greater and more creative civilization. We propose that the American people accept as a universal task the fostering of individual development within a framework of rational and moral values. We propose that they accept as an all-encompassing goal the furtherance of individual growth and learning at every age, in every significant situation, in [143] every conceivable way. By doing so we shall keep faith with our ideal of individual fulfillment and at the same time insure our continued strength and creativity as a society.

If we accept this concern for individual fulfillment as an authentic national preoccupation, the schools and colleges will then be the heart of a national endeavor. They will be committed to the furthering of a national

---

* Christopher Lloyd. *The Voyages of Captain Cook*, Cresset Press, London, 1949.

objective and not—as they now often find themselves—swimming upstream against the interests of a public that thinks everything else more urgent. The schools and colleges will be greatly strengthened if their task is under-girded by such a powerful public conception of the goal to be sought.

And both schools and colleges will be faced with a challenge beyond anything they have yet experienced. We have said that much will depend upon the individual's attitude toward learning and toward his own growth. This defines the task of the schools and colleges. Above all they must equip the individual for a never-ending process of learning; they must gird his mind and spirit for the constant reshaping and re-examination of himself. They cannot content themselves with the time-honored process of stuffing students like sausages or even the possibly more acceptable process of train-ing them like seals. It is the sacred obligation of the schools and colleges to instill in their students the attitudes toward growth and learning and crea-tivity which will in turn shape the society. With other institutions at work on other parts of this task, the schools and colleges must of course give particular attention to the intellectual aspects of growth. This is uniquely their responsibility.

If we accept without reservation these implications of our rational be-lief in individual fulfillment, we shall have enshrined a highly significant purpose at the heart of our [144] national life—a purpose that will lift all American education to a new level of meaning. We shall have accepted a commitment which promises pervasive consequences for our way of think-ing about the purpose of democratic institutions. And we shall have em-braced a philosophy which gives a rich personal meaning to the pursuit of excellence.

NOTES

1. Pasteur. Louis Pasteur (1822-1895), French chemist. His contributions include a theory of fermentation that led to the principle of pasteurization, a method of vaccination against hydrophobia (rabies), and the solution to the prob-lem of the silkworm disease pebrine.

2. Captain Cook. James Cook (1728-1779), English navigator and explorer. The voyage of his *Endeavor* (1768-1781) resulted in the exploration of New Zealand and the east coast of Australia. The expedition of the *Resolution* under his command (1772-1775) discovered New Caledonia. On his last voyage he re-discovered the Sandwich (Hawaiian) Islands; here he was murdered by natives in 1779.

TOPIC FOR DISCUSSION

1. Discuss the ways in which this treatment of education for modern man dif-fers in scope and emphasis from most of the other essays in the book. Identify those points that it does have in common with certain of them. What connection, if any, does Gardner's theory have with the traditions of liberal education? What

goal does it propose for American education as well as for education in general?

2. "The sad truth is that for many of us the learning process comes to an end very early indeed." Does your observation of people bear this out? Do you think that there are any forces or movements in contemporary life which tend to encourage the ideal of learning as a lifelong process? If so, describe them.

3. Gardner speaks about "our [American] rational belief in individual fulfillment." What conception of man does such an ideal necessarily presuppose? What bearing has such a concept on the kind of education our citizens need?

HOWARD MUMFORD JONES

A Joy Forever

Howard Mumford Jones, educator and author (b. 1892), was edu-cated at Wisconsin, the University of Chicago, and Harvard; he has taught at the universities of Texas, North Carolina, and Michigan. In 1936 he joined the Harvard faculty as professor of English. From 1960 to 1962 he was Lawrence Lowell professor of the humanities at Harvard, and since 1962, professor emeritus. During the years 1943-1944 Professor Jones was dean of the Harvard Graduate School of Arts and Sciences. His interest in American literary backgrounds, in education for the modern world, in the nature and condition of the humanities—past and present—is vividly ex-pressed in such works as Ideas in America *(1944),* Education and World Tragedy *(1948),* The Theory of American Literature *(1948),* The Frontier in American Literature *(1956),* The Pursuit of Happiness *(1953),* Guide to American Literature and Its Backgrounds Since 1880 *(1959),* American Humanism *(1957),* Reflections on Learning *(1958), and* One Great Soci-ety *(1959).*

This essay treats briefly certain threats to the "joy of learning." In American Humanism *(New York: Harper & Brothers, 1957) and in* One Great Society *(New York: Harcourt Brace & Company, 1959), Professor Jones deals at length with the nature of the humanities, the history of these studies, and possible answers to the perennial question "But what good are they?" [This selection is taken from Howard Mumford Jones, "A Joy For-ever,"* Reflections on Learning *(New Brunswick, N.J.: Rutgers University Press, 1932), pp. 69-97.]*

[89] . . . Humane learning, it seems to me, has as its principal aim the eludication of what we quaintly [90] call the human predicament, that is, the eternal conflict between the aspirations and the frustrations of man. Its subjects, or rather its companions in this enterprise, are philosophy and art in the widest sense of these two great words. The object of learning is coterminous with the object of philosophy, and the object of art is to seek that stay against confusion, which is joy. I spoke earlier of the happiness that comes from gradually mastering the grammar of any subject, but this happiness cannot come if the skill of the grammarian is exalted above the

power of the creator. It is still true that we murder to dissect, important as dissection must always be. The question of the poet, however, is cogent:

> Think you, 'mid all this mighty sum
> Of things forever speaking,
> Than nothing of itself will come
> But we must still be seeking?

The profound and elusive truth in Wordsworth's[1] poem is one of the most difficult truths to define and to establish, but until we establish it scholarship leads away from, and not into, the work of art. Books were made for men, not men for books, [91] and so likewise were paintings, symphonies, buildings, philosophy, and scholarship. Poems may be the occasion for scholarship, but they should never be merely the excuse for it. Until we realize that humane learning like the god Janus has two faces, we shall not understand what learning is and why its object is joy. Learning is more than information, just as art is more than inspiration. The scholar gets beyond erudition only when, through empathy, he learns to participate in the creation of art; but the artist will not communicate to anybody save himself unless on his side he learns that he belongs to culture and that to this culture (maintained in part by scholarship), in so far as he is an artist, he is in greater or lesser degree responsible. Learning is a union of imagination with fact, the marriage of information and insight, the fusion of scientific accuracy with a passionate sympathy for the human predicament. Learning is about philosophy and the arts; but philosophy and the arts are also about learning.

I owe my title, A Joy Forever, to John Ruskin,[2] whose writings like huge, abandoned caravels[3] lie stranded on the shores of Time. It was under this title that he republished in 1880 the work which [92] appeared a hundred years ago as The Political Economy of Art. This is full of Victorian fallacies, but it is also full of Victorian grandeur, and in it I find this passage: "Observe, there are two great reciprocal duties concerning industry, constantly to be exchanged between the living and the dead. We, as we live and work, are to be always thinking on those who are to come after us; that what we may do may be serviceable, so far as we can make it so, to them, as well as to us . . . each generation will only be happy or powerful to the pitch that it ought to be, in fulfilling these two duties to the Past and the Future. Its own work will never be rightly done, even for itself—never good, or noble, or pleasurable to its own eyes—if it does not prepare it also for the eyes of generations yet to come. And its own possessions will never be enough for it, and its own wisdom never enough for it, unless it avails itself gratefully and tenderly of the treasures and wisdom bequeathed to it by its ancestors."

Never good, or noble, or pleasurable to its own eyes! Its own possessions will never be enough, its own wisdom never enough, unless it avails *itself gratefully and tenderly of the treasures and the wisdom bequeathed by its ancestors!* What can be [93] more eminently nineteenth century? And yet is it not precisely in our sense of the continuity of human wisdom and of human joy that we scholars find delight? Edwin Panofsky[4] reminds us that the cosmos of culture, like the cosmos of nature, is a structure in time and space. What the scholar does, he further points out, is not to erect a rational superstructure on an irrational foundation, but to develop his re-creative experiences so as to conform with the results of his archaeological research. Archaeological research is empty without aesthetic re-creation, but aesthetic re-creation is irrational without archaeological research. Why?

I think Professor Panofsky's answer is still the right one: because we are interested in reality. Reality is a function of explanation, and explanation in turn is a function of that contemplation, that pause for understanding which is the joy of learning. Professor Panofsky puts the matter picturesquely when he says: ". . . The man who is run over by an automobile is run over by mathematics, [94] physics, and chemistry." "It is impossible," he concludes, "to conceive of our world in terms of action alone."

Another distinguished critic of art, Bernard Berenson,[5] points out that learning enables us to appraise objects and artifacts according to their significance: first as to the degree that they enable us to reconstruct the past in general, then to reconstruct the history of a given art, and finally to select and interpret the history of the past which can still vitalize and humanize us. The end of such learning is to seek out "the life-enhancement that results from identifying oneself with the object or putting oneself in its place." His description of this process is too technical for me to quote it here, and he talks principally about historians of art; yet what he says applies in equal measure to the general field of learning. Its purpose is to find the life-enhancing values.

I am, then, persuaded that learning forever has two aspects: the aspect of knowledge *about*, and the aspect of knowledge *of*; that is to say, scholarly information and imaginative empathy. Fused into a harmonious whole, learning is one of the durable satisfactions of life—the joy that arises from the [95] sense of participating in the totality of human experience.

Learning, however, may be travestied in opposite ways. One of these travesties is pedantry—the form of learning without its spirit—and with pedantry we are all supposed to be familiar. The other travesty is, I think, wider spread, less understood, and more difficult to identify. I shall call it appreciationism. It is that approach to art and philosophy which mistakes emotion for insight, the emotion being forever sentimental. Such emotion makes no demand on the individual, matures nobody, offers no challenge to the intellect, and invariably fails us in any crisis. Its transient pleasures are without results upon character, whatever they may do for personality. It is an attempt to teach without intellect, which is supported by the doctrine that even a naïve acquaintance with great minds is better than no acquaintance at all. Perhaps. But do we also hold that a child's notion of electricity is sufficient for the citizen of the atomic age? If this seems to you an extreme or misleading parallel, I remind you that a child's notion of ancient history furnished the drive behind Mussolini's pasteboard empire and that an even [96] more infantile notion of philosophy and biology lay behind the lurid massacres of Hitler's time.

Scholarship like science is difficult; learning like the theory of science is even more exacting; and acquiring a humane point of view is one of the supreme achievements of the mind. I see no more reason to suppose that most of us can rise to the stature of a Goethe or a Burckhardt[6] than to suppose that most of us can rise to the stature of a Darwin or an Einstein.[7] The searching experience, the subtle ideational processes, the revelatory glories of a Beethoven, a Shakespeare, a Michelangelo,[8] a Thomas Aquinas,[9] are not for the holidays of the intellect, a sort of external plaster to be applied when the serious work of science is done for the day and all we want is a little vacation. The humanities are vast and demanding. If the biologist seeks to solve the riddle of the painful earth, so do the metaphysician and the poet. Precisely as the joy of chemistry is not to do parlor tricks but to understand the composition of matter, so the joy of learning is not the ability to solve crossword puzzles and win money on television shows but the capacity to think greatly of man and about him and of the arts that best express him.

[97] Does all this mean that learning is so difficult we should not attempt it in the schools? As well say that because physics is difficult, we should not there attempt it. We do not think that the aim of elementary physics is a vague, pleasant emotion; why then should we think that poetry is merely emotion? We simply cannot be satisfied with an emotional concept of learning, even at elementary levels. Learning is or should be something vital, affirmative, intelligent, and bracing—not the possession of the cultist or the pedant, not the possession of the sentimentalist any more than biology or algebra is to be sentimentally conceived. The concern of learning is with wisdom, with the maturities of thought, with language as the form of thought; and its disciplines must, like the disciplines of science, be exacting. Its aim is comprehension, and in comprehension there lives for those who can catch some glimpse of it a bracing and eternal joy.

NOTES

1. Wordsworth. William Wordsworth (1770-1850), English romantic poet. His "Preface to the Lyrical Ballads" (1799) set forth the principles of the new romantic poetry. His works include "Tintern Abbey," "Ode on Intimations of Immortality," and The Prelude.

2. John Ruskin (1819-1900). English essayist and critic. His aesthetic criticism includes *Modern Painters* (1843-1860), *The Seven Lamps of Architecture* (1849), and *The Stones of Venice* (1881-1883). After 1860 most of his criticism was directed at social conditions, e.g. *Fors Clavigera* (1871-1884).

3. Caravels. Sailing vessels in use in the fifteenth and sixteenth centuries.

4. Edwin Panofsky (1892-   ). Professor and historian of art; Samuel B. Morse Professor, New York University since 1963. His writings include *Albrecht Dürer* (1943), *Renaissance and Renascences in Western Art* (1960), and *Meaning in the Visual Arts* (1955).

5. Bernard Berenson (1865-1959). An art historian and world famous authority on the art of the Italian Renaissance. His works include *Venetian Painters of the Renaissance* (1894), *The Study and Criticism of Italian Art* (1901, 1902, 1915), *Aesthetics and History in the Visual Arts* (1949), and *Rumor and Reflection* (1952).

6. Burckhardt. Jakob Burckhardt (1818-1897), Swiss art historian and archeologist, an originator of the school of cultural history. His greatest work is *The Civilization of the Renaissance in Italy* (1860).

7. Einstein. Albert Einstein (1879-1955), German theoretical physicist who became a naturalized American citizen in 1940. Among his important contributions to science are the theory of relativity and a deduction of the influence of gravity on the propagation of light. He was awarded the 1921 Nobel Prize for Physics; for many years Professor Einstein was a member of the Princeton Institute for Advanced Study.

8. Michelangelo. Michelangelo Buonarroti (1475-1564), Italian sculptor, architect, painter, poet. His sculptures *Moses, David,* the *Pietà di San Pietro;* his paintings, particularly the frescoes in the Sistine Chapel (in particular the *Last Judgment*); his architectural and sculptural work in the Vatican made him the most famous of the great artists of the Italian Renaissance.

9. St. Thomas Aquinas (1225-1274). "The angelic doctor," the greatest of scholastic philosophers; his outstanding work is his *Summa Theologica* (1267-1273). Today, Maritain and Gilson and their followers are carrying on the Thomist tradition in philosophy.

TOPICS FOR DISCUSSION

1. Howard Mumford Jones says that he took the title of this chapter from an essay by John Ruskin. The phrase appears earlier still, however, in the poem "Endymion" by John Keats. Find the "Endymion" reference and discuss the extent to which the meaning of the phrase in that context is relevant here.

2. What is—or should be—the relationship of scholarship and art? Would Jones' opinion on this issue fit in with Barzun's justification of the academic humanities? If so, how?

3. What is meant by the statement "Learning is the union of imagination with fact, the marriage of information and insight, the fusion of scientific accuracy with a passionate sympathy for the human predicament"? Is such a union possible? Probable? Desirable? Will not the "passionate sympathy" reduce or nullify the scientific objectivity necessary for "scientific accuracy"?

4. Discuss the shortcomings of appreciationism.

5. Identify the two elements which should fuse into a harmonious whole in the learning process. Discuss the factors which often prevent such harmonious fusion. What is the "joy of learning"? Is it attainable? Pursuable? Worth the pursuit? How does the author treat this question? What is your opinion?

Topics for Research

SHORT RESEARCH PAPERS

One good way to get started on a research paper is to note the questions that occur as you read. When you find yourself saying *Why? What? To what extent?* about an author's statement, you have taken the first short but definite step in research. The following are some of the questions to which *The Education of Modern Man* offers material on which short research papers could be based. You will find that some of the questions overlap. All are designed to start you formulating questions of your own.

- What are the humanities? What purpose do they serve?
- Are there limitations to science? What are they?
- Are the liberal arts practical arts? Can they be? Should they be?
- Is science one of the liberal arts?
- Can science be humanized? Should it be?
- What is happening to liberal education today? Why?
- What are some of the problems raised by specialization and by professionalism? Why?
- What is the nature of breakdown in communications prevalent in modern society? What are the reasons for it?
- Why does every man today need a knowledge of science?
- Why is scientific training, alone, an inadequate basis for the meaningful life today?
- Which disciplines transmit "values"? What values? Why? (First, define "values.")
- What is a liberal education—in terms of content, aims, and benefits?
- Is education a lifelong process? How? Why?
- Past wisdom or present knowledge—which affords a better basis for the education of modern man? (Don't forget to consider the question: Must one choose between the two?)
- Is it possible to misuse the scientific method? How? In what areas?
- What connection exists between man's nature and his education?
- What connection exists between the education of man and the freedom of man?

Another method of approaching a controlled research paper is to choose the essay in this volume with which you disagree most strongly and to try to find answers to one or more of its main theses in the material offered by the other essays. Or choose one of the recurring general themes (e.g., the nature of a liberally educated person, the importance of science for modern man) and discuss the different ways in which this theme is handled by the essayists represented (or discuss the treatment of the theme by the three or four who seem to you to have handled it best).

If you are particularly interested in the way writers present their material, compare the styles of several of the essayists including as wide a variety of technique as possible.

The questions printed at the end of each essay will give you still other ideas for papers.

LIBRARY RESEARCH PAPERS

Any of the questions under "Short Research Papers" can be used as a starting point for longer papers; the bibliography at the end of the book suggests a number of sources useful in such research, and these sources will in turn lead you to others. Should you need a list of topics rather than a list of questions to begin with, here are a number of suggestions for this sort of library paper:

• Compare C. P. Snow's *Two Cultures* with his *Two Cultures and A Second Look*, and compare both with F. R. Leavis' *Two Cultures? The Significance of C. P. Snow*. Explain to what extent Snow, in the *Second Look*, has modified his views, his emphasis, his tone, and to what extent if any his modifications meet Leavis' objections.

• Trace the course of Thomas Henry Huxley's fight for the inclusion of science in the curriculum of higher education in nineteenth-century England.

• Trace the reasons for the challenge to the liberal arts in American public education in the first half of the twentieth century.

• Outline the goals and methods of liberal education as Plato and/or Aristotle saw them.

• Give an account of the views of some modern admirers of traditional classical learning.

• Give an account of the views of some modern admirers of a new humanism based on science.

• Descrie the evolution of the "Great Books" program; or explain the nature of the program and defend it or criticize it.

• Define humanism, or explain the varying interpretations which have been given to the term.

• Elaborate on the views expressed in one of the essays in *The Educa-*

tion of Modern Man, basing your elaboration on other works by the same author.

• Discuss the special problems of a liberal arts program in a system of public education that attempts to provide education for all.

• Discuss scientific stereotypes, their existence, their weaknesses.

• Explore the question of theory versus practice in humanistic studies.

• Define terms such as "basic education," "general education," "liberal education," and discuss the relationship between them. Which are the newer? When and why did they enter discussions of education?

• Discuss the differences in language and approach between the arts and sciences.

• Compare the role of imagination in science with its role in one or more of the arts.

Suggested Readings

[The headings are not mutually exclusive; entries under one topic may well include material pertinent to the other topics.]

THE LIBERAL ARTS (HUMANITIES): THEIR NATURE, VALUE, GOALS

Arnold, Matthew. "Literature and Science," from *The Portable Matthew Arnold*. New York: The Viking Press, 1962.

Barr, Stringfellow. "Liberal Education: A Common Adventure," *Antioch Review*, XV (September 1955), 300-12.

Barzun, Jacques. *The House of Intellect*. New York: Harper & Brothers, 1959.

———. "Science vs. The Humanities, A Truce to the Nonsense on Both Sides," *The Saturday Evening Post*, CCXXX (May 3, 1955), 26-28 +.

Beesley, Patricia. *The Revival of the Humanities in American Education*. New York: Columbia University Press, 1940.

Bestor, Arthur E. *Educational Wastelands*. Urbana: University of Illinois Press, 1953.

———. *The Restoration of Learning*. New York: Alfred A. Knopf, 1955.

Broudy, Harry S. *Paradox and Promise*. Englewood Cliffs, New Jersey: Prentice-Hall, Inc., 1961.

Bryce, Viscount. "Statement," from Dean Andrew F. West and others (eds.), *Value of the Classics*. Princeton: Princeton University Press, 1917, p. 143.

Bush, Douglas. "Science and the Humanities," from Brand Blanshard (ed.), *Education in the Age of Science*. New York: Basic Books, 1959, pp. 167-87.

Chinard, Gilbert. "Literature and the Humanities," from Theodore Meyer Greene (ed.), *The Meaning of the Humanities*. Princeton: Princeton University Press, 1938, pp. 153-70.

Fadiman, Clifton. "The Case for Basic Education," from James D. Koerner (ed.), *The Case for Basic Education*. Boston: Little, Brown & Company, 1959, pp. 3-14.

Gannon, Robert I., S.J. *The Poor Old Liberal Arts*. New York: Farrar, Straus & Cudahy, 1961.

Gardner, John W. *Excellence*. New York: Harper & Brothers, 1960.

Griswold, A. Whitney. *Essays on Education*. New Haven: Yale University Press, 1954.

———. *Liberal Education and the Democratic Ideal and Other Essays*. New Haven: Yale University Press, 1959.

Hamilton, Edith. "The Lessons of the Past," *The Saturday Evening Post*, CCXXXI (September 27, 1958), 24-25 +.

Hanson, Howard. "The Arts in the Age of Science," *National Education Association Journal*, XLVII (February 1958), 73.

Highet, Gilbert. *Man's Unconquerable Mind*. New York: Columbia University Press, 1954.

Hook, Sidney. *Education for Modern Man*. New York: The Dial Press, 1946.

Hutchins, Robert M. *The Conflict in Education*. New York: Harper & Brothers, 1953.

————. *Education for Freedom*. Baton Rouge: Louisiana State University Press, 1947.

————. *Great Books: The Foundation of a Liberal Education*. New York: Simon & Schuster, 1954.

Huxley, Aldous. *Brave New World Revisited*. New York: Bantam Books, 1960.

Jensen, Arthur E. "Leadership Through the Liberal Arts," *Vital Speeches*, XXIV (July 15, 1958), 601-3.

Jones, Howard Mumford. *American Humanism*. New York: Harper & Brothers, 1957.

————. *One Great Society*. New York: Harcourt Brace & Company, 1959.

————. *Reflections on Learning*. New Brunswick: Rutgers University Press, 1958.

Krutch, Joseph Wood. "Are the Humanities Worth Saving?—I," *Saturday Review*, XXXVIII (June 4, 1955), 22-24.

————. "Are the Humanities Worth Saving?—II," *Saturday Review*, XXXVIII (June 11, 1955), 22-23.

————. *Human Nature and the Human Condition*. New York: Random House, 1959.

————. "If You Don't Mind My Saying So . . . ," *American Scholar*, XXXI (Autumn 1962), 516-19.

————. *The Measure of Man*. New York: Bobbs-Merrill Company, Inc., 1954.

Kuebler, Clark G. "The Special Significance of the Humanities in Liberal Education," from Julian Harris (ed.), *The Humanities*. Baltimore: Waverly Press, 1950.

Livingstone, Richard. "The Rainbow Bridge," *Atlantic Monthly*, CC (November 1957), 174-78.

Maritain, Jacques. *The Education of Man*. Garden City, New York: Doubleday & Company, Inc., 1962.

Newman, John Henry. *The Idea of a University*, edited, with an Introduction and Notes, by Martin J. Svaglic. New York: Rinehart and Company, Inc., 1960.

Ortega y Gasset, José. *The Mission of a University*, translated, with an Introduction by Howard Lee Nostrand. Princeton: Princeton University Press, 1944.

Osgood, Charles Grosvenor. *Creed of a Humanist*. Seattle: University of Washington Press, 1963.

Osler, Sir William. *The Old Humanities and the New Science*. Boston: Houghton Mifflin, 1920.

Perry, Ralph Barton. "A Definition of the Humanities," from Theodore Meyer Greene (ed.), *The Meaning of the Humanities*. Princeton: Princeton University Press, 1938, pp. 3-42.

Pusey, Nathan M. *The Age of the Scholar*. Cambridge: The Belknap Press of Harvard University Press, 1963.

————. "The Centrality of Humanistic Study," from Julian Harris (ed.), *The Humanities*. Baltimore: Waverly Press, 1950, pp. 75-82.

Rickover, H. G. *Education and Freedom*. New York: E. P. Dutton and Co., Inc., 1959.

Shuster, George N. *Education and Moral Wisdom*. New York: Harper & Brothers, 1960.

Ulich, Robert. "The Humanities," from Robert Ulich (ed.), *Education and the Ideal of Mankind*. New York: Harcourt, Brace and World, Inc., 1964, pp. 249-79.

Van Doren, Mark. *Liberal Education*. New York: Books, Inc., distributed by Henry Holt and Company, 1943.

SCIENCE AND SCIENTISTS IN THE MODERN WORLD

Azimov, Isaac. "What Is Science?," from *The Intelligent Man's Guide to Science*. New York: Basic Books, 1960, I, 3-20.

Barzun, Jacques. *Science: The Glorious Entertainment*. New York: Harper & Row, New York, 1964.

Bronowski, J. *Science and Human Values*. New York: Harper & Brothers, 1959.

Conant, James B. *The Citadel of Learning*. New Haven: Yale University Press, 1956.

———. *Science and Common Sense*. New Haven: Yale University Press, 1951.

Dooley, D. J. "Science as Cliché, Fable, and Faith," *Bulletin of the Atomic Scientists*, XV (November 1959), 372-75.

Eddington, Sir Arthur. *New Pathways in Science*. New York: The Macmillan Company, 1935.

Eiseley, Loren. *The Firmament of Time*. New York: Atheneum Publishers, 1960.

Glass, Bentley. *Science and Liberal Education*. Baton Rouge: Louisiana State University Press, 1959.

Green, Martin. "A Literary Defense of the Two Cultures," *Kenyon Review*, XXIV (Autumn 1962), 731-39.

Heisenberg, W. "Atoms with Hooks and Eyes," translated by R. Winston and C. Winston, *Atlantic Monthly*, CXCIX (March 1957), 121-24.

Holton, G. "Modern Science and the Intellectual," *Science*, CXXXI (April 22, 1960), 1187-93.

Huxley, Julian (ed.). *The Humanist Frame*. New York: Harper & Brothers, 1961.

Jeans, Sir James. *The Mysterious Universe*. Cambridge: The University Press, 1948.

Leavis, F. R. *Two Cultures? The Significance of C. P. Snow*, and Michael Yudkin, *An Essay on Sir Charles Snow's Rede Lecture*. New York: Pantheon Books, 1963, pp. 13-50.

Le Corbeiller, Philippe. "The Crisis in Science Education," from Brand Blanshard (ed.), *Education in the Age of Science*. New York: Basic Books, 1951, pp. 229-35.

Lilienthal, David E. "Skeptical Look at 'Scientific Experts,' " *The New York Times Magazine* (September 29, 1963), pp. 23 +.

Nagel, Ernest. "Science and the Humanities," from Brand Blanshard (ed.), *Education in the Age of Science*. New York: Basic Books, 1959, pp. 188-207.

Oppenheimer, J. Robert. *The Open Mind*. New York: Simon & Schuster, 1955.

———. "Science and the Human Community," from Charles Frankel (ed.), *Issues in University Education*. New York: Harper & Brothers, 1959, pp. 48-62.

Sarton, George. *The History of Science and the New Humanism*. New York: George Braziller, Inc., 1956.

Schilling, Harold K. "A Human Enterprise," *Science,* CXXVII (June 6, 1958), 1324-27.

Snow, C. P. *The Two Cultures and the Scientific Revolution.* New York: Cambridge University Press, 1960.

————. *The Two Cultures and a Second Look.* New York: Cambridge University Press, 1964.

Standen, Anthony. *Science Is a Sacred Cow.* New York: E. P. Dutton and Company, Inc., 1950.

Toulmin, Stephen. *Foresight and Understanding.* Bloomington: Indiana University Press, 1961.

Stevenson, L. "Scientists with Half-closed Minds, *Harper's,* CCXVII (November 1958), 64 +.

Trilling, Lionel. "Science, Literature and Culture: A Comment on the Leavis-Snow Controversy," *Commentary,* XXXIII (June 1962), 461-77.

Weaver, Warren. "Science and Complexity," in Warren Weaver (ed.), *The Scientists Speak.* New York: Boni and Gaer, 1947, pp. 1-13.

Wolheim, Richard. "London Letter," *Partisan Review,* XXIX (Spring 1962), 263-269.

Yudkin, Michael. "Sir Charles Snow's Rede Lecture," from F. R. Leavis, *Two Cultures? The Significance of C. P. Snow* and Michael Yudkin, *An Essay on Sir Charles Snow's Rede Lecture.* New York: Pantheon Books, 1963, pp. 52-64.

THE LANGUAGE AND APPROACH OF SCIENCE AND OF THE ARTS

Bibby, Cyril. "Science: A Tool of Culture," *Saturday Review,* XLVII (June 6, 1964), 803-26.

Campbell, N. R. "Science, Imagination, and Art," *Science,* CXXV (April 26, 1957), 803-6.

Cassidy, Harold Gomes. *The Sciences and the Arts.* New York: Harper & Brothers, 1962.

Huxley, Aldous. *Literature and Science.* New York: Harper & Row, 1963.

————. *The Olive Tree.* New York: Harper & Brothers, 1937.

Levi, Albert William. *Literature, Philosophy and the Imagination.* Bloomington: Indiana University Press, 1962.

Rabi, I. I. "Scientist and Humanist: Can the Minds Meet?," *Atlantic Monthly,* CXCVII (January 1956), 64-67.

SCIENCE AND THE HUMANITIES IN MODERN EDUCATION

Blanshard, Brand. "Introduction," from Brand Blanshard (ed.), *Education in the Age of Science.* New York: Basic Books, 1951, pp. vii-xviii.

Bronowski, J. "Educated Man in 1984," *Science,* CXXIII (April 27, 1956), 710-712.

Conant, James B. *Education in a Divided World.* Cambridge: Harvard University Press, 1948.

Hampshire, Stuart. "Ruinous Conflict," *New Statesman,* LXIII (May 4, 1962), 652-53.

Harvard Committee, Report of the. *General Education in a Free Society,* with an Introduction by James Bryant Conant. Cambridge: Harvard University Press, 1958.

Huxley, Thomas H. "A Liberal Education and Where to Find It," Selected Works of Thomas H. Huxley. Westminster Edition, New York: D. Appleton and Company, 1893, VIII, 76-110.

———. "On Science and Art in Relation to Education," in Ibid., 160-88.

———. "Science and Culture," in Ibid., 134-59.

———. "Scientific Education: Notes of an After-Dinner Speech," in Ibid., 111-33.

———. "Universities: Actual and Ideal," in Ibid., 189-234.

Mill, John Stuart. "Inaugural Address," Dissertations and Discussions: Political, Philosophical and Historical. Boston: William Spences, 1867, IV, 385-460.

Russell, Bertrand. "The Place of Science in Liberal Education," Mysticism and Logic. Garden City, New York: Doubleday Anchor Books, Doubleday & Company, Inc., 1957, pp. 32-43. (The essay was originally published in 1917.)

Thiring, H. "Education for the Age of Science," Bulletin of the Atomic Scientists, XV (March 23, 1960), 293-97.

Weaver, Warren. "Science for Everybody," Saturday Review, XLV (July 7, 1962), 45-46.

Whitehead, A. N. The Aims of Education. New York: The Macmillan Company, 1959.